WOMEN STEADFAST IN CHRIST

WOMEN STEADFAST IN CHRIST

Talks Selected from the
1991 Women's Conference
Co-sponsored by
Brigham Young University
and the Relief Society

Edited by
Dawn Hall Anderson
and Marie Cornwall

Deseret Book Company
Salt Lake City, Utah

Library of Congress Cataloging-in-Publication Data

Women steadfast in Christ / edited by Dawn Hall Anderson and Marie
    Cornwall.
      p. cm.
    Papers presented at the 1991 BYU Women's Conference.
    Includes bibliographical references and index.
    ISBN 0-87579-597-8
    1. Women Mormon — Religious life — Congresses.   I. Anderson, Dawn
Hall. II. Cornwall, Marie, 1949–   III. Brigham Young
University. IV. BYU Women's Conference (1991)
BX8641.W67 1992
289.3'32'082 — dc20   91-47724
                                               CIP

Printed in the United States of America

10   9   8   7   6   5   4   3   2   1

Contents

Contents

This book is the sixth in the series from the annual Women's Conference, co-sponsored by Brigham Young University and the Relief Society. Selections in this volume were presented in the 1991 conference.

We are grateful to Carol Lee Hawkins, who was chair of the conference. She and her planning committee spent long hours planning and coordinating the conference presentations and discussions. We are also grateful to the BYU administration and faculty and to the Relief Society general presidency for making the conference possible.

We thank the staff of the Women's Research Institute, who helped create this volume. Tracey Wilkinson Sparks transcribed hours of audio tape and coordinated transcripts between the authors and the editors. Kae Sawyer checked quotations and citations. Suzanne Brady of Deseret Book provided the fine tuning.

Of course, the volume is possible only because of the willingness of the authors to prepare their conference presentations for publication. We thank them for taking the time to give voice to their experiences and to share their lives with our readers.

PRESSING FORWARD, BEING STILL

We can press forward with hope in Christ, like green shoots growing upward toward the sun, only if we have within us the peace and stillness that are the rich seedbed of such growth and progress.

—Elouise Bell

"A Steadfastness in Christ"

CAROL LEE HAWKINS

Those of us from the Relief Society and Brigham Young University who have planned this conference during the past ten months have done so hoping to enrich your lives. By placing you in an atmosphere of inquiry, we want to aid your personal quest of pressing forward with a steadfastness in Christ and demonstrate several ways to help achieve the perfect brightness of hope to which Nephi referred in 2 Nephi 31:20:

"Wherefore, ye must press forward with a steadfastness in Christ, having a perfect brightness of hope, and a love of God and of all men. Wherefore, if ye shall press forward, feasting upon the word of Christ, and endure to the end, behold, thus saith the Father: Ye shall have eternal life."

Our goal was a conference that emphasized intellectual stimulation, cultural enrichment, and spiritual affirmation. In trying to achieve such purposes — and then appeal to a varied audience of women and men, young and old, married and single, parents and children — we recognized a need to offer a full spectrum of subjects using insights from a diversified slate of participants.

We realized the impossibility — even the undesirability — of a consensus emerging from the many ideas that would be presented in a two-day conference. While we have encouraged contrasting ideas, we have wanted you to realize that a unity

Carol Lee Hawkins has served as chair of the women's conference at Brigham Young University and as a member of the Relief Society general board. She has lived in various parts of the world with her anthropologist husband, John P. Hawkins, and their four children. Sister Hawkins has assisted in research projects dealing with women and families in Guatemala, Mexico, and Germany.

3

of purpose actually binds all of us in the family of Christ. This kind of unity can transcend differences in perspective.

A year ago at this same conference, President Rex E. Lee said he would be surprised, even a bit disappointed, if his audience agreed with everything said during the conference. He encouraged us, "in the finest tradition of the gospel and the free and open society guaranteed by our Constitution, to approach each experience not only as an evaluator" of what we heard but also as a student with the opportunity "to learn from new ideas and new points of view." As he encouraged spiritual and intellectual investigation, he said he expected us to "come away . . . with new questions as well as new insights and answers."[1]

We submit that new insights are best sought by linking both scholarship and faith with a bridge of tolerance and acceptance. If you do no more than reaffirm the beliefs you bring with you to this conference, we will have failed. Our intention is to open your minds and hearts beyond your own experience.

It has pleased me in past conferences to observe some of you learning not only from presenters but also from each other in the lunch halls and in sincere discussions between sessions. I have also been heartened by the caring acceptance I have seen among many of you. This conference should provide a place for an affectionate sisterhood that moves into the deepest realms of charity: charity of thought, understanding, sympathy, support, and empathy.

While I encourage you to "deal frankly with each other" — as counseled more than a century ago by Emma Smith — I also advise you to "knit your hearts as one" with "measures that promote union in the society."[2]

We as sisters need each other desperately. As explained by BYU history professor Mary Stovall, "Each of us will experience over our lifetime physical pain, emotional anguish, heartache, grief, even betrayal in one form or another. If we attempt to deny the problem or to cover it with a facade of forced sweetness and light, we imperil both ourselves and each other—

4

ourselves because we deny the healing that can result from the love, strength, and insights of true friends, and each other because people then assume we *are* our facades and feel even more isolated with *their* problems."[3]

To these words we add the loving guidance of Lucy Mack Smith, who recommended that we "cherish one another, watch over one another, comfort one another and gain instruction, that we may all sit down in heaven together."[4] At the same period, her son Joseph Smith reminded us that "by a union of feeling we obtain power with God."[5]

Our hope is that we will leave the conference having been challenged to think deeply and redirect, where necessary, our outlooks. Much as the rays of the sun burst from a common center into many angles that suffuse their warmth, so should we, from our common center, feel free to use our diverse gifts and strengths to build the kingdom of God. May our common faith in Christ steady us all as we "press forward with a . . . brightness of hope."

Notes

1. Rex E. Lee, "The Power Within: To See Life Steadily and See It Whole," *Women and the Power Within: To See Life Steadily and See It Whole*, ed. Dawn Hall Anderson and Marie Cornwall (Salt Lake City: Deseret Book Co., 1991), pp. 3–4.
2. Emma Hale Smith, "A Record of the Organization and Proceedings of the Female Relief Society of Nauvoo," 17 March 1842, microfilm of holograph, LDS Church Archives, Salt Lake City, Utah; hereafter cited as "Record."
3. Mary E. Stovall, "Preface," *As Women of Faith*, ed. Mary E. Stovall and Carol Cornwall Madsen (Salt Lake City: Deseret Book Co., 1989), p. viii.
4. Lucy Mack Smith, "Record," 24 March 1842.
5. "Record," 9 June 1842.

A Perfect Brightness of Hope

ELAINE L. JACK

If I asked you what your favorite word was, what would you say? I once asked a number of friends to share with me their favorite word. What began as a point of conversation soon became a period of testimony, for my friends suggested such words as *commitment, family, love.*

I have thought since that time about what my own favorite word might be. *Rejoice* is a major contender, but I think *hope* wins. To me hope embodies happy feelings, anticipation of good things, the best of the gospel, and zest for life. The word *hope* is embedded in the instructions of Nephi to followers of Christ: "Wherefore, ye must press forward with a steadfastness in Christ, having a perfect brightness of hope, and a love of God and of all men." (2 Nephi 31:20.)

In this women's conference, we celebrate "a perfect brightness of hope." What a light, ebullient phrase that is. I have stood on a mountaintop at sunrise and thought of that phrase, it warms and moves me so. *Hope*—what it does to my soul when I feel it. *Hope*—what it does for the world when we act upon it.

Since my call to be general president of the Relief Society, I've met hundreds of you sisters, received sheaves of letters, and attended meetings in many places with and about Latter-day Saint women. I've learned a lot. One most important insight

Elaine L. Jack was called as general president of the Relief Society in March 1990. She has also served in the Young Women general presidency and as a volunteer in civic organizations. She attended the University of Utah as an English major and is an avid reader. Reared in Canada, she and her husband, Joseph E. Jack, are the parents of four sons.

I have gained is that many of our sisters have lost hope. I see and hear evidences of that far too often—and it grieves me.

Some women have said:

"How many dates do I have to go on to find an eternal partner?"

"I am no longer needed. My family is gone. What good am I?"

"I don't get any support from my husband. I have to take care of everything related to Church and children myself."

These are only a few of the feelings of discouragement and frustration I have heard. They make me sad, because a life without hope is not life—not in the gospel sense. After Moroni had witnessed the destruction of his own family and all his friends and people, he wrote to the Lamanites: "And except ye have charity ye can in nowise be saved in the kingdom of God; neither can ye be saved in the kingdom of God if ye have not faith; neither can ye if ye have no hope. And if ye have no hope ye must needs be in despair." (Moroni 10:21–22.)

For me, to live in despair is not to live. I cannot imagine life without hope. Perhaps that is because I learned early that hope is a personal quality essential for righteous living. In fact, hope is one of the personality traits of godlike men and women. Paul explained that Church members who wish to live "acceptable unto God" are in part characterized as those "not slothful in business; fervent in spirit; serving the Lord; rejoicing in hope; patient in tribulation; continuing instant in prayer." (Romans 12:1, 11–12.)

Recently I read an article about a Cambodian family who endured unimaginable suffering at the hands of the Khmer Rouge. At the end of a particularly arduous day, the mother gathered the family together and taught, "Remember, children, . . . hate does not end with more hate but with love. And from that we take hope. Without love and hope, our lives will be empty."[1] What a wise mother!

My own dear mother taught me a lot about love and hope. She was ill for many years, yet she was always a bright, hopeful person. She taught me that in any circumstance those who are "acceptable unto God" can be recognized because their belief is evident in their attitudes and actions. Mother knew that hope helps us rebound.

To me it is very important that "rejoicing in hope" is on the list of godlike characteristics, especially because we benefit so much from the comfort and happy expectation of hope in tumultuous times. (Romans 12:12.)

Karen's children are close in age. Since her son Brad, now six, nearly drowned two years ago, he has required much extra care. Her father-in-law died about the time her own mother entered a nursing home. Shortly after her mother died, her father remarried. And during all of this, her husband has been starting up his own business.

As Karen knows, as all of you know, daily living can be draining. The demands on women seem to multiply. Personal lives can be in such chaos. Yet, hope stands as a beacon—warm, steady, and inviting. It is reassuring to me that this quality I enjoy so much is also requisite for those who would follow the light and life of the Savior of the world.

Hope Matters

My dear sisters, hope matters. I repeat, *your* hope matters. May I suggest three reasons why.

First: Hope, charity, and faith are very closely related. Paul concluded his treatise on charity with the words: "And now abideth faith, hope, charity, these three." (1 Corinthians 13:13.) An early revelation received by Joseph Smith states, "And faith, hope, charity and love, with an eye single to the glory of God, qualify him [or her] for the work." (D&C 4:5.) Moroni explained, "Wherefore, there must needs be faith; and if there must be faith there must also be hope; and if there must be hope there must also be charity." (Moroni 10:20.) Alma exhorted, "And see that ye have faith, hope, and charity, and then ye will always abound in good works." (Alma 7:24.)

These three good friends—faith, hope, and charity—become stronger through their association with each other. Perhaps what is most important about them is that they only exist together. The charitable woman is also the hopeful, faithful woman. Hence, when a woman loses hope, she will also lose faith and charity. I have known women who have let go of hope and yet claimed to maintain faith. But it appears from the interlacing of these qualities that if we lack one, we shall soon lack the others. Sisters, let us cling to our faith, our hope, our charity, remembering that upon this trio hangs our well-being, now and forever.

Second: Without hope, we despair. Moroni wrote that "if ye have no hope ye must needs be in despair." He then added, "and despair cometh because of iniquity." (Moroni 10:22.) It seems clear, then, that when hope leaves us, despair ensues. And to me despair is no better an alternative than iniquity. The woman living close to God rebounds from despair; in righteousness lies resilience.

Several years ago I watched a woman experience a brief, unhappy marriage. At age thirty-two, after many years of longing for marriage and children, she finally did marry in the temple. She discovered on her honeymoon that this man for whom she had faithfully prepared all her life had not faithfully prepared for her. He wanted the appearance of marriage. But he had no intention of living its realities. What he had said before marriage was not what he intended to do after marriage. On their honeymoon he divulged that he had chosen her only because she seemed strong and self-sufficient—able to provide for herself financially and emotionally.

She was devastated. She despaired. She wondered if her whole heart had been crushed irreparably, along with her girlhood dreams. The world was black, and everything went poorly for many months.

But a remarkable thing happened. She was still very much alive; she just didn't know it for a time. During this period of intense difficulty, I watched the law of hope take its course. My friend desired righteousness all the while she struggled

9

with choices, questions, and personal pain. Her hopeful desire, often unexpressed during those many months, began to work in her. In her fertile soul, dormant seeds of hope, which she had forgotten she'd planted, began to sprout. Then they began to grow. She felt them and, as she was able, nurtured those volunteer tendrils.

It wasn't easy, but hope, faith, and charity are powerful. Once growing, they are not easily dissuaded—if the soil is right. Those tendrils strengthened. Ever so gradually, her anger, disappointment, pain, and even despair were replaced by fresh, fragrant plants of compassion, understanding, and patience, of faith, hope, and charity. My friend lived the biblical teaching that "[she] that ploweth should plow in hope; and that [she] that thresheth in hope should be partaker of [her] hope." (1 Corinthians 9:10.)

It is undeniable that life can bring each of us heartache, devastation, and despair. It is undeniable that the gospel brings us hope, which, when well planted, grows into a magnificent garden.

In 1991 I visited Ricks College for Women's Week. There I met Aja, a beautiful, self-assured woman who was receiving the Woman of the Year Award. I was impressed by her maturity and positive comments about her own future. When I commented on this to one of the leaders, she explained that Aja had won those feelings out of a real struggle. Aja, her twin sister, and their mother had been abandoned by her father many years earlier. Aja's mother had raised the sisters close to each other and to the Church. Tragically, her mother died when Aja was just sixteen years old. The twins were not only orphaned but also destitute. They lived with friends, worked hard, scrimped, and now, four years later, Aja stood on the brink of graduation and marriage. Hers is a story about the resilience of hope well planted and well cultivated.

Third: Hope is an anchor to the soul. Hebrews 6:18–19 says that "we might have a strong consolation, who have fled for

10

refuge to lay hold upon the hope set before us: which hope we have as an anchor of the soul, both sure and stedfast."

Little in life is sure. I became particularly conscious of this fact during the Mideast crisis, for our son Dave was serving in Saudi Arabia. During the most intense part of the conflict, including the bombing raids and the entire ground war, I was traveling in the Pacific. I was very anxious for news but found it was hard to get. When I could, I studied newspapers while I was waiting for airplanes, but television and radio news was almost inaccessible. I learned as I stood up to speak in Brisbane, Australia, that the ground war had started. I learned of the cease-fire as I left for a meeting in Papeete, Tahiti.

Throughout those weeks when I had no way of knowing where or how Dave was, I prayed a lot, and I prayed hard. Dave was always on my mind, and I longed for his well-being and for that of his wife and baby, who were waiting for him in the States. I wondered many times each day if he were all right. It was a frightening few weeks for me.

What anchored me during that time was my hope. I have great hopes for Dave and great faith in him. I also know how sensible and spiritual his wife is. I felt good about them and their spiritual preparation for such a time. Most of all, I felt good about our mutual faith in the gospel. I knew that each member of our family—whether in Salt Lake, or Boston, or Walnut Creek, or Riyahd, or Brisbane—would pray, would expect the best, would prepare for the worst, and would live each day with hope.

Hope is a steadying influence. As an anchor it can keep us from drifting aimlessly, or getting caught in whirlpools, or running into sandbars. Hope, the anchor, is essential in this world so full of tidal waves. Sometimes those waves slap us from behind. Sometimes we see them coming but cannot stop them or get out of the way. In all cases, hope ties us to safety. The waves come and go in their fury or playfulness, but hope is always there, if we will but use this sure anchor.

How to Obtain Hope

How can we obtain hope? In all our circumstances, we can benefit from answering this question.

First and foremost, we look to Christ with joyous expectation. As Paul began his first epistle to Timothy, he identifed himself in this wonderful way, "Paul, an apostle of Jesus Christ by the commandment of God our Saviour, and Lord Jesus Christ, which is our hope." (1 Timothy 1:1.) Truly, the Lord Jesus Christ is our hope. And what type of hope should we have? "A lively hope." (1 Peter 1:3.)

I was truly complimented when an Australian stake Relief Society president said, "Sister Jack, you're real." I couldn't have been more pleased, especially since this wonderful sister had wanted things to be so perfect for my visit that she had bought new hose because she was concerned I'd disapprove of a snagged pair.

I am real—and realistic. I know faith and hope are not a placebo meant to placate the questions and desires of our hearts. They are realities. My hope and my joy in life are based upon the atonement of our Savior and the restoration of his gospel in these days. I base my life on it; therefore, I have reason for my hope.

My sisters and my friends, our Savior lives, and he loves us. This gospel is one of light and joy, warmth and belonging. Just consider these confirming evidences: The angel declared at our Savior's birth, "I bring you good tidings of great joy, which shall be to all people." (Luke 2:10.) The prophets describe our Lord as he who "inviteth . . . all to come unto him and partake of his goodness; and he denieth none that come unto him, black and white, bond and free, male and female; and he remembereth the heathen; and all are alike unto God." (2 Nephi 26:33.) The Savior introduced himself as "Jesus Christ . . . the light and life of the world." (3 Nephi 11:10–11.)

Dear sisters, our joy, our hope, begins and ends in our Savior. A letter I received from Susan, a sister who had been struggling with the loneliness of single parenting, illustrates this hope in Christ:

"Not long ago I was feeling sorry for myself. . . . I've been struggling . . . to pay bills. Upon retiring to bed one night feeling the worse for the daily battle . . . , I lay in my bed moaning to myself. . . . It was then that I looked up to the picture I have of the Savior on my wall, and I felt his eyes come to life. They seemed to look into my very soul, and at the same time these words came to my mind: 'I am here. I've always been by your side, taking the pain you feel as well. I drank the bitter cup for you and I gladly did so. I love you. I always will, and I'll always be here with you every step of the way.'

"As tears streamed down my face, I felt like the Savior's arms had circled my body and were hugging me. I felt so secure, so loved, and wanted—a feeling I can still feel as I write this on paper. The feeling of loneliness left me immediately."

As I read this letter, I thought, "How blessed Susan is to have a personal knowledge of the Savior." What could be more joyous?

Don't defer hope. Proverbs 13:12 states, "Hope deferred maketh the heart sick." Physically, emotionally, and spiritually, hope deferred sickens our hearts. To prevent illness, grab on to, hold on to your hope.

I ask you, as Joseph Smith asked the Church in 1842, the year Relief Society was founded: "And again, what do we hear? Glad tidings from Cumorah! Moroni, an angel from heaven, declaring the fulfillment of the prophets . . . giving us consolation by holding forth that which is to come, confirming our hope!" (D&C 128:20–21.)

Sisters, daily confirm your hope. Some of you feel troubled, I know. Perhaps the source of your concern is your perception of how the Church is run. Others of you may be troubled to your core by the injustices of the world. You may wonder why so many undeserving people live in abundance while so many innocents suffer. Some of you are the innocents. You bear emotional scars because of the abuse of others. Still others of you carry a personal problem that weighs on your soul even as you sleep. May I gently speak to your hearts — don't defer hope even when you feel most hopeless. Confirm your hope every way you can.

My friend who found herself so unhappily married told me that it was the smallest things that kept her going during those first weeks when all her world looked black. A bunch of crocus burst through the snow and then announced their victory with purple blooms. The robins whistled from their nest in her front-yard tree. The sun broke over the horizon every morning. People in her office lived their quiet routines. A person spoke kindly to her at the grocery store. Her little niece hugged her around the legs. Each small, loving, daily detail confirmed her hope. They showed that life still was good. She didn't feel it, but she did not defer her hope. She focused instead on every confirmation that God lives. And if God lives, life could still be sweet, and she could feel hope again.

What to Hope For

What should we hope for? Sisters, let us hope for a better world. To hope for a better world means that we invest in it now. Our investment of hope is measured in the sum of small things.

My neighbor Amy planted a spring garden every year of her adult life. Her own failing health did not dampen her need to plant the flowers she knew she might not live to see.

Every mother invests daily. One mother I know pinned a note on her two-year-old each morning. It said, "Don't give up. I will turn 3." That's hope!

I admire people who read to the blind or take a neighbor to the store, who organize a neighborhood crime watch or local recycling program or tree planting in the park. I admire people who hug each family member daily or remember their aunts' birthdays, those who take neighbors' children with them on trips, and those who can be silly with their friends. I know a widow confined to a wheelchair who crochets dishcloths for all her Relief Society sisters. She takes great personal interest in their homes, children, and all their concerns. She asks her visiting teachers to deliver her gifts at church to the sisters celebrating their birthdays. On each cloth is a note kindly but definitely reminding the sister that cleanliness is next to godliness. Sisters, all our efforts, in the home, the workplace, and the community are investments in a better, kinder world. The prophet Ether taught, "Whoso believeth in God might with surety hope for a better world, yea, even a place at the right hand of God, which hope cometh of faith, maketh an anchor to the souls of [women and] men, which would make them sure and steadfast, always abounding in good works, being led to glorify God." (Ether 12:4.)

Just think of all the small ways you live with hope for your world. Each day that you take a vitamin with iron, you are planning for the future. Every time you spring clean, you probably say, "Whew, I'm glad that's over. I won't have to do it for a year." You bottle fruit so there will be cherry pie next winter. You pore over the atlas, studying the roads you'll drive on your next family vacation. Whether you recognize it or not, your days are full of a hundred acts born from your personal perfect brightness of hope.

Alfred, Lord Tennyson's poem "Ulysses" helps me understand hopeful investments in the world. You remember the story of Ulysses, the Greek hero of Homer's *Odyssey*. Through Tennyson's words we see Ulysses as an old man, still looking out to sea, still seeking the adventures of his youth. He knows full well his age, his position, his responsibilities, his experience. And having recounted them, he then says:

> How dull it is to pause, to make an end,
> To rust unburnished, not to shine in use!
> . . . .
> . . . Come, my friends.
> 'Tis not too late to seek a newer world.

15

Push off, and sitting well in order smite
The sounding furrows. . . .
. . . .
We are not now that strength which in old days
Moved earth and heaven, that which we are, we are—
One equal temper of heroic hearts,
Made weak by time and fate, but strong in will
To strive, to seek, to find, and not to yield.[2]

I enjoy thinking about Tennyson's ideas. I like the phrase, "How dull it is to pause . . . to rust unburnished." I met a spry eighty-one-year-old woman in Perth, Australia, who has been deaf since she was two. We communicated through written notes and her own quick, descriptive hand movements. When I asked her what she loved to do most, she wrote in big letters, "DRIVE A CAR." Then she added that she didn't like to drive in Perth because it was too dull. She missed driving in Sydney where the traffic is heavy, the lanes are narrow, and the motorists drive like Evel Knievel. This woman was definitely not rusting away.

I also love these earlier lines from Tennyson's poem:

I am a part of all that I have met;
Yet all experience is an arch wherethrough
Gleams that untraveled world whose margin fades
Forever and forever when I move.

More than ever, I find my favorite archway is the one on my own front door. My home is the source of my fondest dreams and best hopes—also some of my finest adventures. What better archway to look through than the one through which I'll find the people I love best in the world?

What's glorious about my stage in life is realizing how meaningful my investment in relationships has become. I am grateful for my relationship with the Lord. I'm glad for every moment I've spent in prayer, in study, in service. I'm grateful for every friend I've made, for my husband, for every child

I've had, for every person with whom I've shared a gospel experience. And I am happy to know that those relationships can get even better.

Nothing has ever been as satisfying to me as my relationships. Note that I did not say easy. I said satisfying. It's not perfect out there, I know. And it's not perfect through the archway into my home. Still, it's mostly good, and my relationships always give me hope.

The thirteenth Article of Faith reminds us, "We hope all things." I asked some of my friends and family what they hope for. Here's a short list:

My sister says, "I hope my family continues to love each other and to be good friends."

My elderly neighbor says, "I hope I'll endure independent to the end."

My son Eric says, "I hope my CPA practice will grow."

I say, "I hope the sisters will understand the joys of the gospel."

My single friend says, "I hope I'll get married and have a family of my own."

My physician husband says, "I hope my patients recover quickly, without complications."

My teenage neighbor says, "I hope our baseball team takes state."

My niece says, "I hope my children grow up remembering a happy home in which they felt secure."

We do hope all things, don't we? How much happier our lives are when we daily add the conscious optimism of hope. Emily Dickinson wrote:

> "Hope" is the thing with feathers —
> That perches in the soul —
> And sings the tune without the words —
> And never stops — at all —[3]

I think of hope as a basket full of glorious spring flowers, each blossom representing one part of what my family, friends, and I hope for. Together these hopes are a radiant, abundant, fragrant bouquet. Whatever our metaphor for it, hope remains an effervescent, expectant, happy part of life. My dear friends, my dear sisters, hope matters. May we "press forward with a steadfastness in Christ, having a perfect brightness of hope." (2 Nephi 31:20.)

Notes

1. Sheldon Kelly, "The Rebirth of Sichan Siv," *Reader's Digest*, Feb. 1991, p. 138.
2. Alfred, Lord Tennyson, "Ulysses," in *The Victorian Age: Prose, Poetry, and Drama*, 2d ed., ed. John Wilson Bowyer and John Lee Brooks (New York: Appleton-Century-Crofts, 1954), p. 86.
3. Emily Dickinson, *Final Harvest: Emily Dickinson's Poems*, ed. by Thomas H. Johnson (Boston and Toronto: Little, Brown and Co., 1961), p. 34.

"Peace, Be Still"

I have a colleague who is convinced that we teach the
things we ourselves most need to know. I have always agreed
with this idea in general, but I have come to understand how
it applies to me in particular only recently.

Months ago, Carol Lee Hawkins invited me to be part of
the BYU-Relief Society women's conference. She invited me
on a Monday, and on Tuesday she asked me for a title for my
speech. (That's how it's done these days, you know. People
invite you to speak at an event six months from now, and with
the optimism of the long view, you say yes. After all, you have
six months to prepare. But twenty-four hours later, they ask
you for a title for the speech. And writers, unlike pregnant
mothers, don't have sonic scanners to tell them in advance the
general anatomy of the unborn baby!) In this case, however,
when Carol Lee asked me for a title, I knew the general anatomy:
"Peace, Be Still." In my mind at that time, I had the idea that
I would preach "Be Still" by way of balance for the admonition
to "Press Forward" that was stated in the conference theme:
"Press forward with a steadfastness in Christ, having a perfect
brightness of hope." (2 Nephi 31:20.) Something in me very
much wanted to say to all of you, "Don't press." I did not want
one woman to leave this conference anxious about how to fit
more chores into her daily planner; I did not want to be part
of adding the least shred of guilt to anyone's psyche; I did not

Elouise Bell, professor of English and associate dean of general and
honors education at Brigham Young University, has served as a
member of the Young Women general board. She is the author of
Only When I Laugh, a collection of essays, and Aunt Patty Remembers,
a one-woman show, which she also performs, that is based on the
journals of Mormon pioneer midwife Patty Bartlett Sessions.

want to have our theme, "Press Forward," result in pressing that is painful: *de*pressing, *re*pressing, *sup*pressing.

After a few conversations with Carol Lee, however, I realized that she was as concerned as I not to say, "You're not doing enough; work harder." I felt much better after these conversations, and I began to think more deeply about the balance between pressing forward and being still. I came to believe that pressing forward and being still are not contradictory or mutually exclusive, either-or actions that needed to be "balanced," as I had initially thought, but different ends of a single continuum, different positions on a single line, different moments in one life.

Then quite recently, I found myself viewing these two phrases in yet another way, one which I'd like to explain in some detail. To begin with, you need to know that this past year has been a full one for me, a very fulfilling one, an uncommonly busy one. And I have loved it. I feel gratitude to many people for the rewards of this past year. But along with those rewards, I have had a planner full of commitments and have given far too many talks. A few weeks ago, after giving a speech that, frankly, hadn't been very good, I began to understand that, for the moment at least, I was an empty bucket.

That's when the title of my speech, selected months ago in response to Carol Lee's deadline, came to my rescue. More than anything I might need to tell *you*, "peace be still" is what I needed to tell *myself*. Peace and stillness were what I needed to fill my bucket. At that point, I moved to a more complete understanding of the relationship between pressing forward and being still. They are not contraries or opposites; but neither are they truly different positions on the same continuum. Peace and stillness constitute the fuel that drives our forward motion. Peace and stillness make *possible* that progress. To change the metaphor, we can press forward with hope in Christ, like green shoots growing upward toward the sun, only if we have within us the peace and stillness that are the rich seedbed of such growth and progress.

20

Peace and stillness helped me fill my bucket, as I will explain, but maybe your problem right now isn't burnout or the empty bucket so much as a confusion about the next step you are to take. Many aspects of women's lives are changing in this generation, and although the great truths and values remain constant, many of us are honestly, sincerely puzzled about how to make the practical choices that will implement those truths. Very little is simple for today's woman, whether she be twenty or forty or sixty or eighty. (I think when you hit one hundred, maybe it gets simple again!) Simplistic axioms and glib catch-phrases don't solve the dilemmas we face. The solutions come, I believe, in our moments of stillness and silent searching. Only after we have sought in silence and in trust can we press forward with hope and in confidence that our particular path, however different from another's, is the appropriate path for us, for now.

In *Pilgrim at Tinker Creek*, the wise and reverent Annie Dillard writes of a transition time such as many of us are facing. She is actually writing about the death of the Self, or what we might call the death of ego, and she says: "It is waiting like a hollow bell with stilled tongue. The waiting itself is the thing."[1] That is what I want to say: sometimes being still itself is the thing. Being the hollow bell is the experience we need.

Being the hollow bell, being still and waiting, is hard — hard for many women, and especially hard for me. There are many reasons: there's too much to do; I have too many responsibilities; there's not enough time; there's no convenient place to enjoy solitude; I can't sit down and do nothing while the list of today's duties nags at my conscience. You can add to the list, I know. There are cultural reasons for our avoidance of stillness and solitude as well: our western culture (as contrasted with the culture of the Far East) doesn't value reflection and meditation; we have long confused stillness with idleness, and we view idleness as of the devil; our culture particularly discourages women from idleness, reflection, and so forth. All these assessments are true, but there is a deeper reason why

I, for one, have a problem with stillness. I think many share it. The great English dictionary-maker, writer, and speaker Samuel Johnson shared my weakness. "It may be laid down," he said, "that when a man cannot bear his own company there is something wrong. He must fly from himself, either because he feels a tediousness in life from . . . an empty mind, . . . or he must be afraid of the intrusion of some unpleasing ideas, and, perhaps, is struggling to escape from the remembrance of a loss, the fear of a calamity, or some other thought of greater horror."[2]

There are a number of fancy names for the feeling Johnson was talking about. It's the same feeling that makes some people so uncomfortable when they are alone, even in their own house or car, that they cannot be still with themselves, but must snap on the television, radio, or stereo. The silence is too oppressive. That oppression is sometimes called the sense of the "existential void," a feeling of emptiness, of loneliness, of being unanchored. I think that is the real reason so many of us simply cannot, or more accurately, will not spend significant amounts of time alone in contemplation. We are frankly uneasy, perhaps even afraid. We may not admit as much to ourselves; we may truly believe it is time or space or other commitments or other people that keep us from being still and cultivating inward peace. But whenever I get too quick with excuses like that, I remind myself that the Savior, despite all the responsibilities he had and all the people who must have wanted him to come here, come there, do this, heal that, explain the other—despite all that and the short period of time he knew he had for his mortal ministry, he still took time regularly to go apart—into the desert, into the mountains, out on the sea—to be alone and silent. Sometimes he took as much as forty days for this activity. Surely he must have seen it as a priority. No, I think my external excuses are not the real reasons I avoid that kind of contemplation.

In a small hotel room in Florence, Italy, one spring, I tried to find out why I felt that way—why, for instance, in that most glorious of all art centers in the world, I was uncomfortable being in my room alone, reading or studying, or why I was ill at ease visiting the art museums alone. I asked for enlightenment, and I received it. By myself, I was told, I felt empty, hollow, void. I was afraid I'd discover I was a permanently empty bucket. I believe it is that way with many of us. The fear is that in the stillness we will discover our own hollowness. T.S. Eliot, the Nobel Prize-winning poet, gave us that label early in this century, when he wrote, "We are the hollow men . . . headpiece filled with straw."³ Joseph Conrad, the great Polish-born novelist, created in *Heart of Darkness* a character neatly dressed in white, but inwardly hollow. He seemed made of papier-maché, as if one could poke a finger right through him and find just sawdust and a little dirt. These two writers were expressing the way many twentieth-century people feel because of the great uprooting of our era. It's important to remember that even though Latter-day Saints have a different philosophy from the prevailing one of our century, we still live and breathe in the same cultural atmosphere, and we absorb many of the same attitudes and anxieties, though we may not be aware of it. There is only one atmosphere, and we all breathe it. And a good many of us have absorbed, one way or another, that feeling of uneasiness and fear of our own emptiness.

But Annie Dillard explains what really happens, if we let it: in stillness we discover our fullness, in her words, our joining with "the great rock heart of the earth." Latter-day Saints would say that we discover our connection to Deity. Psalm 46:10 explains it this way: "Be still, and know that I am God." When we still our fears and wait quietly before him, we know that he is God and that we are eternally connected to him—not abandoned, isolated, empty, disconnected, or at sea, but filled with his Spirit and his love. As the lyrics from the musical *Into the Woods* affirm, "No One Is Alone."

So when I felt empty, the title of my yet unwritten talk gave me a direction to go. I needed to be at peace, to still myself.

23

Even though that stillness and solitude could make me uneasy, that was how I would be replenished. Thus, on a beautiful Sabbath day, with the sky very blue and filled to capacity with great white clouds, and the wind vital and crisp to remind me that the Spirit listeth where it will, I went out into Utah Valley to still myself. I went to Nature, not to find out from Nature what I needed to say to you—I am not a pantheist, and I don't believe Nature *per se* gives revelations—but to see if Nature could remind me, could help me develop from within the ideas that I believe were already there but not yet visible.

Let me explain that last thought. I believe that most of what we need to know is already within us. When N. Eldon Tanner was made president of the West European Mission in the early 1960s, he visited missionaries in France, and I was among those fortunate young people. I remember vividly his telling us that we were not really taking to our investigators new and un-dreamed-of doctrine. "No," he said. "Instead, think of it this way: all these people were exposed to the gospel long before you or they came to this earth. It's all there in their minds and spirits, like undeveloped photographic film. Your job is just to develop the film."

I went out to Nature on that beautiful Sunday to see if I could develop some sharp pictures. I gassed up the van, took the calmest and most companionable of my three dogs, and set out.

First I drove into the canyon east of Provo to an overlook from which I could see the whole valley, the lake in the distance, the surrounding mountains. I parked the van, slid and shuffled my way some yards down the steep hillside, tethered Mickey to a bush, and sat down to wait. To be silent, and to try to be still. Silence is not synonymous with stillness; but it is a good, often a necessary, first step.

I waited. I tried to be receptive. I looked over the valley, the hills and the distant roads, and I waited.

Then I noticed Mickey, who was also looking at the scene, very alertly. His pointed terrier ears were up, and he was sweeping his gaze from one end of the panorama to the other. "What is he seeing?" I wondered. He might see the same objects as I saw, but he did not make the same sense out of them. A plane, a distant car moving on the highway, a puff of smoke, a tiny flag flapping in the breeze — none of these had meaning for him, so far as I knew. But for that matter, just what did *I* see? Had an angel lighted beside me at that moment, she would have seen a picture as different from mine as mine was from Mickey's. Then I realized that if I would sit and look and be quiet, my picture would change and expand. I could begin to see and understand what I saw in a different, a nonroutine way. I might even get the tiniest glimpse of what the angel would perceive. I began to realize that in stillness, we hear. In silence, we see. If we can truly still ourselves and be fully attentive — what a huge *if!* — we can see *now*. Not the past or the future, both of which usually blind us to the present, but the now. We can see what *is*. Not what is not, not what we want, but what *is*. How rarely we see that way!

I know people who look at their children, for instance, and almost never see what they are, right now. The parents see what the children aren't — what they aren't doing, what they aren't producing — and they see what they themselves want — the *A* student or the well-mannered son or the skilled pianist daughter. How much we lose for not seeing what exists in the moment!

I suspect that the young men and women who spent those frightful months in Saudi Arabia this past winter now look at their hometowns in a very different way from the way they did before. They see what *is*. And they see the marvels of a simple home, and a quiet street, or a busy college campus, for the miracles they are. Do you remember Emily, in Thornton Wilder's play *Our Town*? When, after her death as a young mother, Emily is allowed to visit a past moment of her life, she can barely stand the beauty of the simplest day in her mortal life, the day of her sixteenth birthday.

We can learn to see that well, even while we are in mortality.

But we must be still to do so. Some of you have seen the movie *Awakenings.* As is so often the case, the book is better. But the point is well made in the film. Men and women frozen by disease into paralytic states that lasted decades discovered, when they were freed from the paralysis, that they saw life, and every aspect of life, much more sharply and appreciatively than the so-called healthy people who were walking around only half-awake themselves. These awakened patients saw people, nature, music, food — every aspect of life — as infinitely precious, infinitely beautiful. This story, of course, chronicles an unusual and unhealthy stillness, but the narrative dramatizes for us how healthy it is truly to see and revel in the present moment.

In that particular moment when I sat among the brush on the hillside, I was directed to the Psalms, specifically to Psalm 104. Do you feel as I do, that the psalmist was seeing with great clarity, out of a deep well of peace and inner stillness that enabled him to touch and fully know the present moment?

"Bless the Lord, O my soul. O Lord my God, thou art very great; thou art clothed with honour and majesty.

"Who coverest thyself with light as with a garment: who stretchest out the heavens like a curtain:

"Who layeth the beams of his chambers in the waters: who maketh the clouds his chariot: who walketh upon the wings of the wind:

"Who maketh his angels spirits; his ministers a flaming fire:

"Who laid the foundations of the earth, that it should not be removed for ever. . . .

"He appointed the moon for seasons: the sun knoweth his going down.

"Thou makest darkness, and it is night: wherein all the beasts of the forest do creep forth.

"The young lions roar after their prey, and seek their meat from God.

"The sun ariseth, they gather themselves together, and lay them down in their dens.

"Man goeth forth unto his work and to his labour until the evening.

"O Lord, how manifold are thy works! in wisdom hast thou made them all: the earth is full of thy riches. . . .

"Thou sendest forth thy spirit, they are created: and thou renewest the face of the earth.

"The glory of the Lord shall endure for ever: the Lord shall rejoice in his works.

"He looketh on the earth, and it trembleth: he toucheth the hills, and they smoke.

"I will sing unto the Lord as long as I live: I will sing praise to my God while I have my being.

"My meditation of him shall be sweet: I will be glad in the Lord.

"Let the sinners be consumed out of the earth, and let the wicked be no more. Bless thou the Lord, O my soul. Praise ye the Lord." (Psalm 104:1–5, 19–24, 30–35.)

After I had read and savored this psalm, we climbed in the van and drove just east of the Provo Temple. I sat looking at the people strolling on the grounds, at the spire pointing to the heavens, and at the valley stretching to the lake. I sat quietly and waited.

This time I opened to Psalm 130:5–7:

"I wait for the Lord, my soul doth wait, and in his word do I hope.

"My soul waiteth for the Lord more than they that watch for the morning: I say, more than they that watch for the morning.

"Let Israel hope in the Lord: for with the Lord there is mercy, and with him is plenteous redemption."

I know there are many who have endured dark sorrows and much pain and who must occasionally ask, "How long must I wait?" Their cry is certainly understandable. But I think this emphasis misses the point of "waiting for the Lord." I think the appropriate question is not "How *long* must I wait?" but "*How* must I wait?" We customarily think of "waiting" for a period of time, waiting until something happens. But by "wait" the scriptures probably mean "attend," "pay attention to," "listen to," or "heed." When we wait upon the Lord, we listen for direction. Regular stillness, the practice and the discipline of stillness and peaceful waiting, ensures that we will hear those directions when they come.

As I sat there thinking about waiting and attending, I realized that I hear small promptings, sometimes. Sometimes the promptings are so quiet and so gentle that I barely hear them; they are on the threshold of my consciousness only. Sometimes, although I have an awareness that they're there, I still miss them, don't heed them. It's always my loss when I don't. Now, here's a question: why are the promptings so gentle, so quiet? Why not dramatic and unmistakable? The heavens can send dramatic messages, without question. So why is the still small voice so still, so small? I think we are being trained to be sensitive attenders, sensitive listeners, not only to inner voices and divine whisperings but also to outer voices and garbled mutterings, to the messages other people give us indirectly, even silently, because they can give them no other way.

For instance, Jill, a social worker, was meeting one-on-one over a period of weeks with several troubled teens from a poor area of a big city. These interviews were being videotaped for later study. One girl, Louise, was especially hard to reach. She did not respond at all to Jill's overtures. In fact, Jill felt she was getting nowhere and had just about decided to stop working with Louise. One night she reviewed the last videotape. And she saw something she had never seen before. There was Louise, as usual, head down, eyes averted, silent, answering only in grunts and monosyllables. But the video clearly showed Louise with one arm stretched out towards the social worker, silently asking for the help she couldn't ask for directly. At the next session, Jill quietly reached out and took Louise's hand as they talked—and that day the floodgates opened, the tears came, and the talk and the healing began. Jill had heard the silent message.

Our children, our young people, our old people, those we know and love well, and strangers — all at times give us crucial messages in subtle or barely perceptible ways, as we give similar messages to them. I believe one way we learn to hear these messages is by training ourselves in stillness and by attending to the silence.

After attending to the silence above the temple for a while, Mickey and I drove over to campus. West of the Maeser Building where I have my office is a lovely hill; it used to be called Temple Hill, before the temple was built farther north. It is a gently sloping hill with a rich inviting lawn. I lay on the grass and could see, for 360 degrees, the mountains of Zion — Y Mount and Rock Canyon to the east, Mount Nebo and Maple Mountain to the south, West Mountain and the Oquirrhs, and of course, magnificent Timpanogos to the north. It was a day to make Wordsworth sharpen his pen in tranquillity, a day to make the Welsh poet Dylan Thomas young and easy once more.

But as I lay and watched the clouds float by, my thoughts too floated, and they drifted to the future, and they became anxious about one thing and another, one task or another yet undone. I tried to bring my mind back to the present, to attend and wait in peace and in trust. But again my thoughts rushed to the future. As they did, however, a phrase drifted into my mind: "This, too, will be given." With the phrase came understanding: I knew at once what the phrase meant. It meant that in stillness we receive vision and revision; that as well as experiencing the fullness of the present moment, we can receive promptings about the future and the past. Countless times, when I have been fretting and fussing about the outcome of some future event, if I have been able to quiet myself, I have received not only general comfort and reassurance but also specific direction, specific vision for the situation. Many of you have had such experiences. We can have more of them; we can start by asking and listening. And by waiting. We can understand not only the future, but also the past, and by understanding it, change it in crucial ways, if we reflect in stillness and openness. There is much more to be said about changing the past, but that is a subject for another day. "This too will be given."

As the sun moved towards the west, Mickey and I rode west, first going down through the rural areas of the county, down towards Palmyra and Lake Shore, and then turning towards West Mountain. The wind picked up, and the shrubs were whipping as I parked the van and walked the dog along a rocky path.

I began to see the process of contemplation more clearly. Silence can lead to stillness, which facilitates meditation or reflection. Reflection leads often to prayer. Prayer of the most useful sort, I think, leads to receptivity, to attending, to waiting on the Lord. And if we are receptive and hear the whisperings, then we are led to more reflection and meditation, and to an ever deeper stillness.

I began to think that prayer is less a deed than a condition, less something we *do* than something we *are*. To most of us, prayer means asking for something or expressing thanks for something. But there is, of course, more. We are told to pray always. We read of the Savior praying throughout the night. Are we talking here about endless repetition of requests, pleading and repeating our petitions? Or does "pray always" mean to be ever receptive, ever attending, listening, waiting?

Annie Dillard reminds us, "The waiting itself is the thing." Is it possible that the praying itself is the thing, more important than whatever we ask for, whatever we say? I think perhaps so. I have also come to know that some things can be communicated only in silence. The poet John Keats wrote, "Heard melodies are sweet, but those unheard are sweeter."[4] He was drawing our attention to those things communicated only in silence, in stillness.

That Sunday when I went out into the valley because I felt empty, I was ministered to by the earth itself. Joseph Smith

taught that the earth has a spirit; and I have learned that that
spirit is a healing spirit. The poet Gerard Manley Hopkins, a
man of religion, a priest, looked at what was happening to the
world already in his time and saw the fragmenting and the
turmoil that were growing everywhere, but nonetheless he
wrote:

And for all this, nature is never spent;
  There lives the dearest freshness deep down things;
And though the last lights off the black West went
  Oh, morning, at the brown brink eastward, springs—

Because the Holy Ghost over the bent
  World broods with warm breast
    and with ah! bright wings.[5]

There is deep down freshness for those who feel temporarily burned out. There are unfailing springs for those of us
whose buckets are momentarily empty. There is morning for
those whose world seems black. There is peace. And there is
comfort. Mother Earth, as I have said, has a healing spirit. But
we can find that healing stillness in other places as well as in
nature. We can be still and find peace in our own homes (even
if the bathroom is the only sanctuary), or in silent intimate
communication with a spouse, a sister, a friend. Often music
helps to still the chatter within. Balm of Gilead is freely available, a freely given gift.

It is my hope, it is my prayer, that each of you can increasingly discover your own sources of comfort, peace, and reassurance. My prayer is that if inner voices nag at you, telling
you that you do not do enough, try enough, give enough, that
you will still those voices. Silence those voices. Tune out the
static and attend to the voices that speak comfort and love and
assurance, for it is love and confidence, not fear and anxiety,
that will motivate us to press forward with hope in Christ.

Notes
1. Annie Dillard, *Pilgrim at Tinker Creek* (New York: Harper Magazine Press,
   1974), p. 265.

2. Samuel Johnson, "On the Spring," *Rambler,* no. 5, rpt. in *Samuel Johnson: Rasselas, Poems, and Selected Prose*, 3d ed., ed. Bertrand H. Bronson (New York: Holt, Rinehart and Winston, 1958), p. 74.
3. T. S. Eliot, "The Hollow Men," *The Complete Poems and Plays* (New York: Harcourt, Brace and Co., 1952), p. 56.
4. John Keats, "Ode on a Grecian Urn," rpt. in *The Norton Anthology of Poetry*, ed. Arthur M. Eastman (New York: W. W. Norton and Co., 1970), p. 698.
5. Gerard Manley Hopkins, "God's Grandeur," rpt. in *The Norton Anthology of Poetry*, ed. Arthur M. Eastman (New York: W. W. Norton and Co., 1970), p. 887.

VOICES FROM NAUVOO

We must cherish one another, watch over one another, and gain instruction, that we may all sit down in heaven together.

—Lucy Mack Smith

The sacred spirituality that graced the Nauvoo Relief Society is still our birthright.

—Maureen Ursenbach Beecher

Voices of the Sisters

SUSAN ELIZABETH HOWE

The following dramatic reading was presented in the opening session of the 1991 Women's Conference to inaugurate the sesquicentennial celebration of the founding of Relief Society.

NARRATOR: March 17, 1992, will mark 150 years since the formation of the Relief Society. Today we inaugurate a celebration of that society, of the good it has done, by remembering the women of the Church, their trials, their strength, the legacy of love and achievement they have left us.

(Lights on audience go down. To a musical background, a series of slides appear on a large screen, slides featuring women in many different situations: of various ages, races, and occupations, in Church and home life, at work and play. The slides are arranged in reverse chronological order, so that the times featured become earlier and earlier. The last three slides are pictures of Eliza R. Snow, Sarah Kimball, and Emma Smith, and these slides remain on the screen. A spotlight comes up on Eliza, Sarah, and Emma, dressed in costumes of their day and standing around a podium.)

EMMA *(looking at the audience around her)*: My, my, my. All these ladies are members? Sisters, we are overjoyed at the growth of our Society. What an impressive group.

ELIZA: Though I must say, Sister Emma, I take exception to their manner of dress. *(Eliza particularly turns to the women*

Susan Elizabeth Howe, assistant professor of English at Brigham Young University, has been the editor of Exponent II *and managing editor of* The Denver Quarterly. *Her play* Burdens of Earth *has been performed at BYU, and her poems have appeared in* The New Yorker, Shenandoah, Tar River Poetry, Prairie Schooner, *and other journals.*

seated on the stand — the Relief Society general presidency and the Women's Conference officials.) The styles you sisters have succumbed to are highly immodest. I am surprised that no one has urged you to retrench.

EMMA: Now, Eliza, we must remember this is a different age. We are not qualified to sit in judgment on customs so far removed from our own time.

ELIZA: We are always qualified to stand for the highest morality.

EMMA: But when judging others, we are not always qualified to know what the highest morality is.

ELIZA *(showing some agitation):* It is most uncomfortable to have you lecture me about judging others. There was a time when you were quite willing to judge me.

EMMA: Your behavior certainly warranted —

SARAH *(breaking in, gently scolding):* Sisters, this discussion is not exactly to the point. Remember why we have come? To join in celebrating the one hundred fiftieth anniversary of our Female Relief Society?

EMMA *(addressing audience):* Oh, yes, please excuse us.

ELIZA: Emma and I are much more reconciled now than we have been in the past.

EMMA: Though we still have our differences.

SARAH *(hurriedly, again cutting in):* And we are so pleased to be here with you, in this, this — Now what in the world is this facility for? It seems cavernous and distant for a Society meeting. Why would the sisters choose to assemble here?

ELIZA: Perhaps we can ask. *(They turn to the narrator, who rises from her seat.)*

NARRATOR: This is a sports facility.

SARAH: A sports facility? For races and wrestling? You have devoted so many resources to gentlemen's recreation?

NARRATOR: This facility is used for basketball, a game you may not know of. And actually, sports are activities many women also value. We are holding our conference here at

Brigham Young University because the buildings are large enough to accommodate —

EMMA *(breaking in):* Brigham Young University? Wouldn't a gathering of our society be more appropriately convened at a university named after Joseph?

SARAH *(keeping the others on track):* Sister Emma, as you see, there are thousands of women before us, and I assume they would like to hear what we might tell them about the formation of our Society.

ELIZA: And perhaps they could tell us about the state of the Society today.

EMMA: I, too, would be interested in knowing what they have done with the Female Relief Society, how it benefits the Church and the world, what it will contribute in the future. *(To audience)* You see, Sister Eliza and I do agree entirely on some things. *(Emma and Eliza nod to each other.)*

ELIZA: In our time there was much good done by the Society—both in Nauvoo and in our lovely Deseret.

SARAH: The Female Relief Society of Nauvoo was a benevolent, charitable organization, providing help for many poor, as well as contributing much to the comfort of the workers who built the temple. We were very proud of the Society in our day.

ELIZA: As we were of those established later, through the years. By means of the Relief Societies, the ladies have made remarkable contributions to the Church.

SARAH: What no one could do alone, we could accomplish together because of our commitment to the gospel of Jesus Christ as restored by the prophet Joseph.

EMMA: Often the work has been done at personal sacrifice or as women have borne great sorrow.

ELIZA: Sisters, before we begin interrupting each other and confusing our listeners, perhaps we should each take a turn at the pulpit, saying what we have to say. *(Emma and Sarah nod agreement.)*

EMMA: And Sarah, as you were the first to suggest that we

37

organize, we must defer to you. You speak now, and Sister Eliza and I will follow.

SARAH: Thank you.

(A musical interlude begins as Emma and Eliza are seated and Sarah begins to speak. The spotlight continues on Sarah; the slide becomes Sarah alone.)

SARAH: I like to think that our society arose from our own initiative, our own desires to serve. You see, Miss Cook, a maiden lady, was living in my home and working as a seamstress, and one day she said, "I should like to help the temple workers, but I have nothing to give them." I had a bolt of cloth, so I told her I would furnish the material if she would make some shirts for the workmen. Then we wondered if some of our neighbors might wish to combine their means and efforts with ours, so we met together in my parlor and decided to organize. We asked Sister Eliza Snow *(she nods to Eliza)* to prepare a constitution and bylaws, which she did and showed to the prophet. He said they were the best he had ever seen, but that he had something better for us. "I will organize the sisters," he told us, "under the priesthood, after a pattern of the priesthood." So we met above Brother Joseph's store the following Thursday and were organized. He proposed that we elect a presiding officer and that she should choose two counselors to assist her. We chose Sister Emma Smith as our president, and she chose Sarah Cleveland and Mother Elizabeth Ann Whitney as counselors. Brother Joseph was very proud of his beautiful wife. He said, "Let these women preside over this society just as the Presidency presides over the Church." And he offered to instruct us from time to time.

After some discussion, Sister Eliza, whom we naturally selected as our secretary, suggested that the name of our organization be *The Female Relief Society of Nauvoo*, and that motion was unanimously carried. You see, our name became our purpose—to provide relief from want and suffering. We accepted donations from those who had enough and to spare and offered what we collected to anyone in need. It was Brother

Joseph who made the first donation—the considerable sum of five dollars. He told us, "All I shall have to give to the poor, I shall give to this society." He had great faith in us, and we did not let him down. We collected everything from food, flax, and wool to soap, bedding, even jewelry, and distributed our goods to those in need. I remember our providing for a Brother Henderson, a worthy widower with nine children. And once Sister Sessions offered two pairs of pantaloons and a shirt to an unknown man whose appearance revealed how little he had. Sister Woolley gave the red yarn she had been saving for a carpet to make mittens for the temple workers. And we once paid the fare for a destitute sister who had to get to New Orleans. As Sister Peck said in one of our meetings, "We have not said 'be ye warmed and clothed' without trying to do it."

Sisters, do you still remember that the purpose of this society is to care for those in need? Surely there are as many needy in your day as there were in our own. Open your hearts to the Spirit, who will teach you what you can give and how you can give it. Learn to hear how sisters throughout our history have received and given help.[1] *(Near the end of Sarah's speech, a musical background begins. When she finishes speaking, the spotlight dims. Then, accompanied by slides, the following taped voices are heard.)*

ELLEN DOUGLAS[2] *(with English accent):* In 1842 my family and I came from England to be with the saints, but by April of 1844 my husband was dead, and my children and I were very ill. After I'd begun to get well I went down into the city on a visit. A kindly woman where I was staying asked me to make application to the Female Relief Society for some clothing. I refused, but she said I needed something because I had been so long sick, and if I would not go myself, she would do it for me. At last I agreed and we went to one of the sisters. She asked me what I needed most. I told her that I needed many things. While I was sick my children had worn out their clothes because I could not mend them. She said she would do the best she could for me. They came over in a few days with a wagon and fetched me such a present as I have never before received in the world.

CONTEMPORARY SISTER 1[3]: The Christmas after my divorce I was out of work and had little for my family. A sister in the ward stopped by and left six hundred dollars—one hundred for each of my five children and a hundred for me. When I came home and found her gift, I was so overcome I couldn't even call her. I cried for hours until I was finally able to thank her with all my heart. —A sister in California

LUCY MESERVE SMITH[4]: In 1856 I was set apart and blessed to preside over the Relief Society. At October conference news came about the handcart companies. President Young was anxious for fear they would be caught in the snow in the mountains, so we didn't go on with the conference. The sisters stripped off their petticoats, stockings, and everything they could spare, right there in the Tabernacle, and piled the clothing into wagons to send to the saints in the mountains.

That winter we did all we could to comfort the needy as they came in with handcarts. I never took more satisfaction and I might say pleasure in any labor I ever performed in my life, such a unanimity of feeling prevailed. My counselors and I wallowed through the snow until our clothes were wet a foot high to get things together to give. The sisters pieced blocks, carded bats, quilted, and got together I think twenty-seven quilts, besides a great amount of other clothing, in one winter for the needy.

CONTEMPORARY SISTER 2 *(South African accent):* Our homemaking counselor appealed to us to knit squares and put them together as lap rugs for old age homes. What a sweet, warm response when we distributed these rugs and saw the joy these gifts of love brought into the lives of the aged. One blind soul of eighty-six years made me tell her all the colors in her rug and had me run her fingers over it again and again to get the feel of it. How special for us to feel the tangible love and support of each other as we have performed this work. —A sister in Pretoria, South Africa

(A change in the music as the spotlight again shines on Emma, now at the podium, and a picture of Emma is shown on the screen.)

EMMA: A month before we organized the Relief Society and I became president, I gave birth to and lost a son. What a trial it was to me to lose another child. But one thing my own sorrow taught me was compassion; as I observed others I learned that the life of almost everyone is touched by suffering. We have to love and comfort each other in order to gain the strength to turn our energies to the work of the Lord. There were stories from our own Society of sisters in great need, who, though they wanted to give to others, needed help themselves. I was touched to hear Sister Husted's story. As donations were being accepted, she arose in tears and said she had nothing to give. She spoke of the death of her husband in Missouri, and the trouble she was under to get a living. Counselor Whitney comforted this sorrowing sister, telling her it was not her duty to give but rather she should be helped by the Society. Sisters began to offer her what they could—some flour, a bushel of corn, a calico dress. As our beloved Mother Smith said in one of our early meetings, "We must cherish one another, watch over one another, comfort one another, and gain instruction, that we may all sit down in heaven together."

Sisters, we will never progress as a society until we learn to love each other without reservation. Until each member feels she can speak freely in our meetings of her own sin or sorrow and know that her sisters love her and do not condemn, our power to do good will be circumscribed. We must love with the true love of Christ; we must sorrow with those who sorrow and take on the burdens of each other's hearts. I would have us listen to sisters who speak from their own depths, that we may learn to hear. And so you will know of my own need to grow, listen first to what I have finally been able to understand—Sister Eliza's sorrow at the death of one who was beloved of us both. *(During the final part of Emma's speech, a musical background begins. As she stops speaking, the spotlight*

41

turns off, and slides appear on the screen, as the following taped voices are heard.)

ELIZA *(voice only):* After the martyrdom of my husband Joseph, I was prostrate with grief and besought the Lord with all the fervency of my soul to permit me to follow the Prophet at once and not to leave me in so dark and wicked a world. So set was my mind that I could not be comforted, and I could not cease that prayer of my heart. Finally my dear Joseph came to me and told me that I must not continue to supplicate the Lord in that way. Joseph told me that his work upon earth was completed—but mine was not. The Lord desired me, and so did my husband, to live many years and assist in carrying on the great latter-day work. He said I must be of good courage and help to cheer and lighten the burdens of others. And that I must turn my thoughts away from my own loneliness and seek to console our people in their bereavement and sorrow.
—Eliza R. Snow

CONTEMPORARY SISTER 3: The greatest struggle I have right now is to breech an estrangement with a son who feels we don't love him and his family as we do our other five children because fourteen years ago he decided to leave the Church and join his wife's church. For the past three years, no matter how we try, he and his wife keep avoiding us or refusing to talk. I've been praying intensely about this sorrow, and my goal is to meet soon and talk through our differences. —A sister in Oregon

MARTHA CRAGUN COX[5]: January 11, 1871. I received from heaven the gift of a daughter, a mite of a creature weighing seven pounds and eleven ounces. As I looked at the waxen figure beside me on the bed I felt I had all I needed in this life to make up my sum of happiness. Two short days she adorned my life. A lingering difficult birth had done its worst for her and on the morning of the thirteenth the spirit warned me to call the father and family and the elders. They saw no cause for alarm and attributed my uneasiness to the weakened state of my nerves, but to humor me they proceeded to bless and name her. Scarcely was this accomplished when the spirit took its flight. This was my first real sorrow and the bitterest disappointment I had ever known.

CONTEMPORARY SISTER 4: All through my son David's struggle with cancer, Church members helped us in so many ways: with food, visits, phone calls, prayers, the temple prayer roll, hugs. But David's death did not mean an end to love and support. A sister from our ward who had taught David in many of his Primary classes visited us, sometimes two or three times a week, for well over a year. She was so impressed by David's way of handling his illness that she decided to write a book about him. She let us talk and talk, cry and cry, never being judgmental or critical. It was only through her patience and love that we were able to keep our sanity. For many reasons the book was never published, but that isn't important any more. The fact that one person took the time to listen to us and be genuinely concerned for our well-being has left a lasting impression on my husband and me. —Patricia Oparowski, Medford, Massachusetts

ELLIS REYNOLDS SHIPP[6]: November 10, 1875, two o'clock in the morning. What a strange fatality! This morning I start for Philadelphia to attend the Medical College. Oh, Heavenly Father, give me strength to endure the separation from my loved ones, and power to succeed in my endeavors to gain a knowledge of medicine — that my life may be noble and useful upon the earth. Into thy hands, kind Father, do I commit my treasures.

CONTEMPORARY SISTER 5: Never in all my life did I think I would go to China. And yet the day my husband Elliot received a call from BYU asking us if we would teach English at a Chinese university for a year, I felt that this was something we should do. So just two months after the Tiananmen Square massacre, on our forty-second wedding anniversary, we left for Nanjing Forestry University. I had imagined that the year would be a challenge, but I had no idea of how difficult it would become. The food was a great shock; I lost thirty pounds in two months.

I also suffered serious health problems. Soon the weather got cold, and we learned that none of the buildings were heated. We didn't have enough clothes to keep warm, and I became very frightened. And lonely. Hardly anyone at the university spoke English, and Chinese couples both work six days a week. Gradually, as the days went by, I became more and more depressed. I woke up every morning feeling awful, actually sick, hating to face the day. Finally I didn't think I could stand it any longer. The afternoon after my husband had informed everyone of my decision to return home, I again got on my knees to pray while my husband was away teaching his afternoon class. I prayed harder than I ever had before, telling the Lord that I wanted to stay but didn't know how I could. I asked that if he wanted me to stay, he would bless me with a feeling of happiness. Later that day a feeling of calm happiness washed over me, and I knew the Lord wanted me to remain in China. After that things gradually got better, and I even enjoyed the remainder of the year. George Q. Cannon said that after we have passed through trying scenes and endured afflictions, we look back at them and are thankful and say they have been more fruitful to us than any other scenes that we have passed through. So it has been for me: I dearly love the Chinese people. I would not take anything for the experiences I had in China.
—Maralyne Howe, Pleasant Grove, Utah

EMMELINE B. WELLS[7]: Wednesday, September 30, 1874. O how miserable I am in regard to some of my children, almost heart-broken. Every nerve in my whole system is unstrung. All the anguish a mother can feel in seeing her chidren do wrong I feel tonight. My heart is bleeding almost. Misery and darkness, and I have no one to go to for comfort or shelter, no strong arm to lean upon, no bosom bared for me, no protection or comfort in my husband. My little ones are all tenderness—oh, what should I do without them—but they are only weak themselves and need to be nourished by me. O if my husband could only love me even a little and not seem so perfectly indifferent to any sensation of that kind. He cannot know the craving of my nature. He is surrounded with love on every side, and I am cast out. O my poor aching heart. Where shall it rest its burden? Only on the Lord, only to Him can I look. Every other avenue seems closed against me. O help me, Father in Heaven, to overcome and resist temptation in every form or shape.

Thursday, April 1, 1875. Went to the Fast Meeting in the morning. Had an excellent meeting. Went again in the afternoon to our own Relief Society meeting, over which I preside. I feel deeply the great responsibility resting upon me in being called to fill this public office; but hope to be guided and sustained by the Holy Spirit in this calling and duty that I may keep humble and be qualified to do all things that are required of me, and please my husband and gain his good will and favor, as also all with whom I am associated.

CONTEMPORARY SISTER 6: The deep sorrow following my divorce drove me almost to despair. Because of my constant determination to remain active in the Church, I now have the strong conviction that there is no other way than to live the gospel. I have had to overcome the odds of unmerited gossip, my friends not being the same, many ward and stake people not understanding, my children rebelling, having to work full time, and dealing with discouragement and depression and financial difficulty and health problems. But I continued to attend all of my Church meetings, hold down a calling, and attend the temple once a week. In time the negatives began to fade, and I have experienced respect and admiration from my friends and associates. I do not take my children's problems so personally any more. I have less guilt and frustration, more self-confidence and self-esteem. The gospel has become more precious to me and my joy in serving has become greater.
—A sister in California

(The slide becomes Eliza alone; a spotlight rises on her standing at the podium; there is a short musical interlude.)

ELIZA: You sisters will not find a greater example of compassion, and the ability to put aside her own sorrows for the needs of others, than in Sister Emma, beloved of our prophet

Joseph, the first wife of his heart. In her behavior to me, Sister Emma has taught us today that we may best serve the Lord as we ourselves love and forgive.

Today I, too, would like to bless you, both by instruction and by the example of what has been done. When we arrived in the Valley of the Great Salt Lake and began to establish our homes, the domestic responsibilities of the sisters required most of their attention. But by 1868 the time had come for us to act in a larger sphere. President Brigham Young recognized our potential; he said he saw a great amount of talent, and even statesmanship in the community of ladies. He instructed us that if we would trim our minds, contemplate subjects we were likely to pass over, and exercise the rights and privileges that were legitimately ours, we could have an immense influence in guiding, directing, and controlling human affairs. He asked me to direct all the wards in organizing Relief Societies, to help the sisters expand their capacity to serve. To me it was quite a mission, and I took much pleasure in its performance. I remember in the First Ward in our city of Great Salt Lake, Bishop Henry Moon assembled the sisters in the ward school room. He said they were called to be organized into a Female Relief Society according to the true order as instituted by Joseph Smith the Prophet. As he did not understand the order of the society himself, he requested me to take hold in organizing the sisters in a proper manner. The Female Relief Society was no ordinary thing. Our beloved prophet Joseph taught that the organization of the sisters was necessary for the perfection of the Church of Christ in any dispensation.

But many of the sisters were so unsure of themselves as not even to be able to speak out in our meetings. Once a sister said that if she could talk about house cleaning, she might talk, but I answered, "Do not let your president have to say all. Has not God endowed you with the gift of speech? If you are endowed with the spirit of God, no matter how simple your thoughts may be, they will be edifying to those who hear you." It was deeply gratifying to me to see the sisters grow and expand their usefulness in a wide and extensive sphere. We found ample scope for our every power and capability for doing good. And one of the most successful presidents is here with us today—Sister Sarah Kimball, who became president of the Fifteenth Ward Relief Society. She was the first to build a Relief Society Hall, a place for the sisters to meet. The Relief Society meetings were held on the top floor, while the sisters ran a store on the first floor. They sold goods they had manufactured and used their money to assist the poor. And the compassion of Sister Kimball's society was not limited to the Saints or even to the Valley. After the great fire in Chicago in 1871, the Fifteenth Ward Relief Society directed a wide effort to collect money and goods throughout Deseret. They eventually sent some $14,000 to the relief effort.

Then came the challenge Brigham Young set for us to store wheat. Sister Emmeline B. Wells headed the project. The reason it was given to the sisters was explained by her husband, Elder Daniel H. Wells, counselor to Brigham Young. "The men have been tried for years," he said, "but they have continued to let the grain go. Now we want to see if the sisters will be more successful." Well, the sisters were successful. By October 1877, the Fifteenth Ward Relief Society had completed a fireproof granary built of rock, with a tin roof, a brick floor, and a concrete base. It held a thousand bushels. Throughout our settlements, granaries were raised by the Relief Societies. You can see how our sisters were being enlarged in their capacity to serve.

And the influence of our Relief Societies continued to grow. The silk industry in Utah was mostly developed through the Relief Societies. We began a paper, *The Woman's Exponent*, that directed its messages to the sisters for over forty years. We also became responsible for health care, opening hospitals and providing for the training of doctors and nurses. Through these years we could see our power to do good expanding along with our ability to serve the Lord.

So sisters, I would advise you of these things. Do not be content with any limitations on your capacity to serve. Develop your talents; develop your means. Open your hearts to comprehend the needs of the world in your own time. Listen to other sisters and take counsel from what they have to say. *(During the last section of Eliza's speech, again a musical background begins. As she finishes speaking, the spotlight on her fades, slides appear on the screen, and the following voices are heard.)*

EMILY S. RICHARDS[8]: The first time Aunt Eliza asked me to speak in a meeting, I could not. She said, "Never mind, but when you are asked to speak again, try and have something to say," and I did. I learned to speak with more and more ease until finally, in 1889, I addressed the annual convention of the National Woman Suffrage Association in Washington, D.C. One journalist even wrote that I was "reserved, self-possessed, dignified, as pure and sweet as an angel." She also said this: "It was not the words themselves but the gentle spirit that went with the words and carried winning grace to every heart."

CONTEMPORARY SISTER 7: I'm older (eighty-one), though I don't spend much time thinking about it, for I still expect myself to do as much and as well as the younger ones. I guess I've always expected too much, and because of that attitude, I have not had the best opinion of myself. This morning I was playing the organ in the temple, and instead of agonizing because I'm not as fine an organist as Bonnie Goodliffe, I just sat there being thankful that I could produce beautiful music and that I was doing what the Lord wanted me to do. I realized I was doing the Lord's work as much as very prominent Church leaders, and I began to feel that I am of great worth. — Pauline Atkinson, Provo, Utah

ELIZA R. SNOW *(voice only):* In August 1878, Mrs. Emmeline B. Wells and I, after attending a conference of the Relief Society in Farmington, Davis County, dined with Mrs. Aurelia Rogers. During our conversation, Mrs. Rogers expressed a desire that something more could be effected for the cultivation and improvement of the children morally and spiritually than was being done through the influence of day and Sunday Schools.

After consulting together a few moments, I asked Mrs. Rogers if she was willing to take the responsibility and labor on herself of presiding over the children of that settlement, provided the Bishop of the Ward sanctioned the movement. She replied in the affirmative. — Eliza R. Snow

AURELIA S. ROGERS[9]: While thinking over what had to be done for the best good of the children, I seemed to be carried away in the spirit, or at least I experienced a feeling of untold happiness which lasted three days and nights. During that time nothing could worry or irritate me; if my little ones were fretful, or the work went wrong, I had patience, could control in kindness, and manage my household affairs easily. This was a testimony to me that what was being done was of God.

CONTEMPORARY SISTER 8: I used to be a visiting teacher to a sister whom I was never successful in reaching. I always felt unwelcome, and that she was annoyed at our intrusion. When I was called as Relief Society president, I assigned her to another set of visiting teachers. Several months had passed when I began having thoughts of her come into my mind, along with the words "Tell my daughter that I love her." This continued for two weeks, and each time I thought it, I dismissed it. I could just imagine the reaction I might receive if I told her such a thing. One Friday afternoon, I was walking into my home with my arms full of groceries, and with a force I can't describe, a picture of her face came to my mind with the words *"I told you to tell my daughter I love her!"* I set the groceries on the floor, ran to the car, and drove to see her. When I arrived, her house was in great disarray and her two young daughters were cavorting wildly around the living room. The sister was agitated and extremely dejected. With all of the confusion in the house, I asked her if she would walk out to my car with me because I wanted to share something with her. *I was afraid!* I did not know how this remote, often aggravated sister would react to the message I had for her. I began by saying, "I know you will probably think this is crazy, but I have a message for you from Heavenly Father. He said to tell you that He loves you." This sweet sister started to weep. She cried and I cried, and we held one another. When she could finally speak, she told me that her husband had left her two weeks before. He told her that he didn't love her any more and moved to a distant state. During the following two weeks, she had prayed and prayed for help and none came. She decided that no one loved her, that her mother could be a better mother to her daughters than she could be, and so she had decided to end it all. As we talked that evening and on many future occasions, she was overwhelmed that the Lord loved her, heard her prayers, and sent someone to help. —A sister in Georgia

AMY BROWN LYMAN[10]: Women have a very acute sense of situations and are often, through this, able to cope successfully with very difficult problems. They have sympathy, imagination, patience, a spontaneous eagerness to help, and a warm good will, all of which are real assets and help them to find their way easily into the hearts of those who suffer.

CONTEMPORARY SISTER 9: Dear President Elaine Jack, my name is Sister Chudyba from Poland. I was at your office in May. At that time I was the Relief Society president in Warsaw. I now have the honor to write to you and let you know that I am in Moscow as a missionary, and that we have Relief Society here in Moscow. Nina Lejontieva is the president. She was baptized this summer. Now we have five baptized women here and every Sunday from twenty to twenty-five new investigators. It is nice to watch people singing hymns in Russian and having the same organization as everywhere. —Sister Chudyba

SUSA YOUNG GATES[11]: For years we have toiled and joyed together in this glorious work of love and amelioration of suffering which we call Relief Society work. Wherever our people have gone, there have been Relief Society workers gathering up their means from each other's scanty stores to minister to those who were sick or in want, giving encouragement to the weary and heartsick, while warning the wayward and thoughtless. We have nursed the sick of our people, robed the dying for their last resting-place, fed the hungry, visited the orphan, and succored the needy. This, sisters, is, has been, and ever will be the true spirit and genius of this whole organization. We charge you to keep this spirit burning bright in your bosoms.

CONTEMPORARY SISTER 10: My gratitude goes to my Heavenly Father for the opportunity of being a witness to this unique historic day, when the Relief Society in the First Surulere Branch has grown to the stage of organizing a bazaar and social. This occasion makes us reflect on the counsel of our early missionaries, who encouraged us to remember that we are the pioneer sisters in this country, that if the sisters focus their thoughts on the struggles of the pioneer sisters in Nauvoo, remembering that the Relief Society membership, which now runs in millions, was started by a few dedicated sisters, and that if we emulate their actions and work and live like Latter-day Saint women, very soon we will experience a wonderful rapid growth of the Church in this land and the membership of the Relief Society. Today I feel great joy being a witness to the manifestation of that vision. —Cecilia C. Ogbonna, Lagos, Nigeria Mission *(Music ends; slide returns to Eliza; spotlight on Eliza at the podium.)*

ELIZA[12]: May I be the voice for the three of us to thank you for letting us come to your gathering today. We leave you our blessings and our love. Let your first business be to perform your duties at home. But, inasmuch as you are wise stewards, you will find time for social duties, because these are incumbent upon us as daughters and mothers in Zion. By seeking to perform every duty you will find that your capacity will increase, and you will be astonished at what you can accomplish. I do not pretend to know where you should devote your efforts, but I assume that your wonderful Relief Society president knows. Listen to her counsel as she speaks to you now. The Lord help us. The Lord is with his Saints, and inasmuch as we continue faithful, we shall be those that will be crowned in the presence of God and the Lamb. You, my sisters, if you are faithful, will become Queens of Queens, and Priestesses unto the Most High God. These are your callings. We have only to discharge our duties. By and by our labors will be past, and our names will be crowned with everlasting honor, and be had in everlasting remembrance among the Saints of the Most High God.

Notes

1. Information on the early history of Relief Society and the lives of Sarah Kimball, Emma Smith, and Eliza R. Snow was obtained from Maureen Ursenbach Beecher and Jill Mulvay Derr. For a fuller account, see Jill Mulvay Derr, Janath R. Cannon, and Maureen Ursenbach Beecher, *Women of Covenant: The Story of Relief Society, 1842–1992* (Salt Lake City: Deseret Book Co., 1992). See also Maureen Ursenbach Beecher's *Eliza and Her Sisters* (Salt Lake City: Aspen Books, 1991).
2. Ellen Douglas [Parker], letter to "Father and Mother," 2 June 1842, typescript, LDS Church Archives, Salt Lake City, Utah.
3. The words of the contemporary sisters have been taken from actual letters and questionnaires received by the author and by Relief Society General President Elaine Jack. The names of certain sisters have been omitted and their home addresses changed to ensure their privacy.
4. "Lucy Meserve Smith (1817–1892)," *Women's Voices: An Untold History of the Latter-day Saints, 1830–1900*, ed. Kenneth W. Godfrey, Audrey M. Godfrey, Jill Mulvay Derr (Salt Lake City: Deseret Book Co., 1982), pp. 268–69; hereafter cited as *Women's Voices*.
5. "Martha Cragun Cox (1852–1932)," *Women's Voices*, p. 281.
6. *While Others Slept: Autobiography and Journal of Ellis Reynolds Shipp, M.D.*, ed. Ellis Shipp Musser (Salt Lake City: Bookcraft, 1985), pp. 172–73.
7. "Emmeline B. Wells (1829–1921)," *Women's Voices*, pp. 298, 306.
8. "General Conference: Relief Society," *Woman's Exponent* 30 (December 1901): 54.
9. Aurelia Spencer Rogers, *Life Sketches of Orson Spencer and Others, and History of Primary Work* (Salt Lake City: George Q. Cannon & Sons Co., 1898), p. 212.
10. *The Relief Society Magazine: A Legacy Remembered, 1914–1970*, ed. Carol L. Clark (Salt Lake City: Deseret Book, Co., 1982), p. 36.
11. Ibid., p. 49.
12. *Millennial Star* 36 (13 January 1874): 21.

From Nauvoo: Sisterhood and the Spirit

MAUREEN URSENBACH BEECHER

Being adult, female, and Latter-day Saint did not always, as it does now, dictate membership in Relief Society; nevertheless those who grew up Mormon have all felt the Society's impact on their lives. Perhaps it was for you, as it was for me, a note warning us kids away from the tempting dessert on the table: "Don't touch! This is for Relief Society." Or the sympathy in our Scottish neighbor's voice as she spotted me playing alone in the yard: "Today's your mother's Relief, is it?" Not until I delved seriously, with Janath Cannon and Jill Mulvay Derr, into the details of Relief Society history did I realize how much a part of that history is me, and how much I am, as are all LDS women, part of that history.[1]

As were many of you, I was reared under quilt frames. During and following World War II, when there was so much to do not only to support the war effort but to provide relief packages for European Saints, Relief Society mothers would secure their preschoolers in the circle of their chairs to play while the women quilted. Well do I remember that prison of lisle-stockinged knees. I hated Relief Society then. My mother, for as long as I can remember, was president of her ward society and would drag me along on her visiting teaching rounds—she seemed always to have assigned herself the remotest calls, five miles beyond the end of the street car line. War refugees—D.P.'s, we called them, with scorn in our voices

Maureen Ursenbach Beecher is a professor of English and senior research historian in the Joseph Fielding Smith Institute for Church History at Brigham Young University. She is a coauthor of Women of Covenant: The Story of Relief Society, 1842–1992. *Canadian by birth, she is married to Dale F. Beecher and is the mother of two children.*

53

for their strange clothing and stranger accents — packed our communities. More than once Mother filled our basement bedroom with whole families. I have no memory of where she put everybody when the Perrys came from Wales — triplets, twins, and a single at each end of the family. I learned through her open heart the route through tolerance to acceptance to love.

The hours Mom spent on the telephone seemed to me a malicious avoidance of my needs; in fact, she was recording blood types and procuring donors for Red Cross clinics, or gathering volunteers to roll bandages, or ascertaining what nursing skills could be mobilized among the women if need arose. After the war, the women's habits of economy and making-do remained: often, of a Saturday morning, on word from the fruit wholesaler, she would call to tell the women that there were peaches, or pears, or some other perishable fruit available at half price. I could always tell at church Sunday which women had sat up half the night canning fruit: their heavy eyelids and stained thumbs gave them away. And the hand-me-downs. Most of my Mormon friends dressed, as I did, in made-overs, not always well tailored. As Mae Turner would say of the ungainly sweaters donated by first-time knitters for shipment to Europe, "We'll accept them all, then press the hell out of them!" Relief Society's history is a latter-day woman's history, and LDS women, wherever they serve, are the Relief Society.

From our combined memories, we could compile a history of Relief Society, at least in this century. But underlying the whole enterprise is a foundation laid before we were born; that undergirding preceded even the 1842 *annus mirabilis* when the Society took on shape. Its earliest recorded expression may well be the 1830 revelation to Emma Hale Smith, now canonized as Doctrine and Covenants 25, in which the Lord clarified for his daughter, and for all his daughters, their potential as contributing members of his church. Emma was to be set apart "to expound scriptures, and to exhort the church," the Lord instructed, "according as it shall be given thee by my Spirit." (V. 7.) An "elect lady" (v. 3), she was to find fulfillment of this promise in her role as president of the first Relief Society, twelve years later.[2]

Women of the Restoration were spiritually gifted, as were their brothers, and they were also full voting members of the organized Church of Christ. As Margaret Smoot commented in 1870, "I have always sought to vote in conference, and then I felt I had done all I desired to do."[3] The sisters' sense of equality with their brethren was reinforced, as Carol Madsen has pointed out, in the texts of patriarchal and other blessings women were given: "Thou shalt be blessed with spiritual gifts," one was promised; "Great wisdom from the Lord to decide the most difficult questions," received another. "Thou shalt have power given unto thee to heal the sick, and to cast out evil spirits, and . . . power to keep the destroyer from thy household," another woman was assured. "The spirit of prophecy and revelation shall rest upon you, and the light of the Lord shall dwell within you and wisdom shall be given unto you to enable you to become perfected in the Lord," was the promise to yet another woman.[4] In matters of the Spirit, women received with men from the Lord's store of gifts.

By 1842, the exercise of their gifts, spiritual and temporal, for the benefit of all was a commonplace among women, as was the notion that they could be more effective working in tandem than singly. By the time of the founding of Relief Society, American women had been organizing themselves for four decades. That a chance conversation in Sarah Kimball's Nauvoo home should lead towards a sewing society for benevolent purposes reflected the pattern of women in a hundred other American communities. How this organization differed, why it should have persisted a century and a half, and why it is today the largest extant women's organization are serious and complex questions.

For me, however, the question of greatest significance and challenge has been an ecclesiastical one. What is the religious significance of the Relief Society to individual women, and how does its being essentially a religious entity affect the Relief Society?

Eliza R. Snow's request of the Prophet Joseph Smith that he pass judgment on her constitution and bylaws forced him to consider the place of women in the Church's structure. The minutes of the first meeting, held 17 March 1842, record his instructions to the women in procedural matters. That task was easy—they had already recognized the need for statutes and were aware of appropriate organizational deportment. Where their organization would fit into the Churchwide structure of governing quorums of priesthood, however, would evolve more gradually.

The Prophet had said that he hoped the society "might be built up to the Most High in an acceptable manner," that it should "move according to the ancient Priesthood."[5] By the sixth meeting of the society, held 28 April 1842, he was ready to reveal the place of the newborn entity in that organization. He began that most significant discourse by announcing that he would "make observations respecting the Priesthood, and give instructions for the benefit of the Society." What follows connects the female organization with priesthood quorums in three particulars: doctrine, organization, and practice.

"Let every man stand in his own office, and labor in his own calling," Joseph Smith had charged Church members in 1832. (D&C 84:109.) Now he gave the women "instructions respecting the different offices, and the necessity of every individual acting in the sphere allotted him or her; and filling the several offices to which they were appointed."[6] Not only would Relief Society have a presidency of three but "he would ordain them to preside over the Society—and let them preside just as the Presidency, preside over the church." The female presidency were to call officers "to carry out the designs of the Institution," and he added that they "be appointed and set apart, as Deacons, Teachers &c. are among us."[7] It is not surprising that the sisters in the Utah reorganization of Relief Society referred to their order as a quorum.

Joseph also taught the sisters the same doctrines of the priesthood he had taught the priesthood quorums, as recorded in Doctrine and Covenants 84 and 121.[8] Perhaps the most significant is the familiar injunction from section 121, affirming to priesthood holders that "the rights of the priesthood are inseparably connected with the powers of heaven, and that the powers of heaven cannot be controlled nor handled only upon the principles of righteousness." That is, he had clarified, "by persuasion, by long-suffering, by gentleness and meekness, and by love unfeigned." (D&C 121:35–37.) Joseph now acknowledged to the sisters that it is "natural" for them to have "feelings of charity." He reminded them of "those sympathies which God has planted in [their] bosoms," of their innocence and purity. Then he charged the sisters that "not war, not jangle, not contradiction, but meekness, love, purity, these are the things that should magnify us." "If you live up to these principles," he promised, "how great and glorious! — if you live up to your privilege, the angels cannot be restrain'd from being your associates."[9]

The principle of authority had long been affirmed to priesthood quorums: both the divine power with which each holder had been ordained, and the right of quorum officers to conduct group business. The same organizational principle was to obtain with the Relief Society: women were to be given certain "keys." In his 28 April 1842 sermon the Prophet approached that topic indirectly. He shared with the sisters his foreboding of his own impending death: "He said as he had this opportunity, he was going to instruct the Society and point out the way for them to conduct, that they might act according to the will of God — that he did not know as he should have many opportunities of teaching them — that they were going to be left to themselves, — they would not long have him to instruct them — that the church would not have his instruction long, and the world would not be troubled with him a great while, and would not have his teachings." In that spirit of urgency which characterized so much of the Prophet's last months, "he

spoke of delivering the keys to this Society and to the church —
that according to his prayers God had appointed him elsewhere."[10] He admonished the sisters to sustain their presidency, "to concentrate their faith and prayers for, and place
confidence [in] those whom God has appointed to honor,
whom God has plac'd at the head to lead." "The keys are about
to be given them," he promised, "that they may be able to
detect every thing false, as well as to the Elders." "This Society
is to get instruction thro' the order which God has established,"
he reiterated, "thro the medium of those appointed to lead."
Then, he emphatically declared, "I now turn the key to you in
the name of God." The promise was to follow: "This Society
shall rejoice and knowledge and intelligence shall flow down
from this time — this is the beginning of better days to this
Society."[11]

Elder Bruce R. McConkie clarified in a 1950 commentary
what that key meant and how it would function in the twentieth-
century Church. "By turning the key," he wrote, "the Prophet
delegated to the duly appointed officers of the new organization a portion of the keys of the kingdom. Under the Priesthood they were now authorized to direct, control, and govern
the affairs of the society. They thus became legal administrators
holding the keys of presidency. Under this appointment their
lawful acts would be recognized by the Lord and he would
work with them in the rolling forth of the kingdom in the
sphere assigned them."[12]

What becomes apparent in reflection is how perfectly the
inclusion of women within the structure of Church organization reflected the divine pattern of the perfect union of man
and woman as seen in temple ordinances. It seems not mere
coincidence that the initial impetus for their organization came
from the women's desire to assist in the building of the temple.
Their craving for the "knowledge and intelligence" promised
them by the Prophet would connect them continually with that
holy house. That principle of union, of "neither ... the man
without the woman, neither the woman without the man, in

the Lord" (1 Corinthians 11:11), would become increasingly clear to the sisters of the Nauvoo Relief Society when the temple ordinances were extended to women in 1843. In a meeting prior to that time, Newel K. Whitney, himself recently endowed, clarified for the sisters their importance in the eternal plan: "In the beginning," he explained, "God created man male and female and bestow'd upon man certain blessings peculiar to a man of God, of which woman partook, so that without the female all things cannot be restor'd to the earth — it takes all to restore the Priesthood."[13] With the organization of the Relief Society, the Lord had moved women, proven worthy by their faith and obedience, towards that final restoration. Inside the holy temple, as they ministered one to another, they would confirm their righteous receipt of the authority thus restored. On 20 September 1843 Emma Smith became the first woman of this dispensation to receive her endowment; before the Saints left Nauvoo, nearly three thousand women would be so blessed.

The essential element of the Relief Society, the only immutable part, is its spiritual core, maintained by shared sisterhood and confirmed by divine daughterhood. Through 150 years of change, that essence has remained. It is manifest in different ways as Latter-day Saint women have matured in the faith, but its gifts have been felt as women have reached for them. The nineteenth-century practice of women physically blessing each other and blessing their children is seldom seen in our time, but the Spirit that prompted those practices remains. The sisterhood so strengthened by the early practices can be found in the Church now as women find their connections as daughters of eternal parents.

In 1979 Spencer W. Kimball, then president of the Church, prepared a talk for the women of the Church. When time came for its delivery in the second satellite-broadcast women's meetings, he was too ill to deliver it. Perhaps you remember that his wife, Camilla, read the talk. I was struck by a particular parallel, one which I yet ponder. President Kimball wrote then of men "being given the tremendous responsibilities of fatherhood and the priesthood" and women "being given many tremendous responsibilities of motherhood and sisterhood."[14] His paradigm makes two obvious parallels: motherhood is analogous to fatherhood, and sisterhood is analogous to priesthood. I was struck by the implied importance that parallel gives to sisterhood, to our importance to each other. I am not certain President Kimball interpreted his diagram in exactly the way I did. My experience in Relief Society, however, and my study of its history have led me to believe that there is a great strength in our sisterhood that in our century we have not yet fully tapped. It is there in potential. We see glimmers of it. We feel moments of it. Perhaps study of our history will help us more fully realize the potential power in our sisterhood.

One seemingly unexceptional Nauvoo Relief Society meeting has particular meaning for me. It was an ad hoc gathering; neither Joseph nor Emma Smith was present, and probably few of the members. Zina Diantha Jacobs, recently enrolled, had communicated to her sister Presendia her enthusiasm for the new society. Presendia lived in Lima, about thirty miles from Nauvoo. Despite, or perhaps because of, her discomfort with her disaffected husband and her ill health — she had lost three of her five children, and was again pregnant — she craved the solace of the sisterhood.

Counselor Sarah Cleveland conducted the meeting. She had been the oldest woman present at the organizational meeting, wife to a nonmember husband. She would soon be forced to follow him from Nauvoo, bidding her sisters a poignant farewell, which would close with the endearment, "Yours in the bands of the gospel."[15] To the women now gathered, she announced that, there being "not much business to be attended to therefore we might spend the time in religious exercises before the Lord," a familiar invitation to testimony bearing. Sister Cleveland first spoke of "the happiness she felt in the present associations of other females." Presendia followed. As the minutes record, she "arose and said she rejoiced in the opportunity, that she considered it a great privilege. She felt that the spirit of the Lord was with the Society, and rejoic'd to become a member altho' residing at a distance and could not attend the meetings."

Sister Durfee then bore testimony to "the great blessing she received when administered to after the close of the last meeting, by Prest. E. Smith & Councillors Cleveland and Whitney." She had never realized more benefit through any administration, she acknowledged, and "that she was heal'd." (Predictably, the administration raised questions among the Nauvoo women not present, but at the next official meeting President Joseph Smith would lay them to rest: "there could be no devils in [women administering] if God gave his sanction by healing," adding, "if he had common sympathies, [he] would rejoice that the sick could be heal'd.") Blessings followed through the course of the current meeting, and the gift of tongues was manifest. "The spirit of the Lord like a purifying stream, refreshed every heart," concluded the minute-taker.[16]

The sacred spirituality that graced the Nauvoo Relief Society is still our birthright. It is generated among us, in answer to our own needs. In our sisterhood we teach one another, testify to one another, bless one another by our love and our faith.

Relief Society came to an abrupt and deliberate end in Nauvoo. There is a lesson for us in learning why. We have long preferred to believe the organization simply did not survive the move West, but the documents indicate otherwise. The Nauvoo Relief Society was terminated before Joseph Smith was martyred. The circumstances surrounding its demise must have caused both Joseph and Emma great pain. From the time the principle was first introduced, Emma Smith had been an outspoken opponent of plural marriage. In her attempt to prove her faith, she had for one brief time assented to her husband's taking other wives, but the burden had been too heavy. With the most powerful weapon she had, her position as president of the Relief Society, she campaigned against the practice her husband was promoting. In four successive meetings on 9 and

61

16 March 1844, in veiled references obvious to those who were informed and involved, she disavowed the practice. She "wanted to see a reformation in boath men & women," she insisted. With each presentation, her tirade against plural marriage became more vehement, finally requiring the women to examine "the conduct of the leaders in this society—that you may sit in judgement on their heads." And then, in final argument, she claimed that "if their ever was any Authourity on the Earth she had it—and had yet."[17]

The seeds of discord were sown, tares among the greening gospel wheat. The misuse of authority signifies the end of that authority. The Society was disbanded, although details of how and by whom are not recorded. The women forgave Emma; Eliza Snow seems even to have exonerated her later by suggesting that she "gave it up so as not to lead the society in erro[r]."[18] Despite her behavior, Emma Smith's sisters did not vilify her in retrospect. Their forgiveness is exemplary. The most important principle to be learned here, however, is one that Eliza articulated when Brigham Young called her to revive Relief Society in Utah: "Without order we have no claim to the Spirit. We must have the spirit or we cannot remain organized," she taught the sisters then.[19] Unity in gospel action is essential. "If ye are not one ye are not mine," said the Lord. (D&C 38:27.)

Through the long winter of the Saints' discontent, their expulsion from their city beautiful and their journey towards the western Zion, the women were bereft of their beloved Society. Its organization was proscribed; there were no meetings, no callings, no members to be admitted, none of the familiar apparatus. Even their charity work was taken over by bishops, though women participated individually to meet each other's needs. But the most significant elements remained: sisterhood and the Spirit. And because of those attributes, Eliza Snow, who in August 1846 wrote that "it is a growling, grumbling, devilish, sickly time with us now," would by the following spring record, "This is truly a glorious time with the mothers & daughters in Zion."[20] As their bodies had weakened in the wilderness, the women had grown in their spirits. They learned to share whatever they had, "dividing" with one another, lending strength to each other, and they practiced the gifts of the Spirit. They blessed one another in whatever ways they could. Wrote one woman of a sister who came to visit: "She possessed such a good influence and asked me if I would sing. I had such a bad cold I could not sing so she arose, came to me and placed her hands upon my head and blessed me. . . . This was a great comfort to me."[21] The essence of Relief Society remained. Writing later of the Relief Society, Emmeline B. Wells observed, "During all this time the sisters never lost sight of this institution as it had been established, nor of the promises made to them of its further greatness, by the Prophet Joseph Smith."[22]

Eight years passed while the Saints established themselves safely in the Valley. Their families' basic needs met, a group of sisters gathered one winter afternoon in 1854 to sew clothing for Indian women and children whom they had noticed were poorly clad against the cold. A decade after Relief Society's demise, Matilda Dudley thus brought the Society forth from its own ashes, a phoenix that would not die. President Brigham Young acknowledged the spontaneous regeneration with favor. "We are going to propose to the sisters . . . to make clothes, &c for the Indians," he announced soon after. Under his direction each bishop was to organize the women in his ward.[23] "It is a laudable undertaking," wrote Wilford Woodruff three years later, as the expanding Relief Society over which his wife Phebe presided met in his Fifteenth Ward home. "There were about 50 present, sewing, knitting, sewing carpet rags, making quilts, &c." Their function soon expanded beyond the temporal and charitable into the added commission the Prophet Joseph had given them: to save souls. While the women worked they listened to guest speakers, in this case Elder Woodruff and Robert Campbell. Another precedent was being set, which would come into full realization with yet another generation of Relief Society.

I have noticed while tracing Relief Society's history that its times of regeneration have occurred during periods of religious reawakening among the people. During such times Relief Society would spring up like volunteer tulips in March. The construction of the temple moving towards completion and Joseph Smith's preparation to introduce the endowment prodded the first incarnation of the Society in Nauvoo. The 1850s Utah societies emerged as prelude to or connected with the spiritual reawakening known to historians as the "Reformation." Latter-day Saints then culminated their self-examination by rebaptism and reconfirmation. But like its Nauvoo precedent, that reborn society also did not last: the dislocation of homes and families at the threatened invasion of Johnston's Army disrupted most of the young societies, and since no central church leadership existed to encourage their continuation once the threat passed, most of them vanished.

With the mid-1860s came another reawakening among the Saints. Wilford Woodruff reflected in his journal the renewing of temple ordinances, and Brigham Young pleaded with the Saints for increased piety in the face of the oncoming Gentile intrusion occasioned by the coming of the railroad. Eliza R. Snow in her autobiography records President Young's calling her then to provide churchwide leadership for yet a third generation of Relief Society. This time, largely because of the energetic and forward-thinking leadership she gave, the organization survived. Her two decades were the halcyon years of Relief Society expansion. Between 1867 and 1887 Relief Society fostered programs still functioning: Young Women, Primary, stake organization, and women's political involvement. Even more programs that evolved under her direction met temporary needs: wheat storage, cooperative stores, sericulture, a centennial celebration fair, a newspaper, medical training and services for women, Relief Society halls and granaries.

"Aunt Eliza," as she was lovingly called, was succeeded by Aunt Zina D. H. Young, then by Aunt Bathsheba W. Smith, and

"Aunt Em," Emmeline B. Wells. All these presidents, whose administrations took the Society to 1921, shared the Nauvoo vision of the work. Then in the twentieth century—with the calling of Clarissa Williams, succeeded by Louise Y. Robison, Amy Brown Lyman, and culminating in the nearly thirty-year administration of Belle S. Spafford—Relief Society moved into a new gear. The period known to historians as the Progressive Era turned the "aunts'" mode of intimate leadership into a "presidents'" pattern of business administration. Professionalism and efficiency made it possible for the Society to deal effectively with a Church membership that was growing exponentially. Presidents Barbara B. Smith, Barbara Winder, and now Elaine Jack inherited in their turn a position of administrative complexity that demanded of them understanding beyond the realm of the aunts, or, for that matter, of most women of this or the last century.

Through 150 years of organization, consolidation, refinement, redirection, further expansion, retraction, and correlation, the Relief Society has emerged as we know it. Its present outward form, with the exception of visiting teaching and the testimony segment of Fast Sunday meetings, would be unrecognizable to our Nauvoo foremothers. But where we have nurtured them, the sisterhood and the Spirit have remained, the sturdy, enduring roots of our modern association.

As it was in the Female Relief Society of Nauvoo, so in our ward Relief Societies, diversity among the sisters is characteristic and in some cases predominant. Last year at this conference Karen Lynn Davidson told of her California Relief Society, which included, among others, a nightclub singer who gets up early every morning to teach seminary. "Only in California!" she could hear us say. Cathy Stokes told us a while ago of her Hyde Park, Chicago, ward where 25 percent of the Relief Society members are single mothers who have been in the Church fewer than five years. From Manhattan we hear of a lesson devoted to teaching women how to ride safely on the subway. We listen to Olga Kovářová and Edith Krause tell about our sisters in Czechoslovakia and in Germany, and from Moscow the Relief Society presidency write of their joy in celebrating the sesquicentennial of an organization that until recently had not existed for them. In our diversity, sisterhood, among those who choose to foster it, remains a dominant theme in Relief Society worldwide.

And so also does the Spirit. Relief Society could conceivably continue as a totally secular association, without spiritual direction or affirmation. But when both sisterhood and the Spirit are present, Relief Society becomes an entity unique among women's associations and will fulfill the Prophet Joseph's "promises . . . of its further greatness."[24] The following account from a contemporary Relief Society president illustrates:

"Ruth was dying of cancer. Her husband Al was staying with her in the hospital, and the family members were visiting daily. I was on my way home one evening and found my car swinging up the hill towards the hospital. It was after visiting hours, but I slipped in anyway, trying to be inconspicuous. I knew there was a 'Family Only' sign on the door, but I wanted to check on Al to see if we could bring a meal by or anything for him. A nurse came out as I approached. 'May I see Mr. Roberts?' I asked. He overheard and signaled me to come in. We visited a bit, and I made my offers of help. He seemed okay. Then we went over to the bed. His wife lay in a light coma. Ruth, who had been so strikingly attractive, now slept with open mouth, teeth removed, hair thin and dull, complexion sallow. As we talked, Al and I rubbed her arms. 'She seems to like that,' he said. Across the room the phone rang. Al went to answer. I stood alone with Ruth, smoothing her hair. I thought of the women of another era who would have given her a blessing, and I wished I felt it appropriate now. As though wish were deed, I felt in my deepest soul the blessing that was Ruth's. It was as though I were the conduit through which the love the Lord had for Ruth was passing. I knew the message: whether Ruth was here with us or had already left us was inconsequential. She was with God, and she was His.

Her offering was accepted, and He loved her. I was bathed in the warmth, the indescribable comfort of the Spirit. Though my hand still rested on Ruth's head, I realized that it was not the form that mattered. The Spirit will dictate its own forms. All I needed to do was to be willing and to be there."[25]

Sisterhood and the Spirit are the timeless legacy of the Nauvoo Relief Society, and all its daughters, to us. May we infuse into our Relief Societies and our lives those two elusive but inestimable qualities, that we may receive the promise uttered by the prophet Joel: "And it shall come to pass afterward, that I will pour out my spirit upon all flesh; and your sons and your daughters shall prophesy, your old men shall dream dreams, your young men shall see visions: and also upon the servants and upon the handmaids in those days will I pour out my spirit." (Joel 2:28–29.)

Notes

1. The Relief Society history, *Women of Covenant: The Story of Relief Society, 1842–1992*, forthcoming in 1992 from Deseret Book, was commissioned in 1979 by Relief Society General President Barbara Smith. Its authors are Jill Mulvay Derr, Janath Cannon, and Maureen Ursenbach Beecher.
2. That Emma Smith's blessing extends beyond her is clarified in the Prophet's explanation that "not she alone, but others, may attain to the same blessings." Minutes of the Female Relief Society of Nauvoo, 17 March 1842, holograph, LDS Church Archives. This and all other citations from documents housed in the Church Archives are used with permission.
3. Riverside Stake Fifteenth Ward Relief Society Minutes, 6 January 1868 to 4 September 1873, 19 February 1870, LDS Church Archives.
4. For a full discussion of the significance of women's blessings, see Carol Cornwall Madsen, "Mothers in Israel: Sarah's Legacy," *Women of Wisdom and Knowledge*, ed. Marie Cornwall and Susan Howe (Salt Lake City: Deseret Book Co., 1990), pp. 189–91.
5. Record of the Female Relief Society of Nauvoo, holograph, LDS Church Archives, 30 March 1842.
6. Nauvoo Relief Society Minutes, 28 April 1842.
7. Nauvoo Relief Society Minutes, 17 March 1842.
8. For a more complete and perceptive discussion of these ideas, see

Kathryn H. Shirts, "Priesthood and Salvation: Is D&C 84 a Revelation to Women Too?" *Sunstone* 15 (September 1991): 20–27.

9. Nauvoo Relief Society Minutes, 28 April 1842.

10. Other suggestions of Joseph Smith's sense of urgency are developed in Ronald K. Esplin, "Joseph Smith's Mission and Timetable: 'God Will Protect Me Until My Work Is Done,' " *The Prophet Joseph: Essays on the Life and Mission of Joseph Smith*, ed. Larry C. Porter and Susan Easton Black (Salt Lake City: Deseret Book Co., 1988), pp. 280–319.

11. Nauvoo Relief Society Minutes, 28 April 1842.

12. Bruce R. McConkie, "The Relief Society and the Keys of the Kingdom," *Relief Society Magazine* 37 (March 1950): 151.

13. Nauvoo Relief Society Minutes, 27 May 1842.

14. Spencer W. Kimball, "The Role of Righteous Women," *Ensign*, Nov. 1979, p. 102.

15. Sarah Cleveland, *Times and Seasons* 4 (1 May 1843): 187.

16. Nauvoo Relief Society Minutes, 19 and 28 April 1842.

17. Nauvoo Relief Society Minutes, 9 and 16 March 1844.

18. Relief Society Minutes, West Jordan Ward, 7 September 1869, LDS Church Archives; *Woman's Exponent* 8 (1 November 1879): 85.

19. Eleventh Ward Relief Society Minutes, 3 March 1869, LDS Church Archives.

20. Eliza R. Snow, Diary, 10 August 1846, 1 June 1847, holograph, Huntington Libraries, San Marino, California.

21. "Sketch of Julia Parks Lindsay," *Woman's Exponent* 39 (March 1911): 163.

22. Emmeline B. Wells, "History of the Relief Society," *Woman's Exponent* 32 (July 1903): 6.

23. Minutes of Meeting, Parowan Ward, 21 May 1854, Thomas Bullock Minutes Collection, LDS Church Archives, as quoted in Richard L. Jensen, "Forgotten Relief Societies, 1844–1867," *Dialogue: A Journal of Mormon Thought* 16 (Spring 1983): 111.

24. Emmeline B. Wells, "History of the Relief Society," *Woman's Exponent* 32 (July 1903): 6.

25. For reasons of privacy, the names have been changed. Original in the author's file.

Voices in Print:
The Woman's Exponent, *1872–1914*

CAROL CORNWALL MADSEN

In 1855, from his distant but perceptive vantage point in England, American author Nathaniel Hawthorne disdainfully noted the commercial success of a growing contingent of female novelists: "America is now given over to a damned mob of scribbling women, and I should have no chance of success while the public taste is occupied with their trash—and should be ashamed of myself if I did succeed."[1] Despite his sour grapes, Hawthorne's retreat in the face of this female literary invasion confirmed the strength of women's presence in the American literary field in the nineteenth century. The development of the steam-powered printing press, which corresponded with a rise in literacy among women, initiated an explosion of newspapers, periodicals, and popular fiction, and women not only constituted a major segment of nationwide readers but of literary contributors as well. Publisher Lewis A. Godey of the popular *Godey's Lady's Book* was one of the first to offer his female contributors more than a forum for their writing. "We were the first to introduce the system of calling forth the slumbering talent of our country by offering an equivalent for the efforts of genius," he claimed in 1840.[2] With fortune as well as fame in the offing, women were in the literary marketplace to stay.

As early as 1820, women's names began to appear not only

Carol Cornwall Madsen is an associate professor of history and senior research historian with the Joseph Fielding Smith Institute for Church History at Brigham Young University. She is working on a biography of Emmeline B. Wells, suffragist, editor, and fifth general president of the Relief Society. She and her husband, Gordon A. Madsen, are the parents of six children.

as contributors to but as editors of a variety of newspapers and magazines, and by 1850 a substantial number of women's publications had begun to make their appearance in cities across the country, including the far West.[3] Salt Lake City was one of them. In 1871, Edward L. Sloan, editor of the *Salt Lake Herald*, meeting resistance to the idea of a woman's column, decided to initiate a woman's paper, for which he felt there was a significant need.[4] His choice for editor was Louisa (Lula) Greene, a twenty-two-year-old woman from Smithfield, Utah, who had contributed several poems to his paper. Hesitant to accept the offer on her own, Louisa sought the sanction of Eliza R. Snow and the blessing of Brigham Young before finally acquiescing. Early in 1872 she moved to the home of her great-uncle Lorenzo Dow Young in Salt Lake City to assume her new post. A small room in the Young home became the *Exponent* office, furnished only with a table, writing materials, a few books and magazines, some chairs — and a bed. It was to be home to the *Exponent's* editor as well.[5] It was only temporary housing for the *Exponent*, however, which moved its office more than ten times during its forty-two year history, the office later serving as a meeting room for the Relief Society board and other women's committees. Until 1889 a yearly subscription to the biweekly paper cost two dollars, dropping to one dollar thereafter. Circulation probably did not exceed three or four thousand copies, but its sphere of influence was much broader through an exchange program with other women's newspapers throughout the country.

Aside from a loosely associated network of agents and correspondents who attempted to increase circulation and a brief period in which a "Consulting Committee" met to supervise its publication, the *Woman's Exponent* never had a formal editorial staff. The editorials, many of the articles, most of the biographical sketches, the poetry, and the fiction were written primarily by the editors themselves, first Louisa Greene, who served until 1877, and then Emmeline B. Wells, who served until the demise of the paper in 1914. In addition, with only occasional help, they handled the financial accounts, the correspondence, and the mailing. "I never supposed when I commenced working on the paper," Emmeline Wells confided to her diary in 1878, "that I would have to do everything for myself. I feel sometimes my burden is too heavy."[6]

Announcement of the forthcoming paper, composed of eight quarto-sized pages, appeared in the *Herald* in April 1872: "The women of Utah are today unquestionably more the subject of comment than those of any other portion of the country, or indeed of the world. As they have long exercised the right to think and act for themselves, so they now claim the right to speak for themselves through the potent medium of the types."[7]

The public practice of polygamy (more correctly, polygyny) was drawing increased attention to Mormons, and the newspaper was intended to provide a forum for articulate LDS women to explain themselves and their beliefs. It was not to be a strident voice for any cause. In fact, the editor promised her readers that there would be no need to promote woman suffrage, since Utah women had been enfranchised in 1870, to contend against any wrongs, or champion any claim.[8] By the second issue, however, the paper's goal to "speak freely on every topic of current interest to women" elicited articles and editorials strongly endorsing woman suffrage, contending against the discrimination of women in politics, education, and the workplace, and defending and championing Mormonism, especially the practice of plural marriage.

But the paper was not just a polemic. Over its forty-two-year span, the *Exponent* addressed a wide variety of topics of interest to women. Promising at the outset to include a "brief and graphic summary of current news, local and general," especially anything relating to nontraditional women, it also featured articles on home and family life, religious doctrine, home manufacturing, travel, and cultural events, and included biographical sketches of the "leading sisters" as well as short life sketches and obituaries of lesser-known women. A major feature was the printed reports of the Relief Society, the Primary, and Young Women's associations and minutes of various women's groups such as the Retrenchment Society, the Reapers Club, and the Women's Press Club. Poetry found its way into every issue along with popular moralistic short stories of virtuous women reforming wayward men. Domesticity received less attention, because the paper's mission was to broaden the knowledge and interests of its readers. A categorical breakdown of the editorial content reflects the *Exponent's* emphasis. More than 20 percent of the editorials addressed the subject of woman's rights, another 20 percent discussed Church and Relief Society news, 10 percent defended polygamy, and 7 percent supported woman suffrage. If nothing else, the *Woman's Exponent* confirmed the extent to which LDS women were in tune with the dynamics of the broader society of their time and their knowledge of the issues that affected them as women.

Each decade of its forty-two-year run seems to have been characterized by a dominant theme relating to the public, collective experience of Mormon women. The first decade was, in many ways, a golden era for their public expression and contribution. Having been given the vote in 1870, they were proud of their participation in the political process, well before most other American women, and voiced their opinions on the volatile question of women's rights. Editor Richards was convinced that LDS women enjoyed such rights well ahead of their American sisters because of the broad-minded policies of Brigham Young: "President Young," she wrote, "proves himself [the] most genuine, impartial and practical 'Woman's Rights man' upon the American continent, as he has ever done; his counsels, instructions and advice to women being always directed toward their progress and advancement in usefulness and the possession of valuable knowledge."[9] Utah women did indeed enjoy not only political rights but educational and vocational opportunities, Utah being among the earliest territories or states, for example, to admit women to practice law.

That fact elicited another exuberant comment from the editor: "Here in Utah, decried, abused and maligned as it has been, women enjoy more of what is contended for as woman's rights than they do in any State in the Federal Union; and that they appreciate their position and are seeking to qualify themselves for spheres of usefulness to which their sisters in other parts of the country can only yet look in prospective."[10]

One avenue of qualification was the Relief Society, through which their abilities, talents, and public interests could be expressed and developed. "The organization of the Relief Society...," wrote Emmeline Wells, "has given to woman, in its rise and progress, influence on almost all subjects that pertain to her welfare and happiness, and opportunities for expressing her own thoughts, views and opinions; all of which has had a tendency to make her intelligent in regard to matters which before were considered incompatible with 'woman's sphere,' and unintelligible to her 'weaker' mind."[11] Charter member Sarah Kimball agreed and further believed that "the sure foundations of the suffrage cause were deeply and permanently laid" at the organization of the Relief Society. Editor Wells opined that when Joseph "turned the key to women," men no longer "had the same absolute sway."[12]

Because they participated in politics and managed and controlled numerous economic projects assigned them through the Relief Society, LDS women had reason to feel that Mormonism, through both its theology and temporal enterprises, offered them broader opportunities for advancement and individual achievement than were available to women outside the Church. A heightened self-image developed from these social and religious concepts, fervently expressed by Eliza R. Snow, who often reminded her LDS sisters that they occupied "a more important position than is occupied by any other women on the earth. Associated, as they are, with apostles and prophets ... —with them sharing in the gifts and powers of the holy Priesthood ... —participating in those sacred ordinances, without which we could never be prepared to dwell in the presence of the Holy Ones."[13]

Louisa Greene endorsed this sentiment. "There is no greater freedom than the Gospel gives to woman," she wrote. "And it is this that makes Mormon women conscious of their power. They have suffered and become strong; experience has matured them, and given them a higher order of attainment than a mere mental education."[14] An anonymous writer claimed that no where else "in all the broad land do women enjoy such freedom" as do Mormon women. "Where are they looked upon by their husbands as their equal?" she asked. "How beautiful to contemplate the restitution of all things in these the last days. The Gospel breaks the fetters wherewith woman is bound, takes her by the hand and says, 'Woman, know thyself.'"[15]

When the next decade broke with all its anti-polygamy fury upon the lives of Mormon women, this elevated self-image helped sustain them against repeated federal and societal assault. The eighties became a time for "circling the wagons," closing in to meet the attack, sometimes with defiance, other times with pleas for understanding, and finally with resignation. Their defiant posture was provoked by the organization in 1878 in Salt Lake City of the Anti-Polygamy Society, whose agenda was immediate prohibition of polygamy. Rallying to their own defense, Mormon women met the challenge with assurance and conviction. "We never thought that woman could rise up against woman," declared Emmeline Wells in astonishment at this female attack on their religious rights. "The time has come when we can no longer be silent, as we are assailed, and that too by our own sex. . . .

"... we must meet it [the challenge]; and we intend to meet it with all the energy and fortitude we possess, and it will be 'diamond cut diamond' rest assured."[16]

While men were arguing the politics of continued practice, women argued the moral and feminist implications of it. "The world says Polygamy makes women inferior to men — we think differently," asserted one editorial. "Polygamy, gives women more time for thought, for mental culture, more freedom of action, a broader field of labor, inculcates liberality and generosity, develops more fully the spiritual elements of life, fosters purity of thought and gives wider scope to benevolence."[17] Affirming its benefits, another article claimed that LDS women "by self-sacrifice, or say by laying aside selfishness and becoming endowed with that nobility of character, which will grasp the higher good for the larger number, ... have shown themselves equal to the effort [required of the practice]."[18]

By the time the federal anti-polygamy Edmunds-Tucker Act became law in 1887, escheating Church property and crippling its economic base as well as disenfranchising polygamists and all Utah women, many Saints had become disheartened and apprehensive. In response, the *Exponent* attempted to rally the spirits of its readers, reminding them that "again and again in ancient and modern revelation has the Lord said He would have a tried people." It cautioned them "that the Lord's ways are not as man's ways, and that great things never come about as even *wise* men anticipate." Thus, it advised, "the Saints should not murmur as did ancient Israel lest they lose sight of 'the prize of the high calling.' "[19]

Whatever the manner individual women chose to use to respond to the 1890 Manifesto suspending the practice of plural marriage, the *Woman's Exponent* by its third decade seemed eager to lay aside past differences and support efforts to unite LDS and gentile women under the common rubric of "Utah women." Linking leadership and resources, many women from both camps decided it was time for Utah women, in a decade-long spirit of detente, to replicate the community action of their American sisters. Celebrating a commingling of LDS and non-LDS women in the local federation of women's clubs, organized in 1892, the *Woman's Exponent* reported its annual meetings and public works, including lobbying for libraries, playgrounds, and recreation centers in Utah towns and cities, all public enterprises of mutual benefit.[20]

Detente, the theme of this conciliatory era of the *Woman's Exponent*, also surfaced in the area of education. With Protestant denominational schools vying for recruits from the LDS "ward" schools, the establishment of a public school system in 1890 helped to soften the critical edges and separatist attitudes of the earlier systems. It also paved the way for cooperative action to achieve mutual educational goals. One of these was establishing a kindergarten, an educational goal of that time, which became a major catalyst for Mormon-Gentile unity when the two groups merged their independent associations into a single Utah State Kindergarten Association in 1896. The *Exponent* enthusiastically reported its achievements. Their cooperative efforts, supported by the lobbying committee of the state federation of women's clubs, resulted in passage of a bill in 1903 providing that at least one kindergarten be opened and maintained in every Utah town of 2500 inhabitants, a major achievement of Utah women.

Although the nation as a whole did not yet consider politics appropriate for women's participation, in Utah, where women had had the vote from 1870 to 1887, politics were high on women's public agenda and were followed closely by the *Woman's Exponent*. Utah politics dramatically changed when preparation for statehood, attained in 1896, required a new configuration of alliances as Utah residents dissolved their local, religiously defined political parties to adopt the national two-party system. LDS and gentile women refranchised at statehood found that new political allegiances could transcend religious differences as they declared themselves Democrats or Republicans and actively supported candidates based on political rather than religious preference.[21]

The most dramatic evidence of the spirit of detente that found detailed coverage in the *Woman's Exponent* was the great Columbian Exhibition and World's Fair held in Chicago in 1893. A national Board of Lady Managers was appointed to head a Woman's Commission, with a local board in each state to supervise a monumental display of the industrial, artistic, and domestic talents of the women of America. The Utah Board of Lady Managers consisted of both Mormon and non-Mormon women, and Utah's representation in the Woman's Building reflected more than a combined physical and organizational effort. It was a union of hearts and spirits in a single cause: to show the world that Utah women were as advanced, as cultured, as educated, and as talented as women anywhere else. Moreover, Utah women gained something themselves from the experience: a newly forged sisterhood that had somehow weathered the bitterness of earlier times and found a comfortable peace in promoting women's culture. Proud of this achievement, territorial manager Emily Richards reported to the *Exponent:* "While this work is divided between the territory, county and individual, it will all go to make one great whole and will be looked upon by visitors at the World's Fair as an exhibit from the women of Utah."[22] Though coming midway in the decade, the Columbian Exhibition was a pinnacle of achievement for the entire decade, uniting women in a fragile but valued bond of common purpose.

At the turn of the century, the *Exponent* entered its fourth and final phase. Interest had waned, circulation had dropped, the editions were becoming sporadic, editor Emmeline B. Wells had turned her attention to the Relief Society, which she then headed, and the causes that had breathed life and purpose into its pages gradually passed into history. With many volatile issues laid to rest, editor Wells, urged by Brigham Young years earlier to record the lives of LDS women, used this period of relative quiescence to complete that charge. In her thirty-seven years as editor, she wrote or edited 319 biographical sketches, twenty-five major life stories, and many collective biographies (women in music, literature, journalism, etc.) as well as brief obituaries for scores of LDS women. "The *Woman's Exponent*," she wrote in a late issue, "will furnish good material for future historians who will, it is ardently hoped, remember the women of Zion when compiling the history of this Western land."[23]

Though generally ignored by most historians until recently,

the *Exponent* is a major source of Mormon women's history. Not only has it preserved the lives of individual women but it has also preserved a record of their organizations and contributions through the reports of their organizations, their clubs and societies, and their individual achievements.

To twentieth-century readers, the *Woman's Exponent* is like a window framing a forty-two-year spectrum of views into another life and time. It chronicles the intellectual, religious, economic, and social history of LDS women during a dynamic period of Mormonism, covering a third of its history and registering women's responses to the events that defined their lives. For forty-two years, women had a forum, free of authoritative or formal constraints, to explain themselves to the world and to express their own ideas and feelings on issues important to them. It provided a network for LDS women, linking them together through the unifying strands of their lives while allowing for the diversity of experience and thought each one represented. Through their concentrated efforts to present themselves favorably to the world through the medium of the *Exponent*, Mormon women reinforced their own faith in themselves and their commitment to their beliefs. This unity of effort and common conviction offset the demoralizing effects of the anti-Mormon crusade and developed a strength in that unity that helped preserve an instrumental self-concept.

Moreover, the *Woman's Exponent* proved to be a continuing connection for LDS women with the forces of the woman's movement of that time, to which they were vitally and imperatively attached. All of the principal issues of the "woman question" of the nineteenth century interfaced to an appreciable extent with Mormonism, and even the most apathetic woman could hardly escape the consequences of that connection.

Finally, by its own account, the *Woman's Exponent* preserved a segment of LDS history little noted and never studied until recently. "There has been no great work during these years commenced by women," editor Wells claimed in 1911, "that has not been considered and helped by this little paper."[24]

Indeed, for LDS women's history, the *Woman's Exponent* is a pearl of great price. In a final editorial, Emmeline Wells appraised its worth for its own time and for ours: "For women, it [the *Woman's Exponent*] has been a standard bearer, proclaiming their worth and just claims throughout the long years of its existence. . . . It has surely performed a mission in the midst of Zion for the women of Zion, holding as it does within its leaves the history of their work."[25] Through the *Woman's Exponent* LDS women have a claim on their past. It is a voice from that past that echoes resoundingly today.

Notes

1. As quoted in Fred Lewis Pattee, *The Feminine Fifties* (New York: Appleton-Century Co., 1940), p. 110.
2. As quoted in Fred Lewis Pattee, *The Development of the American Short Story* (New York: Harper and Brothers Publishers, 1923), p. 72.
3. A book-length study of nineteenth-century female editors is Sherilyn Cox Bennion, *Equal to the Occasion, Women Editors of the Nineteenth-Century West* (Reno and Las Vegas: University of Nevada Press, 1990).
4. Information for this article has been drawn chiefly from Carol Cornwall Madsen, " 'Remember the Women of Zion': A Study of the Editorial Content of the *Woman's Exponent*, A Mormon Woman's Journal" (M.A. thesis, University of Utah, 1977).
5. Lula [Louisa] Greene Richards, "How the *Exponent* Was Started," *Relief Society Magazine* 14 (December 1928): 607.
6. Emmeline B. Wells, Diary, 18 January 1878, Special Collections, Harold B. Lee Library, Brigham Young University, Provo, Utah.
7. Salt Lake *Herald,* 9 April 1872.
8. *Woman's Exponent* 1 (1 June 1872): 4.
9. "Work for Women," *Woman's Exponent* 1 (15 April 1873): 172.
10. "Lady Lawyers," *Woman's Exponent* 1 (1 October 1872): 68.
11. "Women's Organizations," *Woman's Exponent* 8 (15 January 1880): 122.
12. "Woman Suffrage Leaflet" (Salt Lake City, January 1892), 3, LDS Church Archives, Salt Lake City, Utah; "A Wonderful Age," *Woman's Exponent* 27 (1 February 1899): 100.
13. "Position and Duties," *Woman's Exponent* 3 (15 July 1874): 28.
14. "Reveries of a Woman," *Woman's Exponent* 5 (1 May 1877): 180.
15. *Woman's Exponent* 16 (15 September 1887): 63.
16. *Woman's Exponent* 7 (1 December 1878): 102–3.

Voices from Nauvoo

17. "Women Talkers and Women Writers," *Woman's Exponent* 5 (15 August 1876): 44.
18. "A Plea for Utah," *Woman's Exponent* 10 (1 December 1881): 100.
19. "Fear Not for Zion," *Woman's Exponent* 20 (15 November 1891): 76.
20. An earlier expression of the value of united effort is "Bear Ye One Another's Burdens," *Woman's Exponent* 2 (1 March 1874): 146. For examples of a cross-over in membership of the various clubs, see *Woman's Exponent* 24 (15 June 1895): 12; 25 (1 June 1896): 18; 25 (15 December 1896): 73.
21. "Women's Work and Duty," *Woman's Exponent* 24 (1 March 1896): 122; 25 (1, 15 November 1896): 69.
22. *Woman's Exponent* 21 (15 November 1892): 74.
23. *Woman's Exponent* 40 (July 1911): 4.
24. Ibid.
25. "Heartfelt Farewell," *Woman's Exponent* 41 (February 1914): 100.

The Relief Society Magazine, *1914–1970*

CAROL L. CLARK

In December 1970, after a fifty-seven-year history, publication of the *Relief Society Magazine* came to an end. Although many of the subscribers looked forward to the inauguration of the *Ensign*, there were those who could not help but look back. The *Relief Society Magazine* had been an outgrowth of the *Woman's Exponent*, and together they had spanned a period of nearly one hundred years. Such a tradition for women did not end without a measure of sadness. One eighty-four-year-old woman unknowingly expressed the feelings of many Relief Society sisters when she bade the magazine farewell for reasons of her own early in 1969: "Dear Relief Society Magazine: It is with regret and tears that I must say good-bye. My sight is so bad and no repairs can be given it, so I cannot read you any more. For thirty years and more I have enjoyed you, but now I am unable to read the wonderful stories and articles. Good-bye Magazine. I hate so to see you go."[1]

Marianne Clark Sharp, the *Magazine*'s editor in 1970 wrote, "Changing times have brought the end of the journey to the *Relief Society Magazine*. The times were different when it began in 1914 — and that time was the end of the journey for the *Woman's Exponent*. . . . Everyone has worked unselfishly for its [the *Magazine*'s] success, which is attested by the subscription numbers of 301,000 as of August 1970, which would have been greatly increased by the end of the year had the Magazine continued."[2]

Carol L. Clark has served as a member of the Relief Society general board and as administrative assistant to the general presidency of the Relief Society. She has held prominent positions in business, education, and government and has written and edited several books, including The Relief Society Magazine: A Legacy Remembered.

In the November issue, Relief Society general president Belle Spafford said: "We must remember... that with the growth and expansion of the Church, changes must be anticipated, accepted, and adjustments to new ways and new programs made with willingness and faith in the inspiration that guides our leaders."[3]

Surely but reluctantly, Relief Society leaders closed the last page of their beloved magazine.

The *Relief Society Magazine* is still to be loved, for it celebrates the promise and legacy of Relief Society. It is perhaps the single best barometer of the temperaments and attitudes, joys and woes of generations of Mormon women in this century. It was the repository of the articulation of Relief Society's goals, modus operandi, and developing curriculum.

Originally the *Magazine*'s major purpose was to provide a forum for lessons. In 1914 the *Relief Society Guide* and *Relief Society Bulletin* introduced the first uniform Relief Society "guide" lessons written at Church headquarters. Interestingly, the lessons are reminiscent of Church lessons today—short outlines.

The curricula were published in the *Magazine* throughout its history, but the *Magazine*'s purposes expanded as did its circulation. When it formally began in January 1915, Emmeline B. Wells was the general president of the Relief Society. She was the literal link with the past, and having lived through the Nauvoo period, she provided much of the continuity and ballast needed as the fledgling *Relief Society Magazine* embarked. Susa Young Gates, Brigham Young's daughter and the first editor of the *Magazine*, brought fresh energy to the *Magazine*. In the first issue she wrote: "It is impossible for us to be sure what any child of ours may become. How much more impossible, then, to forecast what shall be the future, the final character, of this literary infant, newly-born. . . . We [wish to] make of this magazine a beacon light of hope, beauty, and charity. . . . It is, therefore, the spirit and genius of the Gospel which we would like to develop and expound brightly, attractively, cheerfully, and hopefully, to the readers of the *Relief Society Magazine*."[4]

The *Magazine* did bring much hope and cheer to its readers, although it seldom contained much fine-quality literature. But then it was never intended to. In 1922 editor Gates explained: "As between a cold, spiritless, finished story, and a halting, crudely-told tale, breathing a testimony of the gospel from start to finish, we choose the inspired story."[5]

And Relief Society leaders did publish much that represented the conscience of thousands of Latter-day Saint women. The *Magazine* became a forum, a place where Latter-day Saint women could publish their poetry and articles, receive credit for their good works, read serialized stories (such as the "Prince of Ur" by Homespun), feel part of their sisterhood, and learn gospel truths.

The *Relief Society Magazine* bonded the sisters, in part because it was often contemporary and spoke knowingly to many issues, fashion among them. Evidence comes from the first issue, in " 'Clothing for the Woman Past Forty,' by the Two Sarahs": "When we are approaching the autumn of life, greater care and attention should be given to our appearance than ever before. . . . Dark greens, greys, purples, navy blue, and seal brown are appropriate shades for the woman of forty. . . . Avoid black, when possible, as it is trying at this time of life."[6]

Amusing as that 1915 passage might sound to us now, the *Magazine* still speaks vitally to today's readers, for the women at the helm of the *Magazine* believed theirs was a divine mission and the *Magazine* should reflect timeless truths. This sense of mission is evident in the articles, poems, and lessons, which were meant to be teaching tools and sources of inspiration for the sisters.

To read the *Relief Society Magazine* is to watch the sisters expand Relief Society into education. We must remember that Relief Society was not established as an educational organization. It was a charitable organization. The general board struggled for years with the Society's educational identity. They may not have clearly defined it, but they stood for the value of education, both secular and religious, and they let the curriculum evolve according to the knowledge and interests of the time.

An example of how Latter-day Saint women brought the best of secular and religious instruction together is found in the story of the first Relief Society lessons developed at Church headquarters. Ida Smoot Dusenberry, the driving force behind Mother Education lessons, demonstrates how one person's knowledge and expertise can change Church policy. In fact, her formative influence on Relief Society education makes her perhaps the most important educational leader Relief Society has ever had. An instructor at Brigham Young Academy, she was also second counselor in the Relief Society general presidency from 1901 to 1910. Her Relief Society position allowed her to help move Relief Society into a new role as a formal educator of its members.

Sister Dusenberry's significance to Relief Society began in 1892 when Colonel Francis Parker visited Provo to lecture on the Quincy System, a new child-centered method of teaching children. She became an avid supporter of kindergartens, not then part of the public education system, after she heard Parker's lectures, and her involvement with the movement went beyond the Academy and into state, national, and international levels. Her great interest in the education of young children led her to Boston and New York, where she studied with John Dewey and other national educational leaders. Sister Dusenberry carried her zeal for early childhood education into the Mother's Classes—the first formalized Relief Society curriculum.

A woman of vision and ability, Ida Smoot Dusenberry did more, perhaps, than anyone else to move Relief Society into a Churchwide curriculum. In 1915 the *Relief Society Magazine* began including lessons that were written for the Church as a whole. These Relief Society lessons exhibit wonderful variety, particularly in the teens and twenties of this century:

RELIEF SOCIETY LESSON TITLES

1915

First Meeting	Work and Business
Second Meeting	Theology and Testimony (Orson F. Whitney's *Gospel Themes*)
Third Meeting	Genealogy (Genealogical Society of Utah lesson book)
Fourth Meeting	Home Ethics
	Art (Alice M. Horne's *Devotees and Their Shrines*)

1925

First Meeting	Theology and Testimony (dispensations when the gospel was on the earth)
Second Meeting	Work and Business
Third Meeting	Literature (American)
Fourth Meeting	Social Service (a variety of topics including problem children and social aspects of education)

As the educational curriculum developed, other regular features grew, too. Through the years the *Relief Society Magazine* published countless stories and poems. Women received special encouragement to write creatively through the *Magazine*'s competitions. In fact, the Relief Society poem contest, which began in 1923 as the Eliza R. Snow Memorial poem contest, is the oldest writing competition in the Church. The *Magazine*'s poems generally dealt with matters of testimony and relationships, especially motherhood. A sample poem is "Discrimination," by Olive McHugh:

> "Your mother is a lovely rose,"
> I hear my neighbor say.
> She senses not variety;
> My mother is a choice bouquet.[7]

85

"Notes to the Field" was a regular column in which the general board instructed sisters in various aspects of Relief Society work. Even after the *Magazine*'s demise, "Notes to the Field" were sent to Relief Society workers for several years. Instructions might include policy decisions, as this notable item from World War I: "No Knitting During Meetings":

"The recent decision of the General Board was that knitting shall not be done during our meeting hours except at the regular work meetings. The inattention which is an accompaniment of active fingers is not polite to the speaker or class teacher, nor does it permit the members to get the most out of their lesson work. Our sisters will have plenty of time at home and in the work meetings to do all the knitting for which they can obtain yarn and thus assist the Red Cross cause."[8]

The *Magazine* also regularly featured reports of Relief Society Conference addresses, where Relief Society and priesthood leaders testified, counseled, and advised. Readers might hear from their president, in this instance, Belle S. Spafford: "There is within this society a great life-giving element—a spirit which reaches out to women . . . of all nationalities into a great sisterhood, unifying them in purpose and impelling them on to worthy accomplishment. This life-giving spirit is the spirit of the gospel; it is this which makes Relief Society different from other women's organizations the world over. It is this that gives to Relief Society its strength as well as its heart and soul."[9]

Or from priesthood leaders, such as Bishop LeGrand Richards: "I say, If you want anything done give it to the Relief Society. They never fail."[10]

More than any other section of the *Magazine*, "Notes from the Field," which ran from the first to the last issue, demonstrated that "charity never faileth" was more than a motto to thousands of Relief Society women. In the throes of depression and war, in the midst of abundance and peace, in struggling branches and burgeoning wards, Relief Society work went forward. Sometimes humorous, sometimes tragic, the accounts in "Notes from the Field," sent to Church headquarters by sisters, focused attention on the bazaars, visiting teaching, quilting, homemaking, singing mothers, socials, and compassionate service that were so much a part of Relief Society.

From the Netherlands Mission, 1940: "[Sister Zippro, president of the Relief Society in Holland] says she has never seen so many men marching, so many tanks, airplanes, and tractors, which caused a tremendous destruction of life. . . . She found many families in Rotterdam who had had their homes, furniture, and all earthly belongings completely destroyed and had gone to live with other members temporarily. The old hall in Rotterdam had been completely destroyed, but the new chapel over-mass was still intact, and the members were planning to hold Sunday School there."[11]

And from the East German Mission, Leipzig District, 1952: "Sister Lena Glaus, President, East German Mission Relief Society, reports the many problems and opportunities for service in the East German Mission: 'We think our mission is the best mission in the whole Church. Do you know why? Because no other mission has as many problems as we have.' "[12]

Relief Society did expand many a woman's sphere. The column entitled "Woman's Sphere," which appeared in the last decades of the *Magazine,* included selections that spoke to numerous areas in which women make positive contributions. Relief Society sisters felt it a privilege as well as a duty to contribute by making their homes and communities better places to live. Articles recount Relief Society's struggles against disease, fight for the vote, sponsorship of health and sanitation legislation, efforts for the Red Cross, and shipment of carloads of clothing to war-torn Europe.

While Latter-day Saint women looked forward in their community activities, they also looked back. Early on, the *Magazine* told stories of yesterday's women in a biographical series based on the lives of well-known Relief Society leaders. In later years the *Magazine* added tributes to lesser-known women whose private lives were filled with faith and courage.

How-to homemaking tips were also found in every issue of the *Magazine,* often a combination of the practical and the spiritual. The common themes included dedication to principles of providence, love of culture, and devotion to children.

Committed, thoughtful women wrote for the *Relief Society Magazine.* Their insights and inspirations on subjects ranging from gardening to dealing with stress show clearly that woman's sphere is indeed limitless and that Latter-day Saint women showed their faith through their works. Those who loved and tended the *Magazine* felt well rewarded for what it added to the lives of generations of Latter-day Saint women.

Notes

1. *Relief Society Magazine* 3 (March 1969): 162. All subsequent references are to the *Relief Society Magazine.*
2. 12 (December 1970): 894–95.
3. 11 (November 1970): 817.
4. 1 (January 1915): 38.
5. 1 (January 1922): 49.
6. 1 (January 1915): 22.
7. 5 (May 1940): 352.
8. 2 (February 1918): 101.
9. 3 (March 1949): 148.
10. 2 (February 1949): 75–76.
11. 9 (September 1940): 626.
12. 6 (June 1952): 409.

CHOOSING THE GOOD PART

There are important differences between the Savior and ourselves to be overcome during our mortal existence, but gender is not one of them. Being female is not something we have to repent of.

—Kathryn H. Shirts

Women in the Image of the Son:
Being Female and Being Like Christ

KATHRYN H. SHIRTS

In the popular children's book *The Neverending Story*, by German author Michael Ende, a young boy reading in an attic is magically drawn into the story and becomes one of the characters. The appeal is irresistible. What reader has not wanted, at some time or another, to pass from observer into participant and to share the adventures and friendships of a new world.

Of course, the experience of entering into the story depends upon finding a magic book, connected with powers beyond the printed page. In fantasy tales such books are never advertised publicly. They always seem to be hidden on dusty library shelves, waiting for the right person, with the proper sensitivity and imagination, to come along and discover their worth.

At first glance such stories strike us as delightful but utterly fantastic. We need to remember, however, that some fairy-tale makers have written their stories not for escapist reading but as metaphors for spiritual reality. As the professor in C. S. Lewis's *Chronicles of Narnia* tells the skeptical children when they ask about the possibility of doors into other worlds, "Nothing is more probable."[1]

Lucy Smith recalled that her son Joseph was not the child in the family who read the most but he was the one who pondered most deeply what he had read. When the familiar

Kathryn H. Shirts received her bachelor's degree in history from Stanford University and a master's degree in American church history from Harvard Divinity School. Kathryn, a homemaker, and her husband, Randall, a Brigham Young University chemistry professor, are the parents of six children.

passage from James, "If any of you lack wisdom, let him ask of God" (James 1:5), struck Joseph with uncommon force, he took the initiative and asked, thus moving into the world of the Spirit, which beckoned from the pages of the Bible. What made Joseph Smith unusual was the extent of his willingness to enter into the real "neverending story" by being receptive to messages and messengers from another world.

Not only could Joseph communicate with ancient prophets but he could also identify with them. As he dictated the Book of Mormon under inspiration, he learned of parallels between the Joseph who was sold into Egypt, Joseph the youngest son of Lehi, and a future Joseph who would be the son of another Joseph. (2 Nephi 3.) Thus while preparing the Book of Mormon, Joseph Smith was faced with a remarkable invitation to liken the scriptures unto himself.

In a fascinating paper on the book of Abraham, Machicko Takayama demonstrates some of the ways Joseph became involved in the experiences of earlier prophets. The scriptural narratives revealed through Joseph are presented in the first person, "I, Mormon," "I, Moses," "I, Abraham." Each of the narratives traces the genealogy of the author to earlier inspired writers, and each story refers to earlier stories. The narratives have a nesting structure, like the layers in the skin of an onion or like a series of Russian dolls, one inside the other. As Takayama writes, "The Book of Moses is the book of Noah is the book of Enoch is the book of Adam is the copy of the Book of Remembrance of God."[2] The endowment ceremony that Joseph introduced to the Saints in Nauvoo carried the story back to the very beginning of time where, in dramatic form, he reenacted the experiences of the creation as if he were Adam.

Although Joseph understood that his prophetic calling was unique, he also realized that, like Moses, his mission was to lead *all* the children of Israel into the presence of God. He delegated to others the authority that he received under the hands of heavenly messengers. He extended temple ordinances to ever-widening circles of followers. He inspired others to ask God and receive their own answers, to seek their own spiritual gifts, and to see the fulfillment of ancient prophecy in their own lives.

As the historian Richard Bushman has observed, when Joseph presented the ancient city of Enoch as a model for a new Zion society gathered from all the earth, "the sacred history of the past . . . flowed into the Mormon present." Bushman maintains that even today, "the sacred stories of Enoch, Moses, Nephi, Mormon, and Joseph Smith envelop Mormons in the realities of divine power and the redemption of Christ. . . . In the final analysis, the power of Joseph Smith to breathe new life into the ancient sacred stories, and to make a sacred story out of his own life, was the source of his extraordinary influence."[3]

How are we as a people responding to Joseph's challenge to enter into the sacred stories and transform our own lives? What about us as women? Do the scriptures invite women to participate in the realm of the Spirit as powerfully as they invite men? Is it more difficult for women to relate to the scriptures than it is for men? An experience in my own family made me realize how much more difficult it might be.

In a family home evening lesson several years ago, I brought up the story of Nephi's going to the Lord for instructions on how to build a ship. I asked our children if they thought that the Lord could help them do something practical like that, if they had a special need. My eight-year-old daughter's response was immediate: "No, because I'm a girl." She could not identify with Nephi nor relate to his experience, and the reason was gender.

What was behind her thinking? Perhaps it was that the scriptures record so few experiences of women. Although the Book of Mormon insists that God imparts his word by angels unto women as well as unto men (Alma 32:23), those angelic visits are "off the record." Since the sacred texts are written by male leaders of the spiritual community, it is their expe-

93

riences that are recorded as scriptural, sometimes giving the impression that they have a monopoly on such experiences.

What else was behind my daughter's thought? Perhaps it was the form of our scriptural language. The revelatory language of Joseph Smith's day was Elizabethan English, as represented in the King James Version of the Bible. One of the features of our literary heritage is that when we refer to men and women together, we use masculine nouns and pronouns. To a certain extent, this convention need not be a problem. As Madeleine L'Engle wrote, "I am female, of the species, *man*. Genesis is very explicit that it takes both male and female to make the image of God, and that the generic word, *man*, includes both. . . . When mankind was referred to it never occurred to me that I was not part of it."[4]

On the other hand, while the word *man* can refer generically to a man or to a woman, there are instances where *man* refers only to a male. There are times when it is not appropriate to expand words such as *man* to include a feminine counterpart. Our family learned that when we attempted to read the scriptures together, substituting "man and woman" for "man" or "son and daughter" for "son." We always had to make decisions about whether the inclusive language was appropriate in the context of the passage. Sometimes we found other scriptures that were similar and obviously inclusive to help us decide. Sometimes we found theological arguments. Sometimes we used clues from the passage itself. One of our sons loved to deliberately misuse inclusive language, referring to sizable armies coming down upon the Nephites as "the hosts and the hostesses."

As we tried to determine when inclusive language was appropriate, we became aware of a significant difference in the religious perspectives of men and women. Where men can freely assume the scriptures are speaking to them personally, women must ponder and weigh the evidence. As they read the scriptures, women must constantly make decisions about whether or not to include themselves in the text.

Is there any way to clarify the ambiguities—to affirm the spiritual potential of women and to demonstrate that the gospel, all of it, really does apply to them? Is there anyone with whom women can identify to make them full participants in the story?

What about the concept of a divine Woman, a Heavenly Mother? Joseph Smith suggested that the logic of the revealed gospel requires a Heavenly Mother as well as a Heavenly Father.[5] It is not surprising that Mormon women cherish the concept. A divine Mother represents a final destination for daughters, someone with whom they can identify fully and without ambiguity.

But even though we have the idea of a Heavenly Mother to whom women can relate without ambiguity, we still have a problem. Our concept of the divine Woman is itself ambiguous. Our scriptural stories give no accounts of her activities, no clues to her personality. Our theology contains no doctrine about how to relate to her.

We are tempted to fill the vacuum with images of a heavenly woman drawn from the earthly condition of women. We envision, perhaps, a nurturing figure devoted to innumerable spirit children but withdrawn from the wider realm of cosmic government. I remember a Primary class, in which someone asked the teacher, "If we have a Mother in Heaven, how come we never hear about her?" The teacher's reply was that God was protecting her name from the kinds of slander that human beings direct toward the names of the Father and the Son. It was a clever reply, and, at the time, we all thought it was quite satisfying. None of us realized then that this answer described a lady not quite up to taking care of herself in a tough world, an image drawn purely from certain human conventions and not from divine reality.

There have been attempts to fill out our idea of Heavenly Mother by borrowing from descriptions of goddesses in ancient cultures. Many of these societies revered powerful female figures who were thought to control fertility and the rhythm of the seasons, representing the giving and nurturing of life. As appealing as we might find the concept of dynamic female deities, however, from the perspective of overall morality, the pagan goddesses are ultimately no better role models than are the pagan gods.

So how do we handle the absence of information about our Heavenly Mother, the divine being who could embody the spiritual identity of women? Perhaps it is easier to understand this absence when we realize that we lack a detailed description of our Heavenly Father as well. The Savior spoke of the Father at every turn, but when Philip asked to be shown the Father, Jesus replied that the Father was made manifest through the Son. "Have I been so long time with you, and yet hast thou not known me, Philip? he that hath seen me hath seen the Father; and how sayest thou then, Shew us the Father?" (John 14:9.)

When we ask about the Mother, might not the Lord give us a similar reply? "He that hath seen me hath seen the Mother." We think of the Godhead as united in purpose and similar in character. If we as Mormons are going to assert the existence of a female Deity, shouldn't we assume that her Son mirrors her perfection as well as that of the Father?

When we take this approach, we see that both men and women can enter into the scriptural story and understand their spiritual potential by identifying with the Savior as "the way, the truth, and the life," the divine ideal and the divine mentor. (John 14:6.) But wait, we might ask. Isn't it important for women to have female role models? Can women learn about their own spiritual potential from a male? And can women be as much like Christ as can men?

In answering these questions, we need to consider the scriptural insistence that Jesus was not a man like other men. One of the limitations of human existence is to be locked into one's narrow perspective, based on one's nationality, social status, education, and gender. With perfect compassion the Savior transcended those limitations, descending below all

96

things to be in all things and through all things the light of truth. (D&C 88:6.)

The Gospels record his ability to step outside the perspective of a Jewish male to see women simply as individuals. In a society where women were not allowed to study the scriptures, he taught the Samaritan women at the well and he excused Mary from serving with Martha in order to study things of more value. Women were not permitted to function as legal witnesses, yet he allowed women to be the first witnesses to the resurrection. His parables balanced the shepherd hunting for the lost sheep with the woman hunting for the lost coin.[6]

As Dorothy Sayers wrote, "Perhaps it is no wonder that the women were first at the Cradle and last at the Cross. They had never known a man like this Man — there never has been such another. A prophet and teacher who never nagged at them, never flattered or coaxed or patronized; who never made arch jokes about them . . . who took their questions and arguments seriously; who never mapped out their sphere for them, never urged them to be feminine or jeered at them for being female; who had no axe to grind and no uneasy male dignity to defend."[7]

There have been many questions about whether Jesus was married. Without going into a detailed analysis of the issue, the writers of the gospel portray him as having no mortal wife or child. He is not limited to the role of an earthly husband. He is the bridegroom to the Church. (Matthew 9:14–15; D&C 88:92.) But then again he is the mother hen who would gather her chicks under her wing. (Matthew 23:37; 3 Nephi 10:4–6; D&C 10:65.) The Savior used many images to describe the Atonement — the image of grain being buried in the ground to ensure a harvest, the image of a building being destroyed and rebuilt, the image of a man laying down his life for his friends. (John 12:23–24, 2:19, 15:13.) He also used the image of a woman in labor. (John 16:20–22.)

It is this image of Christ's spiritual suffering to bring forth spiritual life, as a woman suffers physically to bring forth physical life, that reverberates throughout the scriptures. "Inasmuch as ye were born into the world by water, and blood, and the spirit, which I have made, and so became of dust a living soul," God tells Adam, as recorded in the book of Moses, "Even so ye must be born again into the kingdom of heaven, of water, and of the Spirit, and be cleansed by blood, even the blood of mine Only Begotten; that ye might be sanctified from all sin, and enjoy the words of eternal life in this world, and eternal life in the world to come." (Moses 6:59.) King Benjamin declares that because the hearts of his people have been changed through faith in Christ, they have become "the children of Christ, his sons, and his daughters." (Mosiah 5:7.) King Benjamin uses dual imagery. Christ has spiritually begotten them — in other words, he has become their father — and they are born of him, in essence making him their mother as well.

Just as the scriptures describe the Savior using both male and female imagery, the scriptures insist that God is serious about women identifying with Christ. In Genesis, we learn that God created man in his own image, male and female. (Genesis 1:27.) The book of Moses adds "in the image of his own body, male and female, created he them" and also "in the image of mine Only Begotten created I him; male and female created I them." (Moses 6:9, 2:27.) There are important differences between the Savior and ourselves to be overcome during our mortal existence, but gender is not one of them. Being female is not something we have to repent of.

According to the book of Moses account, God brings Moses up into a high mountain to speak with him face to face. In that exalted interview, he declares, "I have a work for thee, Moses, my son; and thou art in the similitude of mine Only Begotten; and mine Only Begotten is and shall be the Savior, for he is full of grace and truth." Moses is profoundly impressed to hear that he is "in the similitude" of Christ. When the presence of God withdraws from Moses and he is left to confront Satan, he asks the adversary, "Who art thou? For behold, I am a son of God, in the similitude of his Only Begotten; and where is thy glory, that I should worship thee?" And Moses insists a second time, "Get thee hence, Satan; deceive me not; for God said unto me: Thou art after the similitude of mine Only Begotten." (Moses 1:6, 13, 16.)

Since all human beings are created in the image of the Savior, as the book of Moses explicitly states (Moses 6:9, 2:27), we can envision God's saying to all of us as he said to Moses: "Thou art after the similitude of mine Only Begotten." Women may thus enter into the story themselves, identifying with the Savior and acknowledging their relationship with him: "For behold, I am a daughter of God, in the similitude of his Only Begotten."

There are other suggestions in the scriptures that, since we can all relate to the Savior, we can all relate to the crucial stories detailing the process of salvation, regardless of whether the stories are told about men or women. The same verse which declares that God created male and female in the image of his own body also states that when God created male and female he called *their* name Adam. This usage reflects the Hebrew '*adam*, which can refer to humanity or mankind in general.[8]

With this collective meaning in mind, we see the story of Adam's baptism in the book of Moses as the story of Eve's baptism as well and therefore as the example for all human beings that it is clearly intended to be. After God has explained the plan of salvation to Adam, Adam is carried away by the Spirit of the Lord and immersed in water. When he has been baptized, the Spirit of God descends upon him and he is born of the Spirit. A voice from heaven then declares: "Thou art baptized with fire, and with the Holy Ghost. This is the record of the Father, and the Son, from henceforth and forever; And thou art after the order of him who was without beginning of days or end of years, from all eternity to all eternity. Behold, thou art one in me, a son of God; and thus may all become my sons." (Moses 6:66–68.)

What God says about Adam as his son, and thus about Eve

as his daughter, at the time of baptism parallels the identifying characteristics of those who receive eternal life as defined in Doctrine and Covenants 76.

• In Moses 6:68 Adam is declared a "son of God." Doctrine and Covenants 76:58 calls those who endure to the end "gods, even the sons of God."

• After his baptism by the water and by the Spirit, God tells Adam, "thou art one in me." (Moses 6:68.) Doctrine and Covenants 76:59 says of those who overcome by faith, "all things are theirs . . . and they are Christ's, and Christ is God's."

• God informs Adam that "he is baptized with fire, and with the Holy Ghost," implying that a member of the Godhead is present with him representing, or bearing record, of the Father and the Son. (Moses 6:66.) Those who are sealed by the Holy Spirit of Promise, according to Doctrine and Covenants 76:62, "dwell in the presence of God and his Christ forever."

• After his baptism, God tells Adam, "Thou art after the order of him who was without beginning of days or end of years, from all eternity to all eternity." (Moses 6:67.) Doctrine and Covenants 76:57 explains that the inhabitants of the celestial world "are after the order of Melchizedek, which was after the order of Enoch, which was after the order of the Only Begotten Son."

To go through the process of salvation, therefore, is to assume a series of identities in relationship to the Savior by obedience to the first principles of the gospel. We are born into the world as children of God, in the image of his Only Begotten Son. When we are born of the water and of the Spirit, we become sons and daughters of Christ through his atonement. Those who endure to the end in the divine tutorial complete the identification. In the words of John, "Beloved, now are we the sons of God, and it doth not yet appear what we shall be: but we know that, when he shall appear, we shall be like him: for we shall see him as he is." (John 3:2.)

It does not yet appear what we shall be because we are in

process, but to be in process at all is to have gone beyond the pages of the scriptures and entered into the story. The Savior becomes not only an ideal but a sustaining presence, not only the text but the interpreter of the text, not only an exemplar but a companion. Thus to read the scriptures is to be open to a divine dialogue, to be speaking with another Character in the story.

In his earthly life, the Savior himself entered into this kind of dialogue as a child growing from grace to grace in the image of a parent. He was instructed in the Law and the Prophets and immersed in the traditions of the Jews, yet it was through his close relationship to the Father that the Savior was able to recognize himself in the scriptures and carry out his divine mission. The role of the Messiah, his own special role, was always present in the scriptures, but it was comprehended through personal inspiration.

As women we have several options in dealing with our own scriptural heritage. One alternative is to object to the male language and male culture saturating the scriptures and reject the scriptures as irrelevant to our needs as women. Another option is, as obedient daughters of God, to accept the scriptures but be overwhelmed by their predominantly male perspective and underestimate our own spiritual potential. Relying on the Savior as a model and as a mentor, however, we have yet another approach. We can immerse ourselves in the scriptures and, at the same time, by being open to the influence of his Spirit, relate them to our own lives and circumstances. In the intercessory prayer recorded in 3 Nephi, the resurrected Lord prays that those who believe in him might be purified, "that I may be in them as thou, Father, art in me." (19:29.) The intimacy of that relationship overcomes the distance that can be created by any particular form of scriptural language and brings women as well as men into the very center of the story.

Notes

1. C. S. Lewis, *The Lion, the Witch, and the Wardrobe* (New York: Macmillan, 1981), p. 46.

2. Machiko Takayama, "The Book of Abraham — A Grammatological Analysis," presented at the Sunstone Symposium. Salt Lake City, Utah, August, 1990, p. 19; copy in possession of author.
3. Richard L. Bushman, *Joseph Smith and the Beginnings of Mormonism* (Urbana: University of Illinois Press, 1984), pp. 186, 188.
4. Madeleine L'Engle, *Walking on Water* (Wheaton, Illinois: Harold Shaw Publishers, 1980), p. 36.
5. "An interesting sidelight is given to this time through a possible glimpse of the thought-kernel which grew into such fragrant bloom in the full-voiced poem of Sister Snow. It was told by Aunt Zina D. Young to the writer as to many others during her life. Father Huntington lost his wife under the most trying circumstances. Her children were left desolate. One day, when her daughter Zina was speaking with the Prophet Joseph Smith concerning the loss of her mother and her intense grief, she asked the question:

" 'Will I know my mother as my mother when I get over on the Other Side?'

" 'Certainly you will,' was the instant reply of the Prophet. 'More than that, you will meet and become acquainted with your eternal Mother, the wife of your Father in Heaven.'

" 'And have I then a Mother in Heaven?' exclaimed the astonished girl.

" 'You assuredly have. How could a Father claim His title unless there were also a Mother to share that parenthood?'

"It was about this time that Sister Snow learned the same glorious truth from the same inspired lips, and at once she was moved to express her own great joy and gratitude in the moving words of the hymn, 'O my Father.' " Susa Young Gates, *History of the Young Ladies' Mutual Improvement Association of the Church of Jesus Christ of Latter-day Saints from November 1869 to June 1910* (Salt Lake City: General Board of the Y.L.M.I.A., 1911), p. 16, footnote.
6. Jolene Edmunds Rockwood, "Jesus and Judaism," 1987 Sunstone New Testament Symposium, 11 August 1987.
7. Dorothy Sayers, *Are Women Human?* (Grand Rapids, Michigan: William B. Eerdmans Publishing Co., 1971), p. 47.
8. Jolene Edmunds Rockwood, "Eve's Role in the Creation and the Fall to Mortality," in *Women and the Power Within: To See Life Steadily and See It Whole*, ed. Dawn Hall Anderson and Marie Cornwall (Salt Lake City: Deseret Book Co., 1991), p. 50.

Choosing the Good Part:
Women from Christ to Paul
JOLENE EDMUNDS ROCKWOOD

There is an interesting story in Luke 10:38–42. Jesus has gone to Bethany, to the home of Mary, Martha, and Lazarus, whom Jesus later would raise from the dead. Mary is sitting with Jesus, listening to his word, when Martha, cumbered about with much serving, comes to him and says, "Lord, dost thou not care that my sister hath left me to serve alone? Bid her therefore that she help me." And Jesus answers her and says, "Martha, Martha, thou art careful and troubled about many things: but one thing is needful: and Mary hath chosen that good part, which shall not be taken away from her."

This story has powerful implications for us as women, for in speaking as he did, Christ departed from the role of women in the Judaic tradition, and in so doing set Christian precedents that are as relevant to us today as they were when they were first uttered.

What was the role of a woman in the society in which Jesus was born and grew up? The Midrash and the Talmud, early Jewish writings dating from about 400 B.C. to the latter part of the first Christian century, indicate that Jews at this time believed that Eve was solely responsible for the transgression in Eden and that, because of her role in the Fall, all women were subject to and inferior to men. Also, because Eve was formed from Adam's rib, women were regarded as a secondary cre-

Jolene Edmunds Rockwood holds a master's degree in theological studies from the Harvard Divinity School and is a widely known lecturer and author on the subject of women and religion. The founder of the Rural Alliance for the Arts in Indiana, Sister Rockwood is a homemaker. She resides with her husband, Fred, and their six children in Indiana.

ation.[1] Although in Judaism a woman was highly honored in her role as mother, she had no role in public worship. In the synagogues, men and women were separated during worship to prevent the women from "distracting" the men, a tradition referring back to the image of Eve as temptress. As woman was the cause of Adam's fall, so also a woman's voice in a religious meeting would tempt a man away from higher worship.[2] It was the woman's duty to listen and not to respond or be seen.

Even some of the religious rituals a woman conducted in the home became her responsibility because of Eve's actions in the Garden of Eden. The woman, for example, was to light the candles to begin the Sabbath observance because it was woman who originally "extinguished the light of man's soul."[3] When she kneaded dough, it was her responsibility to separate out a "heave" offering (the best portions of the sacrificial animal which historically were set aside for Yahweh and the priests before the sacrifice was made) to make amends for Eve's defiling Adam, who was "the heave offering of the world."[4]

A woman "acquired merit" by encouraging her husband and sons to study the Torah, but "whoever teaches his daughter Torah is as though he taught her obscenity." Jews were to "let the words of the Torah rather be destroyed by fire than imparted to women," because "a woman has no learning except in the use of the spindle."[5]

The men were encouraged to leave their wives at home and "go into the marketplace and learn intelligence from other men," because women, by nature of their creation, were intellectually and physically inferior to men.[6] The Midrash records that God deliberated long in deciding which part of the body he would use to make the wife of Adam, but "in spite of the great caution used, woman has all the faults God tried to obviate" — including haughtiness, eavesdropping, wantonness, and jealousy. These characteristics were seen as evident not only in Eve but also in Sarah, "an eavesdropper in her own tent"; Miriam, "a talebearer" who accused Moses; Rachel, who was "envious" of Leah; and Dinah, who was a "gadabout."[7] At

104

their first meeting Adam perceived these pernicious qualities in Eve and knew she would "seek to carry her point with man either by entreaties and tears, or flattery and caresses."[8]

The Midrash also derives other qualities of women from that primeval rib. For example, women need to use perfumes and men do not because "dust of the ground remains the same no matter how long it is kept; flesh, however, requires salt to keep it in good condition." Women's voices are high and "shrill" and men's are not because "when soft viands are cooked, no sound is heard, but let a bone be put in a pot, and at once it crackles." Women are rigid and not easily placated, as men are, because "a few drops of water suffice to soften a clod of earth" but "a bone stays hard" and will not soften in water. It is the man who proposes marriage and not the woman because man lost his rib and must find a woman to retrieve it. And finally, "women precede men in a funeral cortege, because it was woman who brought death into the world."[9]

Jews prayed for sons and celebrated when they were born. No corresponding celebration marked the birth of a daughter. "The world cannot exist without males and females," a rabbinical dictum states, "but happy is he whose children are sons and woe to him whose children are daughters."[10] "The Lord bless thee with sons and keep thee from daughters" were the words of the priestly benediction.[11]

According to Israelite law, after childbirth a woman must not touch any sacred vessel or enter any sacred place until she was "purified." If her child was male, this period was forty days; if a daughter, purification required twice as long, eighty days. And, finally, to be born male was itself reason to give thanks daily: "A man is obliged to offer three benedictions daily; that He has made me an Israelite, that He has not made me a woman, that He has not made me a boor."[12]

Thus in the Jewish writings that emerged between the end of the Old Testament period and the first centuries after Christ, the Genesis Adam and Eve account was used by many com-

105

mentators to justify cultural practices, explain, or even create, sexual characteristics, and define roles of men and women.

The Midrash, Talmud, and apocryphal and pseudepigraphal literature were all in use by the Jews at the time of Christ and shaped the society into which he was born. Jesus Christ was born into a strict Jewish household. His Judaic lineage, his ancestral line back to David and ultimately to Adam, is listed in two different places in the Gospels. (Matthew 1:1–17; Luke 3:23–38.) There are many indications that Joseph and Mary were strict observers of the law of Moses, as were Mary's cousin Elisabeth and Zacharias, the parents of John the Baptist. Zacharias was a Levite and a priest in the temple. (Luke 1:5.) We know that John the Baptist went through the ritual rite of circumcision after eight days and that an angelic visitor attended the circumcision ceremony and gave John a special blessing. (Luke 1:59; D&C 84:28.) Most certainly, Jesus followed this same route, as did all Jewish boys. (Luke 2:21.)

After the ritual forty-day purification period, Joseph and Mary took the baby Jesus to the temple, in accordance with the law of Moses, to offer a sacrifice and present the child. (Luke 2:22–38.) Jesus' education undoubtedly began as a small child, for all Jewish mothers used the psalms and prayers as lullabies. When little boys were three, their fathers began "to teach them . . . scripture, benedictions, and wise sayings. Formal schooling began at five or six, with the Bible as the text."[13] A boy, at seventeen, would then go on to rabbinical academies. The four Gospel accounts of his ministry show that Jesus had a thorough knowledge of Jewish literature, not just the Old Testament, but the Midrash, Talmud, and other Jewish rabbinical writings, which he used to teach his disciples and condemn hypocrisy.

"But the educational system imposed upon Jewish children was more, far more, than formal schooling arrangements," notes Elder Bruce R. McConkie in *The Mortal Messiah*. "It was part and portion of their way of life. . . . [In the home] private prayers were offered both morning and evening. Before every meal they washed and prayed, and after every repast they gave thanks. . . . Every Sabbath was a holy and sanctified day." Jesus Christ was "a product . . . of his environment; and his Father chose to place him in the care and custody, during his formative years, of Jewish Joseph and Jewish Mary and their Jewish home with all its Jewish teachings, practices, and ways of worship."[14]

When he was twelve, his parents took him to the temple, another custom of the time. All Jewish boys were schooled at the local synagogue in the Torah. At the age of twelve or thirteen, they were presented at the temple to be questioned on their knowledge and then to become "a son of the law,"[15] a process very similar to the present-day bar mitzvah. What a surprise they must have had the day Jesus came, for he not only had the entire body of Jewish literature memorized but he also understood its true meanings so completely that he ended up being questioner and teacher of those learned men who were to examine him. No wonder he either stayed or went back to the temple long after his appointed interview time and missed joining the caravan back to Nazareth. We can only imagine what kind of information he gave the learned men at the temple that would forever change them and prepare them for his future ministry. Surely, from that point on, all Sanhedrin eyes were upon the young boy from Nazareth, if they were not already.

And why didn't his parents understand his question, "Wist ye not that I must be about my Father's business?" (Luke 2:49.) When Joseph is called a carpenter in the scriptures, it could mean more than an occupation, for the Hebrew word for *carpenter* was also used frequently in rabbinic literature to mean "scholar, teacher, builder of men." Could it have been Joseph's business to teach as a scholar, or a carpenter of men's souls? We know Jesus meant his Father in Heaven, but how could Mary and Joseph have missed the obvious meaning to his statement, unless there were two meanings?[16]

We know Christ progressed "from grace to grace" until he reached the point that he "could not be taught by any man" and "received a fullness" or a full knowledge of his mission. (D&C 93:13; JST Matthew 3:25; D&C 93:12–13.) He was probably taught by heavenly visitors, in addition to attending school and studying the Torah at the local synagogue with the other boys. In all things, he was the ultimate Jew.[17]

Considering his thorough and complete knowledge of the Law, it is interesting to note not only what the Savior did talk about but also what he omitted in his teachings. In contrast to the Jewish tradition and literature, he did not use the story of Adam and Eve as an explanation for either the origin of sin or the respective roles of men and women. On the contrary, he taught that people were not punished for the previous sins of parents or any ancestors, as we see in the story of the man born blind: "Who did sin?" asked the disciples, "this man, or his parents, that he was born blind?" (John 9:2.) No one's sins were visited on the man, Christ answered. The implications of his answer call into question other Jewish traditions: how, then, could the perceived sin of Eve still be passed on to every Jewish woman?

He demonstrated continually in his actions and words his respect for women as equals to men in the eyes of God. Many women were numbered among his closest associates, including Mary Magdalene, Joanna, Susanna, and others. (Luke 8:1–3.) The disciples referred to them as the "women also of our company." (Luke 24:22.) His relationship with many women was a dear friendship. He loved Martha, Mary, and Lazarus (as it says in John 11:5) and wept openly when he saw the distress of Mary over the death of her brother Lazarus. (John 11:35.)

His gospel was one in which women could fully participate. His doctrines liberated them spiritually, giving them equality. Now let us return to the story of Mary and Martha of Bethany where we see, for the first time, a woman being given full permission to sit at the feet of a rabbi and study the Law. That, remember, was considered heresy in Jewish tradition. And why did Martha appeal to Jesus for help instead of just asking Mary to come and help? Because Jesus was the rabbi, and rabbis didn't teach women. But instead of turning her away, he announced for all to hear that Mary had chosen the good part, that women were to have the same spiritual priorities as men, and that the worldly cares of the world were less important.

When the woman with an issue of blood touched the hem of his garment, according to Jewish laws of purity, he should have rebuked her, for she was unclean and by touching him had made him unclean. (Leviticus 15:19–30.) But instead, he blessed her and healed her and praised her for her great faith. (Mark 5:25–34.) Similarly, it was forbidden to touch the dead body of Jairus's daughter, but Jesus raised her from the dead and blessed her. (Numbers 19:11–22; Mark 5:35–43.) He openly taught the Samaritan woman at the well, despite the rabbinic admonition against a rabbi speaking with a woman in public. "And upon this [scene] came his disciples, and marvelled that he talked with the woman: yet no man said, What seekest thou? or, Why talkest thou with her?" (John 4:27.) Disregarding the Jewish refusal to allow a woman's testimony as a witness in any situation, [18] Jesus appeared first to women as a resurrected being, entrusting the first witnessing of the world's greatest event to women. "Go to my brethren," he told Mary, and tell them. (John 20:17.) When they ran to the apostles and exclaimed the good news, the women's words "seemed to them as idle tales, and they believed them not." (Luke 24:10–11.)

So too, the first to bear news of the Messiah to the Samaritans was the woman at the well, and the people "believed on him" because of the woman's testimony. (John 4:39–40.) It was a prophetess, Anna, who, along with Simeon, declared the divinity of the newborn Messiah when Mary and Joseph took him to the temple. (Luke 2:36–38.) When some of the apostles murmured against Mary for anointing Jesus with expensive ointment, he chastised them, saying that she was the only one among them that recognized his impending death, "for she hath poured this ointment on my body for my burial. And in this thing that she hath done, she shall be blessed; for verily I say unto you, Wheresoever this gospel shall be preached in the whole world, this thing that this woman hath done, shall also be told for a memorial of her." (JST Matthew 26:9–10.)

We see throughout the Gospels an intentional attempt to relate the truths he taught equally to men and women. Women are included as models and examples in just as many parables, miracles, and sermons as men. That is most dramatically seen in the pairing of men-women examples in his teachings, as if to make sure that women as well as men saw his teachings as relevant. For example, in Luke 15:3–7, a male shepherd leaves the ninety and nine to find a lost sheep and, in verses 8–10, a woman loses a coin and searches her home until she finds it. Both rejoice in the finding. The point of both stories is the same: the worth of every individual, male or female, is great, and heaven rejoices over one sinner that repents. Yet they are told sequentially in the text, emphasizing that these truths apply equally to men and women. Another example is found in Luke 7:2–15. Christ heals the centurion's servant and immediately afterward raises the widow's son — one miracle for a man, and the next for a woman. In Matthew 13:31–33 he likens the kingdom of heaven, first, to a grain of mustard seed that a man plants in his garden and, second, to some leaven that a woman puts in her dough, both parables told sequentially and yet having exactly the same message. In Luke 13:10–16, the Savior heals a woman on the Sabbath; in 14:2–6, he heals a man on the Sabbath. In Luke 17:35–36, one man shall be taken from two who are in the field, and one woman shall be taken from two who are grinding. Jesus heals a Gentile's daughter and then a deaf man in Mark 7:24–37, and in Matthew 9:20–30 he heals a woman, raises a girl from the dead, and heals two blind men.

Two examples of great faith are told sequentially in Matthew 9:18–26. The first tells of a ruler whose daughter was dead. He came to Jesus and said in faith, "Come and lay thy hand upon her, and she shall live," as the woman two verses later also said in faith, "If I may but touch his garment, I shall

110

be whole." "Daughter, be of good comfort; thy faith hath made thee whole," he said to her. Other examples of pairing are found throughout the four Gospels; Luke, more than the other evangelists, groups them together, but all the Gospel writers relate numerous examples of healings, parables, and exhortations involving women equally with men.[19]

Christian doctrine that made women full participants in worship must have caused problems for the early converts to the young Church Christ left behind at his death, for all the first converts to Christianity were Jewish, presumably burdened with the traditional attitudes about women. Judaism and Christianity were so intertwined that in the beginning of the missionary effort after Christ's death, the twelve apostles proselyted only among the Jews and did not think that a Gentile should be baptized into the Church.

The Lord gave Peter direct revelation, instructing him that the time had come to baptize non-Jewish Christians. Cornelius, a Roman centurion who was converted to Christ, was told by a heavenly messenger to send for Peter in Joppa. Before Cornelius's men arrived, Peter, while praying, saw the heavens open and all manner of animals descending unto him, animals that were unclean and forbidden according to the Law of Moses. A voice told Peter to kill and eat the animals. "Not so, Lord," he replied, "for I have never eaten anything that is common or unclean." The voice answered, "What God hath cleansed, that call not thou common." When the servants of Cornelius arrived, then, he was prepared to go with them, and when he met Cornelius, he said, "Ye know ... it is an unlawful thing [according to the Jewish Law] for a man that is a Jew to keep company, or come unto one of another nation; but God hath shewed me [using traditional Jewish symbols that he would understand] that I should not call any man common or unclean." (Acts 10:14, 15, 28.)

With the conversion of non-Jews to Christianity came the necessity of determining which of the traditions of the past were compatible with the new faith and which were not. An

111

example of that is seen in Acts 15. A dissension arose in Antioch among the Jews about whether or not a male Gentile convert to the Church had to be circumcised and keep the law of Moses. The apostles gathered in Jerusalem to determine Church policy on the subject. We can only imagine how many of these types of issues must have come up when Gentile converts began joining the Church. As members of the Latter-day Church in this dispensation, we ourselves have had similar challenges in sorting out doctrine and culture, as we have evolved into an international church and taken the gospel message to underdeveloped nations, where Church programs often need to be eliminated or heavily adapted to local situations.

The apostle Paul was particularly sympathetic to the problems involved in separating Jewish culture from Christian doctrine. He was "all things to all" people, that he "might by all means save some." (1 Corinthians 9:22.) Specifically, "unto the Jews I became as a Jew, that I might gain the Jews. . . . to the weak became I as weak, that I might gain the weak." (1 Corinthians 9:20, 22.) Very often Paul had to walk a fine line between Jewish customs and Christian principles. He often used references to the law of Moses and traditions to demonstrate a principle or prove a point to the Jews.

Paul had been a devout defender of Judaism against Christianity. Reared a Pharisee, he had been trained under the renowned Jewish scholar Gamaliel and was, by his own description, a "zealous" observer of the Jewish law. (Acts 22:3.) He was present at the stoning of the Christian disciple Stephen and "was consenting unto his death." (Acts 7:58; 8:1.) Paul was prevented by a miraculous conversion from further persecuting the Christians. (Acts 22.) By the time he wrote those epistles now preserved in the New Testament, he knew both Judaism and Christianity thoroughly.

It is in the epistles of Paul or in letters attributed to him that the status and conduct of women are most discussed. These communications with various units of the Church contained advice, doctrine, and answers to questions that had caused conflicts within individual units of the Church. Before examining these passages, we need to remind ourselves of some things. First, these passages represent a very small portion of Paul's total writings, and so not only must we look at Paul's message as a whole to see how these smaller segments fit in but we also must not let a few passages color the rest of the tremendous doctrinal wisdom and teachings of Paul that include both men and women.

Second, we need to remember that these epistles were answers to specific questions and problems that were troubling the small units of the Church throughout the Christian world. These groups were living far away from the center of the Church in Jerusalem. Eventually they became even more isolated as the leaders of the Church were killed, Christians became openly and viciously persecuted, and Jerusalem's prominence as Church headquarters decreased.

Third, the early converts to the Church brought with them all kinds of baggage from previous beliefs, particularly the Jews who had a totally different view of women's role in worship. That is why we often find Paul referring first to the Law, meaning the law of Moses or the Torah, and then stating a Christian principle to support or refute it. As the Church spread throughout the Roman Empire, Paul also had to deal with influences of Roman and Greek traditions which often stood in contrast to Jewish law.

And fourth, other evidence in the book of Acts and elsewhere in the New Testament clearly indicates that, in general, women were fully participating in the gospel of Christ. There are references to women praying, prophesying, speaking in tongues, and exercising all manner of spiritual gifts along with the men. (1 Corinthians 11:5; 12:8–10.) *All* (both men and women) were filled with the Holy Ghost on the Day of Pentecost. (Acts 2:1–4, 11.) "Quench not the Spirit. Despise not prophesyings" of any member, male or female, the Saints are told in 1 Thessalonians 5:19–20. The four daughters of Philip

113

the evangelist "did prophesy." (Acts 21:9.) Priscilla and her husband, Aquila, are Paul's companions whom he refers to as "my helpers in Christ Jesus: who have for my life laid down their own necks." (Romans 16:3–4.) They taught Apollos, "an eloquent man, and mighty in the scriptures . . . whom when Aquila and Priscilla had heard, they took him unto them, and expounded unto him the way of God more perfectly." (Acts 18:24–26.) Paul's missionary efforts in Thessalonica included a great multitude of devout Greeks, including "of the chief women not a few." The order is reversed a few verses later: "Therefore many of them believed; also of honorable women which were Greeks, and of men, not a few." (Acts 17:4, 12.) Tabitha (or Dorcas), a leading member of the Church in Joppa and a woman filled with good works, died and was raised from the dead by Peter. (Acts 9:36.) In his letter to the Romans, Paul commends Phebe, "our sister" who is a "servant of the church" at Cenchrea, and asks that they receive her and assist her in her business. (Romans 16:1–2.) Many commentators have speculated that because of Phebe's official business, she may have held the office of Deaconess.[20] He also greets "Mary, who bestowed much labour on us," and many other men and women of the local church. (Romans 16:6.) When the Sanhedrin gives Saul letters authorizing the arrests of Christian Jews in Damascus, he states that he is seeking men and women. (Acts 9:1, 2.) He subsequently notes "binding and delivering into prisons both men and women." (Acts 22:4.) It seems very clear that women are playing an important and esteemed role in the gospel in the early Church.

Let us now look at some of the specific passages concerning women that have been problematic. Several of these are found in 1 Corinthians. This letter was written to address problems of the newly formed church in Corinth, a Greek city near Athens. Paul begins his epistle with pleas for unity. "I beseech you, " he says, to "all speak the same thing, and that there be no divisions among you; but that ye be perfectly joined together in the same mind." (1:10.) Apparently the Corinthians' prob-

114

lems were originating from contention and lack of unity: some were followers of Paul, others Apollos, others of Cephas, others of Christ. "Is Christ divided?" he asks. "The Jews require a sign, and the Greeks seek after wisdom: But we preach Christ crucified, unto the Jews a stumbling block, and unto the Greeks foolishness." (1:13, 22, 23.)

In the following chapter Paul then describes what constitutes a true follower of Christ. He talks about the role of the Holy Ghost in revealing truth, the need for the natural man to become spiritual. (2:10–15.) He has fed the Corinthians "with milk, and not with meat," for they are as yet spiritually immature. (3:2.) He chastises them for tolerating sinful practices among the members, including marital infidelity and changing the ordinances of the gospel. (1 Corinthians 5–7, 10.) He returns again and again to his plea for unity among them, using symbols of all members being part of the body of the Church, different, yet working together for the whole. (12:12–31.) Many have interpreted Paul's discussion in chapter 7 of marital fidelity to mean he was advocating celibacy as a higher state than marriage. The Joseph Smith Translation, however, makes an important change that indicates Paul is actually speaking of celibacy for men and women serving missions, not as a general rule. (JST 1 Corinthians 7:29–33.)

Paul's advice involving women was usually a mixture of Jewish customs and Christian doctrine. In 1 Corinthians 11, he responds to a contention among the Corinthians relating to whether a woman should be veiled during worship. It probably represented a conflict between the traditional Judaizers, whose women always wore veils during worship, and the new Hellenistic converts who never wore veils. He tells the Corinthians that he approves of women praying and prophesying in the Church (Christian principle) as long as they cover their heads (Jewish tradition). Paul recites the traditional Jewish interpretation of the Adam and Eve story to make his case: man "is the image and glory of God: but the woman is the glory of the man. For the man is not of the woman; but the woman of the

115

man. Neither was the man created for the woman; but the woman for the man" and, for this reason, "ought the woman to have power [also translated as *veil*] on her head because of the angels." (Vv. 7–10.)

To the Jews, a veil or head-covering served as a sign upon all women of the shame of Eve for bringing sin into the world, and it also protected women, with their weaker wills, from the influence of evil angels. It was also worn by women in synagogues to keep their presence from distracting the men from their worship.[21] Thus Paul presents the classic Jewish interpretation of the rib story in Genesis 2.

Paul then changes the direction of his argument, going beyond Jewish tradition to state a Christian truth: "Nevertheless," he concludes, "[the true principle here is that] neither is the man without the woman, neither the woman without the man, in the Lord. For as the woman is of the man, [as Eve was of Adam], even so is the man also by the woman [as Christ was by Mary]; but all things of God." (1 Corinthians 11:11–12.) Having thus stated both Jewish and Christian viewpoints, he then seems to throw the question back to the askers to answer for themselves: "Judge in yourselves: is it comely that a woman pray unto God uncovered? Doth not even nature itself teach you, that, if a man have long hair, it is a shame unto him? But if a woman have long hair, it is a glory to her: for her hair is given her for a covering." (Vv. 13–15.) But without additional information to help them avoid interpreting the question from within their culture, the questions would, more than likely, simply be heard as rhetorical. He has taken the question and relegated it to the area of etiquette and good taste rather than of doctrine. "If any man seem to be contentious [over this issue], we [the Jews] have no such custom [anymore], neither the [new Christian] churches of God," he concludes. (V. 16.)

The important point here, somewhat obscured by the veil question, is that the women were praying and prophesying in worship services alongside the men, a far cry from the traditional Jewish practice, and that in the Christian Church "neither

116

is the man without the woman, neither the woman without the man, in the Lord." Paul then proceeds to another issue, calling the first a division, but the next one a heresy: changing ordinances and partaking of the sacrament unworthily. (Vv. 19–34.)

Paul continues with his plea for unity in chapters 12, 13, and 14, where he lists the gifts of the Spirit, stressing that each gift is a part of the whole, as each person is a part of the whole body of Christ, or the Church. "For by one Spirit are we all baptized into one body, whether we be Jews or Gentiles, . . . bond or free; . . . for the body is not one member, but many." (1 Corinthians 12:13–14.) All are necessary, including the feeble and the less comely. "That there should be no schism" in the body, the greatest of all spiritual gifts is charity, the pure love of Christ which "never faileth." (1 Corinthians 12:23–25; 13:8.)

Then, in chapter 14, Paul interrupts his lengthy discourse on unity and gifts of the Spirit with a startling and uncharacteristic exclamation: "Let your women keep silence in the churches: for it is not permitted unto them to speak; but they are commanded to be under obedience, as also saith the law. And if they will learn any thing, let them ask their husbands at home: for it is a shame for women to speak in the church." (Vv. 34–35.) These two verses are omitted from official Church lesson manuals, never quoted in Church meetings, and left unexplained in commentaries. These verses are problematic because we know from latter-day revelation that this doctrine is not part of the Gospel of Jesus Christ. Women learn, as do the men, in church. They teach as do the men, they participate fully in the gospel, and, while they are at liberty to ask their husbands doctrinal questions at home, they are fully capable of learning at church as well. Second, these verses disagree with and reverse other doctrinal statements appearing in Paul's writings, such as 1 Corinthians 11, where he states that women could pray and prophesy as long as they had their heads covered (vv. 5–15), or 1 Corinthians 14, where he affirms that *all* [women and men] should speak in tongues, *all* should proph-

117

esy, and *all* should let the gifts of the Spirit flow freely (vv. 5, 24, 31, 39). It also contradicts his earlier pleas for unity and equality among the members of the "body" of the Church. (1 Corinthians 12.) Has Paul completely reversed his stand? Was all his talk about unity and equality in the previous chapters to be undone in two verses? Many New Testament scholars, noting how out of place the verses seem in their context, have concluded that they were not the words of Paul but were inserted later through some scribal error. But, once again, the Joseph Smith Translation clarifies things, for it changes the word *speak* to *rule*, thus putting the issue into the realm of priesthood authority. The question then becomes one of who will preside in the Church. (JST 1 Corinthians 14:34.)

Another explanation for 1 Corinthians 14:34–35 is the possiblity that Paul was quoting, for emphasis, directly from the letter he had received, his intent being to contrast the Corinthian Saints' attitudes with the unity and equality which should be sought among the Church members.[22] If so, the passage in chapter 14 could read thus: "How is it then, brethren? when ye come together, every one of you hath a psalm, hath a doctrine, hath a tongue, hath a revelation, hath an interpretation. Let all things be done unto the edifying [of the whole]. . . . For ye may all prophesy one by one, that all may learn, and all may be comforted. . . . [Now some of you have said] let your women keep silence in the churches: for it is not permitted unto them to speak; but they are commanded to be under obedience, as also saith the law. And if they will learn anything, let them ask their husbands at home: for it is a shame for women to speak in the church. [But I say to you] What? came the word of God out from you? or came it unto you only? If any man think himself to be a prophet, or spiritual, let him acknowledge that the things that I write unto you [that all may prophesy] are the commandments of the Lord. But if any man be ignorant, let him be ignorant. Wherefore, brethren, covet to prophesy, and forbid not [anyone, man or woman] to speak

118

with tongues." (1 Corinthians 14:26, 31, 34–39.) Read this way, the passage makes a lot more sense in its context.

There is other evidence to support regarding these two verses as a quotation. First, ancient Greek used no punctuation or quotation marks, so it was up to others — translators, later readers, and commentators — to determine which passages were quoted and which were not. Unless a statement began with a phrase such as "as it has been said" or "as it was written," a quotation might be overlooked. There are a number of quotations not only in 1 Corinthians but in other epistles as well, so it is very likely that the epistles would refer to or even quote parts of the correspondence the epistles are replying to.[23]

Second, verses 34 and 35 could also have been direct quotations from rabbinic literature. There are many similar statements in the Midrash and Talmud: "the law" referred to in verse 34 is the rabbinic oral law, which did totally silence women in the synagogue. While men usually engaged in questioning and commenting on the text of the rabbi's address, women were in absolute silence.[24] In rabbinic literature the word *shameful* is often used to describe a woman's demeanor and reflects directly back to Eve's shameful sin in Eden.

Third, from the context, the verses that follow 34 and 35 sound like an irritated response to them: "What? Came the word of God out from you?" he exclaims. His reply is one of chastisement. He is shocked at the deviation from Christian principles that he had previously put in place, and he almost dismisses the deviation in a frivolous manner as nonsense, calling the precipitator of such dogma ignorant. "What? Came the word of God out from you? or came it unto you only? [So, now *you* are claiming to receive direction for the Church?] If any man think himself to be a prophet, or spiritual, let him acknowledge that the things that I write unto you are the commandments of the Lord. But if any man be ignorant, let him be ignorant! [If you are truly a man of God, you will know by the Spirit that these things I have written are from the Lord.]" He then concludes the thought and brings in the theme of the previous chapters: "Wherefore ... covet to prophesy, and forbid not [anyone, men or women] to speak with tongues. Let all things be done decently and in order."

Paul ends the epistle with a powerful chapter on the atonement of Christ, and a further plea to stand fast in the faith and do all things with charity. (1 Corinthians 16.) Paul was exceptionally well suited for his difficult mission of helping to integrate the Gentile converts into a new religion where all the first members were Jewish. He was a perfectly trained Jew, a Roman citizen, and a Christian, tutored by the Savior himself. His overall message was the same as Jesus Christ's, one of unity and oneness, and it can be summed up in his message to the Galatians: "For as many of you as have been baptized into Christ have put on Christ. There is neither Jew nor Greek, there is neither bond nor free, there is neither male nor female: for ye are all one in Christ Jesus." (3:27–28.)

It is my sincere hope that in our struggles to find a comfortable place as women in our Church and our society, we will catch the vision of Paul and feel a unity not only with our fellow sisters but also with our brothers as well. May we seek always to accept the liberating doctrine of Jesus Christ and choose the good part in all areas of our lives, focusing on the spiritual needs first and filling ourselves with charity, the pure love of Christ. If we will do that as a first priority, everything else will fall into place and bring us true and everlasting joy. "And Jesus answered and said unto her, Martha, Martha, thou art worried and troubled about many things: but one thing is needful: and Mary hath chosen that good part, which shall not be taken away from her." (Luke 10:41–42.)

Notes

1. For an in-depth commentary on the Genesis Adam and Eve story, see Jolene Edmunds Rockwood, "The Redemption of Eve" in *Sisters in Spirit*, ed. Maureen Ursenbach Beecher and Lavina Fielding Anderson (Urbana and Chicago, Illinois: University of Illinois Press, 1987), pp. 3–36, or

Rockwood, "Eve's Role in the Creation and the Fall to Mortality" in *Women and the Power Within: To See Life Steadily and See It Whole*, ed. Dawn Hall Anderson and Marie Cornwall (Salt Lake City, Utah: Deseret Book Co., 1991), pp. 49–68.

2. Ber 24a and Meg 23a, Talmud, as cited in Constance F. Parvey, "The Theology and Leadership of Women" in *Religion and Sexism: Images of Women in the Jewish and Christian Traditions*, ed. Rosemary Radford Ruether (New York: Simon and Schuster, Touchstone, 1974), p. 129.

3. Louis Ginzberg, *The Legends of the Jews*, 12th ed., 7 vols. (1909; Philadelphia: Jewish Publication Society of America, 1937) 1:67.

4. Ibid.

5. A. Cohen, *Everyman's Talmud* (New York: Schocken Books, 1975), pp. 160, 179.

6. Ibid., p. 161.

7. Ginzberg, 1:66.

8. Ibid., 1:68.

9. Ibid., 1:67

10. Cohen, p. 171.

11. Ibid., p. 172

12. Ibid.

13. Bruce R. McConkie, *The Mortal Messiah* (Salt Lake City, Utah: Deseret Book Co., 1979), 1:223.

14. Ibid., pp. 224, 221.

15. Ibid., p. 375.

16. Geza Vermas, *Jesus the Jew: A Historian's Reading of the Gospels* (New York: Macmillan, 1973), pp. 21–22.

17. McConkie, 1:196, 296.

18. Melodie Moench Charles, "Precedents for Mormon Women from Scriptures," in *Sisters in Spirit*, p. 53.

19. For more information on pairing see Parvey, "Theology and Leadership," pp. 138–42.

20. Charles, "Precedents for Mormon Women," p. 54.

21. Ginzberg, 1:67; Parvey, p. 126.

22. Laurence R. Iannaccone, "Let the Women Be Silent," *Sunstone* (May-June, 1982): 39–45.

23. Ibid., pp. 43–44.

24. Ibid., p. 43.

Old Testament Insights: Women, Wit, Wisdom

AILEEN HALES CLYDE

I was drawn to the poetry of the Old Testament by my literate mother, who often chose to read to me when I was a child, from Genesis, Psalms, 1 Samuel, 1 Kings, and Isaiah. The more common Bible stories were introduced to me not at home but in Sunday School or Primary. Before I could read, I had heard many times, "In the beginning God created the heaven and the earth. . . . And God said, Let there be light: and there was light. And God saw the light, that it was good: and God divided the light from the darkness. . . . And God said, Let the waters under the heaven be gathered together unto one place, and let the dry land appear: and it was so. And God called the dry land Earth; and the gathering together of the waters called he Seas: and God saw that it was good." (Genesis 1:1, 3, 9–10.) And so on through the Creation, with the assurance in each case, "And God saw that it was good." I would hear my mother's voice asserting and confirming as I sat on her lap and sometimes drifted off to sleep, "And God said, Let us make man in our image, after our likeness: and let them have dominion over the fish of the sea, and over the fowl of the air, and over the cattle, and over all the earth, and over every creeping thing that creepeth upon the earth. So God created man in his own image, in the image of God created he him; male and female created he them. . . . And God saw everything

Aileen Hales Clyde has served as second counselor in the Relief Society general presidency. She has also served as a regent of the Utah System of Higher Education and chaired the Utah task force on gender and justice. Sister Clyde received her bachelor's degree in English from Brigham Young University, where she taught part-time for ten years. She and her husband, Hal M. Clyde, are the parents of three sons.

that he had made, and, behold, it was very good."(Genesis 1:26–27, 31.)

That still strikes me as a good beginning. And as a child it impressed upon me that God was my creator and that he saw his work as good. What I heard from the Bible when I was very young rings in my ears still and provided a dependable buttress against the difficult paradoxes that I later discovered abounded in scriptures and also in life.

The household where I grew up included three brothers, no sisters, and parents who encouraged wide-ranging discussions of what was, what should be, and how we each had a part in figuring things out. My identity as a person sprang from these discussions. By the time I was through adolescence and was reading scriptures seriously on my own, I had noted that in the Old Testament a woman's worth was tied to her marital status and that her father was usually the broker in that important arrangement. Women were possessions of their fathers or their husbands. The tenth commandment does not even give the wife first priority in a man's listed possessions. "Thou shalt not covet thy neighbour's house, thou shalt not covet thy neighbour's wife, nor his manservant, nor his maidservant, nor his ox, nor his ass, nor any thing that is thy neighbour's." (Exodus 20:17.) I saw that fertility had very different consequences for women and for men. Childbirth was the key to a woman's worth. Stories of Rachel, Sarah, Samson's mother, and Hannah, all manifest the stigma and disgrace associated with barrenness. As a young woman, this impressed me as very sad and very unfair.

Old Testament references to women are limited, but they provide rich glimpses into female ways. In Genesis 21, for example, after Sarah has weaned her miracle baby Isaac, she tells Abraham to send Hagar and her son Ishmael away. Abraham is deeply grieved until God tells him that Ishmael, too, will lead a great nation. Thus assured that the child will survive, Abraham gives Hagar a bottle of water and some bread and sends her and the child into the wilderness of Beersheba. In the Beersheba desert, dehydration comes quickly. Poor Hagar had been expelled before, but this would be much worse because of the child. After the water is long gone, Hagar, who cannot bear to see her child die, places him under a shrub for some particle of shade and goes "a good way off, as it were a bowshot" in distance, and weeps. (V. 16.) An angel of God "call[s] to Hagar out of heaven" (v. 17) and tells her that God has heard the cries of her son. That detail is more important than I ever before knew. An angel heard Hagar, but God heard the child. For over a year now, I have worked on a state task force on child abuse. In this connection, I have heard harrowing reports of the ritual abuse of children. Some of those small children, who never met one another, independently report that they had help from angels and that despite their pain they had felt God's love. In the case of Ishmael, God opens Hagar's eyes and she sees a well of water. She refills the bottle, gives the lad a drink, and he lives. (Genesis 21:14–20.) In seven short verses we are caused to contemplate banishment, thirst, mother's love, miraculous water, relief, and God's love. This brief passage still evokes various responses from me. I feel the pain of empathy for Hagar, earlier proud and fulfilled, now low and desperate. Then, in a wondrous turn, God's power works in her and she can act and deliver again her son. I feel elation and relief. The wonder in such scripture is the more I look, the more I see.

Having been raised on Bible stories, I appreciate the need to forewarn as well as invite people to search the scriptures. The Old Testament, particularly the book of Genesis, is not for the faint-hearted. As the incident with Hagar suggests, these are families who are capable of harshness, deception, violence, and self-serving.

The story of Jacob reveals an entire family whose members constantly deceive one another. The men do it, and the women do it. There is no gender bias in deception. Jacob, with his mother Rebekah's help, deceives his brother Esau and his father Isaac in order to secure for himself the coveted birthright and its blessing. Later, Jacob's uncle Laban deceives Jacob by substituting Laban's elder daughter Leah for the younger daughter Rachel, whom Jacob loved so much. I find Genesis 29:20 perhaps the loveliest verse in the Old Testament: "And Jacob served seven years for Rachel; and they seemed unto him but a few days, for the love he had to her." Jacob, in turn, deceives Laban over ownership of their livestock. Rachel deceives her father, Laban, over possession of his beloved family icons. Much later, Jacob's own sons deceive him about their younger brother Joseph's disappearance. Jacob's sons, Simeon and Levi, deceive the people of Shechem over the defiling of their sister Dinah, "which thing [the defiling] ought not to be done." (Genesis 34:7.) But what the brothers did, after their father's peaceful negotiation with the people of Shechem, was to roar into the city, brandishing swords. They killed every man, "and all their little ones, and their wives took they captive." (Genesis 34:29.) This in no way restored Dinah's honor. The violence was self-serving and ego-raising. Jacob's son Judah deceives his widowed daughter-in-law Tamar by reneging on his promise to let her marry his last son. Tamar, in turn, deceives her father-in-law Judah to expose his wrongful deception.

In reminding you of these imperfect people, I spared you Sodom and Gomorrah, also in Genesis. When I hear people bemoaning the awful state of the world, implying that things are worse than ever before, I think, "They are not readers of the Old Testament." The Old Testament writers are quite willing to expose their characters' imperfections. This is no whitewashed history. And we should take comfort that while we have not eliminated all their transgressions, most of us know better and do better, much of the time.

Among the Old Testament women are some who were initiators of action and decisions that blessed Israel and bless us, their spiritual descendants. Shiphrah and Puah in Exodus are known to us by their names and also by their occupation. The Egyptian king, fearing a slave revolution, ordered the Hebrew midwives to kill all male babies at birth, "but the midwives feared God, and did not as the king of Egypt commanded them, but saved the men children alive." (Exodus 1:17.) When confronted by the king, they explained that "the Hebrew women are not as the Egyptian women" (v. 19) and are so vigorous in birthing that they and the babies were gone before the midwives arrived to assist. This prevarication was a combination of civil disobedience and divine obedience. Their yes to God's command required a no to the king's command. Their own safety seemed to be of no consideration to them. They dealt with their dilemma and stood accountable before God and the king.

In Judges 11 is a gem of a story that I never heard in church. I still remember the impact that it had when I first read it privately and carefully. It is an account in forty verses of a remarkable young woman, acted upon but also capable of acting. She is known to us as Jephthah's daughter. Her father was "the son of an harlot" (v. 1), surely one of the ten ugliest and most biased labels in any language. Jephthah bore the stigma of that label. Banished not only from his father Gilead's house but from Israel, he lives in Tob, where he becomes known as a man of valor. When the Ammonites make war against Israel, the elders of Gilead seek Jephthah to lead the Israelite army, and he bargains with them to be instated as head of his father's house if he wins. Then he makes what is both an unnecessary and disastrous vow. "And Jephthah vowed a vow unto the Lord, and said, If thou shalt without fail deliver the children of Ammon into mine hands, Then it shall be, that whatsoever cometh forth of the doors of my house to meet me, when I return in peace from the children of Ammon, shall surely be the Lord's, and I will offer it up for a burnt offering." (Vv. 30–31.) The vow was unnecessary, because the spirit of the Lord had already come upon him, and he knew he would be aided to victory. It was clearly disastrous because anyone coming from his home to meet him would be someone whom he loved and who loved him.

After a great slaughter, the children of Ammon were "subdued before the children of Israel." (V. 33.) And who comes out "with timbrels and with dances" (v. 34) to meet her victorious father on his return from battle? Jephthah's daughter, his only child! Now this great warrior, full of victory and power, does not berate himself for this state of affairs. Instead he berates his daughter. "When he saw her, . . . he rent his clothes, and said, Alas, my daughter! thou hast brought me very low, and thou art one of them that trouble me: for I have opened my mouth unto the Lord, and I cannot go back." (V. 35.) In contrast, with remarkable equanimity, she sees what must be and offers herself so that her father can fulfill his vow. We have no record of her fear or of any need for pity or for apology from her father. The record does tell us, though, that she asks for time — time to "bewail her virginity" (v. 37), time to grieve for the family she will not have, two month's time to go into the mountains with her friends before she yields herself as her father's sacrifice. There was no substitution this time. God had not required this act, but Jephthah's daughter submitted herself for her father's honor. That she took comfort with companions suggests strongly to me the importance of and strength in sisterhood. Much later, in Hebrews 11:32–33, the rash Jephthah is remembered for his faith, but I remember his nameless daughter for her courage and for her strength in her friends. Her friends remembered her, too. Judges 11 concludes, "And it was a custom in Israel, that the daughters of Israel went yearly to lament the daughter of Jephthah the Gileadite four days in a year." (Vv. 39–40.)

Tucked immediately after the book of Judges is the short but familiar book of Ruth. The story of Ruth has come to represent for me a remarkable story of conversion. The Moabitess, whose husband, father-in-law, and brother-in-law have died, chooses to follow her mother-in-law to Israel, where she would be exiled in a culture that hated Moabites and where a woman's survival depended on a husband, father, or brother. But she knows God and loves her mother-in-law. Her words in this beautiful Hebraic passage testify of her loyalty to both.

"And Ruth said, Intreat me not to leave thee, or to return from following after thee: for whither thou goest, I will go; and where thou lodgest, I will lodge: thy people shall be my people, and thy God my God: where thou diest, will I die, and there will I be buried: the Lord do so to me, and more also, if ought but death part thee and me." (Ruth 1:16–17.)

When Naomi herself, realistic and wise, saw Ruth's steadfastness, she "left speaking unto her" (v. 18), which does not mean she stopped talking to her but that she quit trying to convince her of the difficulties they would face in Israel. "So Naomi returned, and Ruth the Moabitess, her daughter in law with her, which returned out of the country of Moab: and they came to Beth-lehem in the beginning of barley harvest." (Ruth 1:22.) But barley was not all they harvested.

Those two became a great team. The last three of the four chapters in the book are very adult reading. Boaz, a kinsman of Naomi's husband, allowed Ruth to glean in his field. He was quite quickly stricken by her. "And when she was risen up to glean, Boaz commanded his young men, saying, Let her glean even among the sheaves, and reproach her not: and let fall also some of the handfuls of purpose for her, and leave them, that she may glean them, and rebuke her not." (Ruth 2:15–16.)

A careful reading indicates how greatly complicated it could be for a righteous Israelite man to marry the widow of his kinsman's son, recently from Moab. But Naomi and Ruth helped, and Boaz never quite knew what hit him. "So Boaz took Ruth, and she was his wife: and when he went in unto her, the Lord gave her conception, and she bare a son. And the women said unto Naomi, Blessed be the Lord . . . for thy daughter in law, which loveth thee, which is better to thee than seven sons, hath born [a son]. And Naomi took the child, and laid it in her bosom, and became nurse unto it. And the women her neighbours gave it a name, saying, There is a son born to Naomi; and they called his name Obed: he is the father of Jesse, the father of David." (Ruth 4:13–14.)

In a culture hostile to the leadership of women, these

women worked toward an end the writer carefully emphasizes. Obed is the father of Jesse, the father of David, through whose line — carefully detailed for us in the first chapter of Matthew — came Jesus, who is called Christ.

Following Ruth in the Old Testament is 1 Samuel, which actually predates the book of Ruth by five hundred years. The story of Hannah, a favored wife of Elkanah, is full of detail and marvelous glimpses of human striving to reach and serve God. Elkanah had two wives: Hannah, who was barren, and Peninnah, who was fertile. Once a year Elkanah took his family to the city of Shiloh to worship and to offer "sacrifice unto the Lord of hosts." "And when the time was that Elkanah offered, he gave to Peninnah his wife, and to all her sons and her daughters, portions: But unto Hannah he gave a worthy portion; for he loved Hannah: but the Lord had shut up her womb." And this troubled Hannah greatly, so that she wept and often did not eat. "Then said Elkanah her husband to her, Hannah, why weepest thou? and why eatest thou not? and why is thy heart grieved? am not I better to thee than ten sons?" (1 Samuel 1:2–8.)

One time when they were at Shiloh to make their offering, Hannah waited until all had eaten and drunk and then returned to the temple alone. Eli the priest was seated "by a post of the temple" (v. 9), apparently unnoticed by Hannah. He had his own problems. His two sons, the Priests Phinehas and Hophni, who were supposed to serve the Lord, were "vile" and he knew it. (1 Samuel 3:13.)

"Now Eli was very old, and heard all that his sons did unto all Israel; and how they lay with the women that assembled at the door of the tabernacle of the congregation. And he said unto them, Why do ye such things? for I hear of your evil dealings by all this people. Nay, my sons; for it is no good report that I hear: ye make the Lord's people to transgress." He expressed concern not only for their pernicious example but also for their own souls — to no avail. "If one man sin against another, the judge shall judge him: but if a man sin against the Lord, who shall intreat for him? Notwithstanding they harkened not unto the voice of their father."(1 Samuel 2:22–25.) So perhaps Eli had also come to the temple at a quiet hour with a private grief and petition.

Hannah had returned to this special place of worship to beseech the Lord to hear her prayers for a child. She vowed that if the Lord would give her a son, she would in turn "give him unto the Lord all the days of his life. And it came to pass, as she continued praying before the Lord," we are told, "Eli marked her mouth. Now Hannah, she spake in her heart; only her lips moved, but her voice was not heard: therefore Eli thought she had been drunken." (1 Samuel 1:11–13.)

Here is a biblical case where a priesthood leader misunderstands a woman, and she, in dignity, yet with respect, clarifies for him. "And Hannah answered and said, No, my lord, I am a woman of a sorrowful spirit: I have drunk neither wine nor strong drink, but have poured out my soul before the Lord. Count not thine handmaid for a daughter of Belial: for out of the abundance of my complaint and grief have I spoken." And in a record all too brief, but wonderful nevertheless, Eli hears and understands. Then, exercising the office he is called to, he says, "Go in peace: and the God of Israel grant thee thy petition that thou has asked of him." (1 Samuel 1:15–17.)

Hannah responds with grace and full composure. No doubt Eli's words were full of bright promise, but she seemed immediately restored from sorrow by power beyond both her own hopes and the priest's words. "So the woman went her way, and did eat, and her countenance was no more sad." (1 Samuel 1:18.) Eli's blessing must have been confirmed to Hannah by the Spirit's witness. Later she sings a song of faith and strength, not well enough known by the latter-day daughters of Zion. "There is none holy as the Lord: for there is none beside thee: neither is there any rock like our God. . . . He raiseth up the poor out of the dust, and lifteth up the beggar from the dunghill, to set them among princes, and to make them inherit the throne of glory: for the pillars of the earth are the Lord's, and he hath set the world upon them." (1 Samuel 2:2, 8.)

Too often Hannah is remembered for bargaining with God and then giving her son Samuel to serve in the temple. Her faith and capacity for love and sacrifice deserve more of our emphasis. And surely she could represent an ideal to priesthood leaders who occasionally misread the obvious signs and would delight in clarification as evenhanded and reasonable as Hannah's.

These books are what I call religious. They teach me not only about the people but about God and faith. Other books have other emphases, and as our eighth Article of Faith suggests, we need to read the scriptures to discern such differences. The Prophet Joseph wrote the Articles of Faith in response to a request for a brief history of the Church from a Chicago newspaper editor, John Wentworth. Joseph included in his reply thirteen statements of belief that distinguished some of the similarities and differences between Latter-day Saint doctrine and that of other religions. The eighth article begins, "We believe the Bible to be the word of God as far as it is translated correctly." This qualification—"as far as it is translated correctly"—suggests to me a certain attitude toward scripture. I am not to distrust or dismiss whatever I may find hard to understand or sympathize with; rather, I am to read prayerfully, deeply, and thoughtfully, as did Joseph Smith. I am to read with all my wits about me. I am to ponder and question in order to learn.

Often in scripture we are to learn by negative examples as well as positive ones—and rarely do we encounter characters who are flawless. That is true of Esther and her cousin Mordecai in the book of Esther as well as the more obvious villain Haman, the determined enemy of the Jewish people then scattered and under Persian rule. The author of the book of Esther unfolds the tale of Esther and Mordecai's loyalty to their people with an emphasis that is not primarily religious. The book opens with details of a lavish royal celebration lasting seven days. The men and women are separated during the festivities and on the seventh day when the king Ahasuerus is "merry with wine," he sends his chamberlains to fetch his queen, Vashti, so all can see her beauty—and she refuses to come. The chamberlains who have to report the affront are enraged, and the king is "very wroth, and his anger burn[s] in him." No doubt the liquor lent significantly to the riling, for the offense quickly takes on cataclysmic proportions. A drunk chamberlain offers his own opinion that "Vashti the queen hath not done wrong to the king only, but also to all the princes and to all the people" in all the provinces of Ahasuerus's vast kingdom. (Esther 1:16.) He was sure that when the report of Vashti's refusal got abroad that all women would show disrespect for their husbands. And thus it was decided that Vashti would come before the king no more, that her royal estate would be given to another, and that a decree would be sent throughout the empire commanding that all wives should give their husbands honor. This mandate would also go to every province, translated into the various languages, proclaiming that "every man should bear rule in his own house."

The only verse of even minimal human tenderness in the whole book of Esther begins the next chapter. We see the king and he has sobered up. "After these things, when the wrath of king Ahasuerus was appeased, he remembered Vashti, and what she had done, and what was decreed against her." This hint of a sad morning-after memory is as close to regret as this story of vanity and court intrigue will come. In brief, Esther is rounded up at the behest of her cousin Mordecai for the beauty contest held to replace Vashti. She gains the approval of the king, and, in a tale intricately woven, she becomes the queen. There is much intrigue and much danger in the story, involving Esther, Mordecai, and Haman, an enemy of the Jews. Yet I find it significant that after Esther becomes the queen, and as soon as she gains power, she, who has so recently faced death herself, requires the death of the sons of Haman. "Let Haman's ten sons be hanged upon the gallows," she says. (Esther 9:13.)

Not only has the anti-Semite Haman been defeated in this tale, but no sons will be left to resume his vendetta against the Jews. We can see on close and careful reading what is seldom derived from passages selected without context: the purpose of the book of Esther is mainly to intensify the Jewish people's loyalty to their traditions and religion at a time when they are being threatened by the invasion of Hellenism and national disintegration. The author's message in this book is clearly not religious. God's name appears nowhere in it. There is no mention of prayer. Devotion to one's race takes the place of genuine religious feeling. The vividly drawn characters are all, except perhaps for Vashti, notably designing, revengeful, even cruel.

My growing affinity for life and its diversity in my time is enriched by the human variety and divine connections so memorably recorded in the Old Testament. Reading there for personal meaning is an adventure that has never disappointed me. I have discovered in those books all kinds of lives, and they have taught me much about mine.

Fruits of Faithfulness:
The Saints of Czechoslovakia

OLGA KOVÁŘOVÁ CAMPORA

Introduction by Carol Cornwall Madsen

*In September 1955, after a month of performances on its
first European tour, the Mormon Tabernacle Choir reached
the city of West Berlin. At the end of a long, tense day of traveling
through Russian-occupied East Germany, Choir members were
relieved to arrive in the Allied sector of Berlin. As they descended
the huge stairs of the railroad station, tired and apprehensive,
they were startled to hear the strains of a familiar hymn. As*
Time Magazine *reported, waiting for the Choir on the station
steps was a large group of German people who, upon seeing
the Americans, "burst into the great Mormon hymn, 'Come,
Come, Ye Saints.' The Americans joined in," English merging
with German, "to thunder the final phrase, 'All is well! all is
well!' "[1] Tears of joy and love were their common language.*

*Many of those singers were refugees, fleeing from the es-
calating restrictions imposed by Communist rulers, which were
dramatically enforced six years later by the construction of the
Berlin Wall. Turning an afternoon rehearsal into a free concert, the Tabernacle Choir sang to a hall filled with refugees
and Church members who had been permitted to leave East
Berlin temporarily. Emotions ran high as the Choir sang well
beyond the allotted rehearsal time, closing with the hymn that
had welcomed them. "This was not only music," reported the*
Berlin Telegraf, *"it was the building of a human bridge."[2]*

*A hundred years after it was written, William Clayton's
hymn bridged those years and spoke its message of hope to
another dispossessed people, not only in Germany but throughout Eastern Europe. Like their latter-day forebears, East
European Saints relied on their faith and the promises of the*

134

gospel to support their commitment to the Church during forty years of isolation. For those beleaguered Saints, the words rang true: "Gird up your loins, fresh courage take, Our God will never us forsake."

As this simple Mormon hymn reflected the spirit and endurance of Latter-day Saints long denied religious liberty, so music would also eloquently express the joy of liberation forty years later. On Christmas morning, 1989, in Berlin, culminating a three-day celebration that began with the actual and symbolic opening of the Brandenburg Gate, Leonard Bernstein conducted an international choir and orchestra in a performance of Beethoven's stirring Ninth Symphony before an audience that spilled out of the concert hall into every available space surrounding it. In this majestic musical setting, the powerful poetic expression of universal love, "Ode to Joy," penned by German poet Friedrich von Schiller, magnificently conveyed the significance of that great moment in history. Impulsively changing the word Freude *("joy") to* Freiheit *("freedom") in the chorus, Bernstein declared that "this heaven-sent moment" excused his poetic license because both words expressed the exuberance of the thousands who listened to this celebration of the irrepressible human spirit. As von Schiller had written in his "Ode":*

Millions, bravely sorrow bearing, Suffer for a better time!
See, above the starry clime, God a great reward preparing. . . .
Joy [freedom], of flame celestial fashioned, Daughter of Elysium
Every man a brother plighted, Where thy gentle wings are spread.[3]

Can anyone forget the joyful expressions on the faces of those who crossed unchecked through the openings in the Berlin Wall or stood shoulder to shoulder in Prague's famed Wenceslas Square to celebrate their country's freedom that miraculous winter?

Dr. Olga Kovářová shared in the miracle of those events. She had experienced the debilitating bonds of political oppres-

sion and had given meaning to the phrase "a steadfastness in Christ" by transcending those bonds and advancing His work in a Communist nation. Shortly after her baptism into the Church nine years ago, while still a doctoral student of education and pedagogy in Brno, Czechoslovakia, Olga Kovářová faced a dilemma. She had been taught the gospel of Jesus Christ in secret, she had been baptized under cover of night to avoid detection, and she had met each week with the handful of Saints in her hometown at great risk. Now, she had an opportunity to continue her studies in the free society of Austria, where she had relatives, but she also felt a commitment to remain in her native country. After weeks of prayer, fasting, and counsel with Church leaders, who wisely left the decision to her, she chose to finish her schooling at home.

What an inspired choice that was! Since receiving her Ph.D. in education, Olga has been determined to fill the ethical void in Communist ideology by teaching ethics and morality in her university classes in Brno and introducing such concepts as love and joy and the meaning of life to hundreds of young people at the yoga camps she conducts each summer. To keep those principles alive for her students, she started a newspaper, which she called "The Art of Living," a unique and dangerous venture for this young woman so continually under the scrutiny of Communist censors. "Czechoslovakia is ethically sick and it needs to be made ethically well," she boldly wrote in an early issue and then introduced Christian principles as guides to a better life. But to write about God's love without mentioning his name and to elaborate the theme of her newspaper, "Men are that they might have joy," within the framework of Marxist-Leninist ideology were sometimes, she admits, beyond her powers. She was successful enough, however, to have many readers say to her, "Olga, you must be very happy, because you write such joyful things." Since the 1989 revolution, she has seen her ideas incorporated into a textbook for high school teachers, Self-Education in Ethics and Morality, *which has been adopted by universities throughout her country.*

Her search for a higher moral purpose brought Olga into the Church. The branch she joined was small, its members mainly those faithful ones who had joined before the war. Olga was the first young woman baptized in more than forty years. She decided the branch needed revitalization. Eight years and forty-seven converts later, including her own family, the branch is vigorous, youthful, and growing. It is not difficult to see how that happened. Olga is literally a Latter-day Saint. From her deep-rooted faith to her childlike humility, she radiates the spirit of the gospel. One who knows that best is Elder Martin Pilka, one of her converts and the first missionary from Czechoslovakia in recent times. "Olga," he wrote to me in his hesitant English, "is a very good sister but for most members she is also authority, because she is clean and full of love. I know that God chose her. Through Olga and Otakar Vojkůvka (whom Olga calls her spiritual father) was the Church restored in a big part of our country. Through Olga came to the Church a lot of young people and through Olga and this people the Church is living today." Indeed it is—in Czechoslovakia and throughout the world.

Dear sisters, brothers, and friends, I open my heart in faith to share with you experiences I have had living in East Central Europe in the beautiful country of Czechoslovakia. Until the end of 1989, life in Czechoslovakia was under full Communist control that had lasted forty years. I want to explain what living in these circumstances has meant to me. I believe that among people there is only one language that helps us to understand each other fully: it is the language of our heart, which is the language of love and of the Spirit of God. I am grateful that I can open my heart to you in this love.

Let me begin with an analogy. An Austrian scientist studied the life of crayfish. They, like lobsters, have at the base of their antennae small pockets where sand is deposited. The sand helps give these creatures their sense of equilibrium. If the sand is removed, they become disoriented until it is replaced.

In our bodies, we have a similar need for equilibrium, which comes from filling our hearts with the Spirit of God. If we do not keep that Spirit, we lose our spiritual balance.

In Communist-dominated life, I saw that people lost their individuality, their personality. They became dependent—literally—upon the Communists in all aspects of their lives. Someone was always watching what they did. People came to depend so much upon the leaders of the Communist party that they were reluctant to express their feelings openly. They became incapable of being happy. Only occasionally with trusted family and trusted friends would they show feelings. The Communists taught people to be honest, to be chaste, to work hard, and to be unselfish. They even had special schools to teach Communists how to influence people to live this way. But the Communist leaders were not honest with their people. They had privileges that were denied others, they did not live moral lives, and therefore they could not be models for non-Communists. The younger generations saw that hypocrisy and became very cynical. As a result, all people learned to lead two lives: one a private life, and the other a public life. In the Book of Mormon is a description that fits very well the majority of Communist leaders:

"And it came to pass that they did have their signs, yea, their secret signs, and their secret words; and this that they might distinguish a brother who had entered into the covenant, that whatsoever wickedness his brother should do he should not be injured by his brother, nor by those who did belong to his band, who had taken this covenant.

"And thus they might murder, and plunder, and steal, and commit whoredoms and all manner of wickedness, contrary to the laws of their country and also the laws of their God." (Helaman 6:22–23.)

Heavenly Father has allowed people to have experiences under rulers who not only govern without God's laws but who impose laws contrary to God's laws. Most Czechs grew up without a sense of direction. Nor could they find one. Communists do not believe that the way a person thinks about reality is important. The Marxist-Leninist philosophy places the highest value on material things. For that reason, those living under this ideology found their lives impoverished, lacking spiritual and higher cultural values. Albert Einstein said that the goal of material welfare is the same goal that a drove of pigs has. Our people longed for higher goals.

One year before our revolution, the movie depicting the life of Mahatma Gandhi was shown in Czechoslovakia. I noticed that most young people sat through this film not just once but two or three times. Although Gandhi's ideas are spiritual and most young people in my country do not believe in God, they were touched by Gandhi's idea of nonviolence. During our revolution, I saw in some Czech shop windows displays of nonviolence featuring Jesus Christ and Gandhi. Gandhi was quoted as saying: "Always, whenever I felt despair, I would realize that in the end truth and love always prevail." The Czech hunger for a spiritual and cultural life beyond Communist materialism was clear.

Among the leaders of the Czechoslovak Revolution in 1989 were university students. I find it very meaningful that it was called a Velvet Revolution. I will always remember the two students, very good friends, who came to my office. "Olga," they shouted, "we are bringing excellent news. The mills of the gods have started to grind again." We looked at each other and without another word, tears came to our eyes and we hugged. Two days later our nation came together: in Brno about one hundred thousand people gathered on the main square. We held hands and sang our national anthem. I felt the love of God among all the people so strongly: their hearts began a new beat, their souls began to live, life again had meaning for them. After forty years of an alien history, a history imposed on us by another nation, the history of the Czech people resumed. Then I recalled, in Paul's words: "Where the Spirit of the Lord is, there is liberty." (2 Corinthians 3:17.)

I know that the Velvet Revolution was a miracle of God.

The French author Antoine de St. Exupéry in his book, *The Little Prince*, wrote: "What is essential is invisible to the [human] eye."[4] In America many have told me: "We prayed many years for freedom in your country." Brothers and sisters, I thank you for this gentle yet powerful help and influence. Our Czech youth were the embodiment of God's miracle, for as it is written in Ether 4:12, "Whatsoever thing persuadeth men to do good is of me; for good cometh of none save it be of me."

In many ways God has been persuading men and women toward good in our country. The Czechoslovak Mission was organized in 1929 by Elder John A. Widtsoe, the president of the European Mission. A young elder from the German-Austrian Mission, Arthur Gaeth, was chosen to preside over the mission. He was succeeded by Wallace Toronto, also one of the first missionaries. He and the elders had to leave when the Nazis occupied the country. After World War II, President Toronto returned with a larger number of missionaries, including our current president, Richard W. Winder, and Edwin B. Morrell, later president of the Austria Vienna East Mission. But by 1950, two years after the Communists had come to power, the mission was closed and would not be reopened until July 1990.

During the years of Communism, the Church could not exist publicly, even though a lot of other churches could. The Czech Latter-day Saints could not preach, hold meetings, baptize, or ordain members to the priesthood. The penalty for breaking that Communist law was prison for three to seven years.

Nevertheless, the LDS Church continued to exist. About fifty members were active to the extent that they were in contact one with another. These members — despite Communist repressions and the fear of imprisonment — were faithful, never betraying their innermost ideals. Mostly older members, they gathered from time to time in their own homes because it was dangerous to meet every Sunday.

I joined the Church eight years ago, during this dark period under Communism. In Brno, the second largest city in Czechoslovakia, where I attended the Masaryk University, I met the Vojkůvka family. They had belonged to the Church for more than thirty years, yet that was a well-kept secret. I came in contact with them through my interest in yoga. A schoolmate who knew that I was interested in yoga told me one day, "Olga, I traveled last Sunday to my parents, and I met on the train a wonderful man. He is about seventy-five, and he is an expert in yoga." She had taken his address, so I visited this man. He appeared to me seventy-five in his age but in his heart nearer eighteen and full of joy. This was so unusual in Czechoslovakia at that time of cynicism. We started to speak of life, and I saw that he was not only educated but knew how to live joyfully. I became very good friends with him and with his whole family. The family consisted of the elder Mr. Otakar Vojkůvka, his son, Gád, daughter-in-law, Magda, and their two children, Gád and Miriam, ages fifteen and thirteen. We had many discussions over many months.

The spirit in the Vojkůvka family was something very different for me. When at one point I asked the elder Mr. Vojkůvka about the meaning of their lives, he answered with a single sentence: "God sent us to the earth to sow joy, life, and love into souls and flowers." With this sentence a door opened for me into a different life — a life I had never imagined. I wondered where he learned this philosophy of life. One day I told them, "I have looked for many of the things you tell me in the New Testament, but I do not find them. Where do you read these things?" "Yes, it is true," they admitted. "They are not in the New Testament. We have a different book." They then gave me *A Skeptic Discovers Mormonism,*[5] translated into Czech. Overnight I read the entire book. I returned the next day to the family. Not certain that they were Mormons, I asked them if they knew how I could contact these people, the Mormons, and if I could get a copy of the Book of Mormon. They then gave me a Book of Mormon in Czech. I noted on the binding "Church of Jesus Christ of Latter-day Saints," so later that day I checked in the encyclopedia to find out about this church.

There I read about Joseph Smith and how he was a crazy man —
not normal, the article said — and I read there many other bad
things about this church. Full of curiosity, I began to read the
book anyway, but although I felt a strong spirit in the book, I
did not read far. When I met with the Vojkůvka family again,
I told them, "I could not read all this book because I read one
page and I felt questions." They told me, "It's okay, Olga. It is
good that you have questions." So began a time of questions
and learning the gospel.

Let me share my first clearly spiritual experience. Again it
concerned my search for a higher purpose than materialism.
While reading the Book of Mormon, I came to 2 Nephi 2:25
and read, "Adam fell that men might be; and men are, that
they might have joy." I felt as if I had discovered a lost but
important understanding for which I had been searching over
many years. Yes, women and men are that we might have joy!
That night I suddenly awoke, sat up and saw around me a light,
and felt the same light in my heart. I realized that no longer
did I just believe in God; I *knew* that Heavenly Father and Jesus
Christ exist. I felt their love, not only for me, not only for good
people, but for all people.

After my conversion, I had to wait half a year to be baptized.
It was 1983 and because we had no baptismal font, we needed
to wait until summer when we could be in the woods and not
be noticed. The police would not be expecting a religious
activity in the dark; however, as we neared the reservoir near
Brno at about ten on the evening of my baptism, we noticed
many fishermen. We waited, and the time dragged on — fifteen
minutes, then thirty, then forty-five. I felt very disappointed
and sad, wondering if this unexpected setback meant I was not
sufficiently repentant. I silently questioned Heavenly Father:
"Perhaps I am not well enough prepared, perhaps my testimony
is not strong enough?" Yet, I felt a great desire to be baptized.
Finally, a brother who had been baptized a year or so earlier
suggested, "I think we must pray and ask Heavenly Father to
make it possible for Olga to be baptized." This was my first

miracle with a priesthood prayer. Within a few minutes of our quiet prayer, most of the fishermen left the river's edge, and the three who remained were some distance away. You can imagine my feelings of joy as I came up out of the water.

Then an older brother asked me, "Do you know why there were many fishermen by the water tonight?"

"Yes," I answered, "so that I would better realize my responsibility for my sins."

"Of course," he answered, "but also remember that Jesus, as he walked by the Sea of Galilee, said to Simon Peter and Andrew, who were casting a net into the sea, 'Follow me, and I will make you fishers of men.' " (Matthew 4:19.) I felt his meaning was that I should soon be an instrument in God's hands to bring young people into the Church. In the confirmation blessing the elder Vojkůvka, who had not overheard this conversation, also said that I was the first young woman convert in almost forty years and that through me many people would come to the Church.

I soon realized that I had become one new link in the chain of women who have been significant among Latter-day Saints in Czechoslovakia. In the 1920s, after World War I, the Brodilová family—a mother and two daughters—lived the gospel and prayed for the missionaries to come to Czechoslovakia. Others also became role models for me: Miloslava Krejčí, baptized in the 1930s and ever active in genealogical research, was one of the Brno Branch stalwarts. Olga Šnederflerová, wife of our district president in Prague, shared her quiet, steady faith since joining the Church in the late 1940s. In the early 1980s, Norma Toronto Morrell, wife of President Edwin Morrell and sister of Wallace Toronto, shared her love with us during frequent, supportive visits from Vienna with her husband, who presided over the Czechoslovak and neighboring Latter-day Saints. Four years ago, Barbara Woodhead Winder, then general president of the Relief Society, visited our branches and helped us to feel a part of the greater Church. Now she presides as companion to President Richard W. Winder since the re-opening of the Czechoslovak Mission in July 1990. All these women who preceded me are strong examples of love and patience.

At first, however, I did not know of them, and I was surprised to find at my first Sunday meeting that our Church group consisted of seven old people. They smiled at me with kindness, but I asked myself, "How special is this Church? It is only for old people." In time I would understand the reason. Most young members had escaped Czechoslovakia because all members were persecuted. Brother Vojkůvka, for instance, was questioned many times in secret places. In government documents, it was written of him, "Be careful. This man has a great influence on young people." In these days the Church had, of course, no missionaries. Latter-day Saint families had long been persecuted, questioned by the police, and warned not to teach their children about God and not to baptize them, even out of the country. Therefore, we dared to meet only in the evenings, at first once a month, and later once a week, when it was already dark outside and the neighbors were occupied with doing something other than being interested in people gathering. The blinds were pulled down, the windows had to stay closed, and we did not sing hymns for fear of being overheard. In these meetings, however, we strongly felt the spirit of the Holy Ghost. At first we were only seven; by 1989, we were about sixty in this one room. We had only one Book of Mormon among us; it was over forty years old, from before the time of Communism. The neighbors, noticing the many visitors, wondered why their elderly neighbor Mr. Vojkůvka had so many young friends. One neighbor asked him, "Mr. Vojkůvka, what do you celebrate each Sunday? So many young people are coming to your house." He answered simply, "We learn to be happy." After the revolution, this neighbor returned to say, "I think that I too need your school of life."

So, before the revolution, every Sabbath was for me the happiest day of the week, because I could partake of the sacrament and learn more about the gospel, which would help me during the whole coming week. A few months after my baptism, a friend of mine also joined the Church, and we started to pray and discuss with the Vojkůvka family how we might do member-missionary work. We decided to invite our many university friends to a School of Wisdom, prior to our Sunday meetings, where we would teach the youth about the gospel, about Jesus Christ, and about Heavenly Father.

During those eight years before the Velvet Revolution, there were baptized about fifty young people and a few older people, including my parents, whom I had been afraid to tell about my belief in God. My parents had been Protestants, but in our home we were not spiritually awakened. There was no LDS church in Uherské Hradiště, the town where I was born, and at the Masaryk University, atheism was required. Belief in God was not permitted. Sometime after my conversion, I began yoga lectures in my hometown. At my invitation, my parents attended. After visiting three times, as we sat together at home that day, they asked me, "Olga, what are you doing? This is so special. Where did you learn such wonderful things about life? We didn't tell you anything like this." Then I had the courage to bring out the Book of Mormon and speak to them about the gospel and the Church. My father is now a branch president in Uherské Hradiště, where we now have eighty-two members and four missionaries after only two years of missionary work.

To think this miracle began with something so simple as our School of Wisdom classes — Brother Vojkůvka and a few young members offering gospel education to Czech atheistic youth. We knew that some of those attending the seminars were from the secret police, and before the Velvet Revolution, we could not openly talk about God or Jesus Christ, or even about love. So we taught university students seven ideas: first, admiration for good things in life; second, self-respect; third, being interested in living; fourth, finding joy in living; fifth, expressing gratitude; sixth, loving others (as Jesus intended); and seventh, enthusiasm — finding the burning within. The purpose of these principles was to help the youth build meaningful relationships with others and to bring them to a more spiritual life. We taught through examples, stories, and Bible parables. I was many times questioned by the secret police, but they were kind to me. Sometimes I could tell by their special questions that they knew I was a Church member, but since we did not organize or teach against our government, I was probably safe.

The Vojkůvka family were also experts in yoga. To help youth experience these seven gospel ideas to find spirituality and joy in life, we arranged yoga summer camps where they exercised outdoors, ate well, and learned to live happily together. There were about eighty people at each one-week camp. Even during one week at a camp, a participant's behavior was often changed for the better. We didn't pray or mention Heavenly Father, but we held hands before eating our food and expressed gratitude for being together.

For eight years now, we have held six or seven weeks of camp each summer. Our young LDS members taught at the camp, as if they were full-time missionaries. I am now teaching at the Missionary Training Center in Provo, Utah, and I receive letters from newly baptized LDS youth in Czechoslovakia who tell me how these seven ideas and other associations with us led them from being atheists to becoming believers in God. Each year we taught five to six hundred youth and middle-aged people from all over Czechoslovakia. We see that these people are already partially prepared to receive the new missionaries.

I am so grateful to Heavenly Father that the Czech Mission has been opened once again. We have six branches, and others are soon to be organized. Thirty-six missionaries are at present serving in Czechoslovakia, and eight more are studying at the MTC, among them four sister missionaries and one couple.

Missionary work will help the Czechoslovak people come to a new morality, based upon the eternal principles of the gospel. There is a great need for a new moral order. The president of Czechoslovakia, Václav Havel, speaking on New Year's Day, 1991, said: "Freedom surprisingly opened doors upon undesirable characteristics and showed the depth of moral decay afflicting our souls." Many Czech people are looking for a life full of truth. Who can be better examples of such a life than LDS missionaries? Czechs who seek a better life see the missionaries as positive examples of spiritually minded youth. Czechs also need strong families based upon prayer. We may have freedom, but without spiritual understanding, freedom leads people astray. Austria Vienna East Mission President Dennis Neuenschwander, now a member of the Second Quorum of the Seventy, wrote in a Christmas letter to family and friends in 1990: "Through the gospel, faith in Jesus Christ springs forth where there has been emptiness. Hope abounds where once there was despair. Charity is replacing destructive cynicism. Lives are changed as the light of the gospel penetrates the darkness."

We need more young elders, more sister missionaries to provide positive examples of young women living the Gospel, and more older couples as examples for our families and to help build the branches.

Brothers and sisters, we love you and we need you. To you in America I want to say, as did the Lord, "Arise and shine forth, that thy light may be a standard for the nations." (D&C 115:5.)

Notes

1. "Music from the Tabernacle," *Time*, 19 Sept. 1955, p. 55.
2. Ibid.
3. Friedrich von Schiller, *An Anthology for Our Time* (New York: Frederick Ungar Publishing Co., 1960), pp. 42–45.
4. Antoine de St. Exupéry, *The Little Prince* (New York: Harcourt Brace Jovanovich, 1971), p. 70.
5. Timberline Wales Riggs, *A Skeptic Discovers Mormonism*, 5th ed. (Salt Lake: Deseret Book Co., 1961).

147

She Who Laughs, Lasts

MARY ELLEN EDMUNDS

The thing that makes this presentation difficult is that for me humor is mostly spontaneous . . . so I didn't prepare anything. Well, that's not entirely true. The truth is, I don't know how to start or end, but I've got a few good ideas for the middle. Here they are: She who laughs, lasts! She lasts through paper cuts and budget cuts, dark and stormy nights, losing at Monopoly and losing at love, weight gains and labor pains, braces and glasses, and falling down on the ice in front of a hundred people, and traffic jams and divorce and cancer and single parenthood and everything.

If you can survive all this, you have what's known as a "sense of humor." I like this kind of humor because it is gentle and kind. It breaks the ice and brings down the walls that divide us from each other.

I've cut a lot of articles out of newspapers and magazines about humor and laughter. I'd like to share some of them with you. In 1987 anthropologist Ashley Montagu advised people to "rediscover the childlike playfulness they once enjoyed. People should," he advised, "avoid hardening of the attitudes."[1] Good point.

Other studies show that when people laugh hard, the heart rate speeds up, the circulatory system is stimulated, and the muscles go limp. The body's immune system is stimulated, and

Mary Ellen Edmunds has served as an associate director of training at the Missionary Training Center in Provo, Utah, and as a member of the Relief Society general board. She has taught nursing at Brigham Young University, coordinated the work of health missionaries for the Church, and directed a health project for children in Nigeria. She has also served as a missionary in Taiwan, Hong Kong, the Philippines, and Indonesia.

148

more endorphins — which are natural pain-relieving substances in the brain — are produced during laughter.

So much for the science and body chemistry of it. Now for life. In my life, humor has helped me cut down on competition and envy.

Humor increases peace.

Humor for me is two parts love and three parts courage.

"Be of good cheer" is a commandment, not a suggestion. I work at the Missionary Training Center as an associate director of training. I work with welfare and visitors center missionaries, Southeast Asian languages, and senior missionaries.

Sometimes missionaries come to the MTC almost afraid to smile. How unattractive! Who would want to know more about a religion that turns people into unsmiling, unhappy sales-people?

Elder M. Russell Ballard, speaking to the missionaries at the MTC in September 1985, noted that "lightmindedness offends," but, he added, "if we said you couldn't have a sense of humor, all the Brethren would be in jeopardy."

I receive a lot of letters from missionaries in the field. This one came from Elder and Sister Jankowski, serving in Nigeria, West Africa:

"The only light in our house deep in the rain forest of Nigeria at 4:00 A.M. was a small glow at the end of the hall from an under-powered 40-watt light bulb. As I lay there in my bed, a black object in the hallway caught my eye. To my horror, there — only twelve feet from our bed — was the dreaded Giant Wild African Black Cockroach! Should I wake my faithful, brave husband? I decided I would attempt to rid our house of the menace myself. Each step I took I could feel the terror building inside me. It was too late to turn back now as I could see clearly his huge, three-inch body and his two fangs in the subdued light.

"During what seemed an eternity, I found my way to the kitchen. There on the shelf was the only help I could count

149

on to rid us of this menace: RAID! As I held the can I could feel its power waiting to strike.

"Now I was only three feet away from the black nemesis of the night. My finger shook as I pressed down on the trigger. Like a cobra striking, the spray found the mark again and again. I unleashed the deadly spray until I could see the poison dripping off his two fangs. No black African wild cockroach had ever been given such a deadly, personal, one-on-one dose of RAID!

"I moved quickly to the light switch, and with one single motion I flipped on the lights. There, only six inches away from the electrical outlet, lay a dead three-inch black plug adapter, the two electric prongs dripping RAID profusely."

I believe that "Men are, that they might have joy." They might not, too. (2 Nephi 2:25.) And don't forget *women!*

It's wholesome and healthy to be cheerful and happy. Alma, in speaking to his son Corianton, said that when men and women are "in the gall of bitterness and in the bonds of iniquity" they are in a state "contrary to the nature of God; therefore, they are in a state contrary to the nature of happiness." (Alma 41:11.)

Having a good sense of humor means having the ability to know how to be sensitive to situations and to others' feelings. Humor is laughing *with* people, but never *at* them. Humor is learning to laugh at ourselves, but never at that which is sacred.

Humor is a way to deal with life's inconsistencies.

Are you ready for more clippings yet?

Elder Boyd K. Packer said, "A good sense of humor is a characteristic of a well-balanced person. It has always been apparent that the prophets were men with very alert and pleasing senses of humor."[2]

Elder Richard L. Evans shared the thought that "humor is essential to a full and happy life. It is a reliever and relaxer of pressure and tension, and the saving element in many situations."[3]

During general conference in 1984, President Gordon B.

Hinckley encouraged us, "Enjoy your membership in the Church. Where else in all the world can you find such a society? Enjoy your activity. . . .

"Be happy in that which you do. Cultivate a spirit of gladness in your homes. . . . Let the light of the gospel shine in your faces wherever you go and in whatever you do."[4]

Think of someone you enjoy being around. Is he or she a happy person? Someone who lifts your spirits? So often we just need to be *silly* together. Some friends and I have fun remembering our Primary graduation. We especially enjoy repeating the opening remarks of our leader: "You sweet young girls on the threshold of eternity, keep your standards high! Lower your skirts and *raise your standards!*"

We need to laugh at ourselves. All I have to do for a good laugh is get out my yearbooks.

A friend shared this wonderful piece of silliness with me recently. "The Fourteenth Article of Faith: We believe in meetings — all that have been scheduled, all that are now scheduled, and we believe that there will yet be scheduled many more great and important meetings. We have endured many meetings and hope to be able to endure all meetings. Indeed, we may say that if there is a meeting, we seek after it."

Humor has tied our family closer together.

In our family is a wonderful soul whom we call "Aunt Florence," although I think she's actually my father's second cousin. Aunt Florence, when she was eighty-four, got a letter from a company inviting her to come and see their presentation about condominiums, telling her she'd receive a free gift — a choice between a beautiful twenty-piece set of china or a Homelite XEL chain saw. This was her response (with help from me and my mom):

"Dear Mr. Johnston: I just received your marvelous letter about the unique condominiums that you have in Park City and Hawaii. Living as I do in a nursing home, you can imagine how delighted I'd be to live in Park City or Hawaii instead. I

151

don't know how I was lucky enough to get on your mailing list, but what a thrill!

"One thing I'm *very* excited about is the Homelite XEL chain saw. It's just what I need here at the nursing home when we work on crafts. Maybe they'll let me start coming again when they realize I've got such a nice saw; I had to quit going because I wasn't participating. I've missed it.

"Another thing I need to mention is that when you fly me over to Hawaii, I'll have to go first class. I've had several strokes, and I just can't seem to hold my knees together anymore, so I'll need the extra space.

"Thanks again for thinking of me here in the nursing home. I think that's great! Owning something 'for the rest of my life' (as you put it) sounds terrific since I'm only 84!"

Some months after Florence passed away, a letter from the IRS arrived, saying she hadn't paid her taxes for 1979. Unless she had reasonable cause for delay, she might be liable for penalties. They invited, "If you believe you had reasonable cause for filing late and for paying late, please explain. We have enclosed an envelope for your use. Thank you for your cooperation."

Well, that most certainly deserved a reply, and as our family prepared one, we could hear Florence hooting:

Under the "I did not file the form because," we checked the "Business was closed" box.

In the "Remarks" section we wrote: "Yes, business was closed permanently on 9 June 1980. I'd not had an income for quite some years prior to that because I was in a nursing home. I know this is unusual to be getting a letter from me now that I'm dead, but I didn't want to mess up your records. I know how important that is to you. It was only with very special permission that I was able to send this note from the Other Side. I must say it's a lot more fun here where there aren't any taxes, but despite that I do wish you well in your work. I know a lot of people don't fully appreciate what you do, but now that I've got a new perspective (as they say) I know you work hard. By the way, in case anyone there is interested, everything they say is true—you've got to work there for what you get here, if you know what I mean. Tell the guys in the office to get with it. Thanks again for your inquiry and for providing the envelope."

I love sitting around the dinner table with my family and having someone start a "Remember when . . . ," and then we laugh. Sometimes we only have to say a phrase or a word, and everyone cracks up.

During the years I worked as a nurse, I found it was essential and often helpful to cultivate a sense of humor. One day when I'd been working with a particularly surly and uncooperative patient, I went to his bedside, determined to speak my mind. I said cheerfully, "I know you really like me but have a hard time expressing it." As I said, humor is two parts love, three parts sheer courage. We both started laughing, and we ended up good friends.

Humor has a way of leveling—of helping us experience equality. When the same thing touches or amuses two people, it reaches across a lot of artificial walls and even cuts through language and other communication barriers.

Laughing together is similar to crying or weeping together: it's unifying, it's a tenderizer, and I believe it helps us be more *real* with each other.

There *is* a time to laugh, to be hilarious, just as there is a time to weep, to be tender and sorry and comforting. Balance seems critical to me. We need to feel many things, and not just one emotion all the time. People who are constantly happy make me uneasy or nervous. If they never crash or have a hard day, they don't seem *real*.

Many people I know who are considered funny are also weepy, as I am. Perhaps we use humor to cover the tears and prop up the tenderness. I know I don't feel as lighthearted as I used to be before I lived in Africa and Asia and came face to face and heart to heart with a lot of suffering and pain, incredible unfairness and inequity. There is much in life that is simply not at all funny.

Yet when people say humor is the opposite of spirituality and "seriousness," they are dead wrong. That's like saying faith is the opposite of hope. No, the opposite of good humor is contention. The opposite of happiness is misery. The opposite of cheerfulness is gloom. The opposite of optimism is negativism.

Humor is not the opposite of serious spirituality. It is the opposite of anger, contention, envy, and self-centeredness. A humorless heart is too often a hard heart. The devil wants us to be miserable, and so he tries to take away genuine humor, changing it from *good* humor to something vulgar, crude, and often cruel.

Good humor is never cruel. In fact, I find that humor is often a way to focus on others rather than on yourself. You want to make them laugh, even at the expense of forgetting how hassled or stressed or oh-woe-is-me you may feel.

Wait. I feel another clipping coming on.

It's Brigham Young. "Let us make ourselves capable of doing at least a little good, and this will occupy our minds upon something that is indeed profitable to others, and will somewhat divert our attention from worshipping ourselves and blaming everybody that does not do the same!"[5] He's right: humor helps us cast off self-importance.

Articles, cartoons, books—watch for things that are genuinely funny and share them with others. So often things are even funnier when they're shared with just the right person at just the right time. Humor definitely reduces stress. I've watched this magic over and over. When you find something that would lift someone's spirits, share it. Listen to these great book titles:

How to Be Miserable for the Rest of the Century
Raging Hormones: The Unofficial PMS Survival Guide
Chocolate—The Consuming Passion

Even the titles bring a smile. Share books, articles, and ads — nonsense and sense — with each other.

"Let not your heart be troubled, neither let it be afraid," the scriptures tell us. We sing songs that have phrases like "Born this happy morning" and "Hallelujah!" not "Oh dear me, I'm bored and angry and depressed and discouraged today." Don't make your theme song "Hang down your head, Tom Dooley."

Declarations such as "Joy to the world!" and "Rejoice! the Lord is King" are for all of us, not just a few shepherds on a beautiful night listening to angels sing. The message is for each of us every day.

I hear Brother Joseph: "Happiness is the object and design of our existence."[6] And Moroni: "He that is happy shall be happy still." (Mormon 9:14.) Be happy now so you can be happy forever! There is a way!

May we bring happiness to each other. May your humor be good and kind. God bless you to find good humor amidst all that is troubling you today and all that we'll all face alone and together as the time steadily approaches when Jesus Christ will come again and we will finally rest from all that isn't good and kind. "And then may God grant unto you that your burdens may be light, through the *joy* of his Son. And even all this can ye do if ye will." (Alma 33:23.)

Notes

1. Ashley Montagu, in "Want Health and Wealth? Experts Prescribe Large Doses of Laughter and Play," *Deseret News*, 20 Mar. 1987, p. A-3.
2. Boyd K. Packer, *Teach Ye Diligently*, rev. ed. (Salt Lake City: Deseret Book Co., 1975), p. 249.
3. Richard L. Evans, "The Spoken Word," *Improvement Era*, Feb. 1968, p. 71.
4. Gordon B. Hinckley, "Live the Gospel," *Ensign*, Nov. 1984, p. 86.
5. Brigham Young, 7 June 1863, *Journal of Discourses*, 26 vols. (Liverpool: F. D. Richards, 1855–86), 10:205.
6. Joseph Smith, *Teachings of the Prophet Joseph Smith*, sel. Joseph Fielding Smith (Salt Lake City: Deseret Book Co., 1938), p. 255.

WHERE HAS GREED GOTTEN US?

"Why do ye adorn yourselves with that which hath no life, and yet suffer the hungry, and the needy, and the naked, and sick and the afflicted to pass by you, and notice them not?"

—Mormon 8:39

The Ethics of "I Want"

MARY ANN RASMUSSEN

I grew up in Salt Lake City and graduated from the University of Utah. I married Scott Rasmussen in 1979, and we moved to New York City, where we both graduated from Columbia Law School. After graduation I took a job with a Wall Street law firm, which I greatly enjoyed but which required a number of significant sacrifices.

After six years of practice, during which time our first child was born, my husband and I came to the conclusion that, as much as we enjoyed the excitement, diversity, and vitality of living in New York City, our demanding work schedules and the daily two-hour commutes were not conducive to the type of family life we wanted.

We decided to simplify our lives, and so we moved back to Utah. I am currently a member of the Utah State Bar and practice my specialty, trusts and estates law, on a limited basis. I have restructured my life so that I can spend the bulk of my time with our two children, which has been the most rewarding and enjoyable consequence of our quest for simplification.

Another advantage of this simplification process relates to what we have learned about the emphasis our society places on materialism. As our family dropped from two incomes down to one, and as we voluntarily restricted our ability to acquire things, we became more acutely aware that one of the few things that can be said with certainty about our society is that it is extremely materialistic. As we drive or walk along urban streets, we often see T-shirts and bumper stickers proclaiming

Mary Ann Rasmussen practiced law for six years with large New York City firms. She and her husband, Scott, returned to Salt Lake City, where she has practiced her specialty in trusts and estates law on a limited basis so that she can spend more time with their two children.

slogans such as "Shop until you drop," "When the going gets tough, the tough go shopping," "Whoever dies with the most toys wins," or one slogan that probably makes the philosopher Descartes turn over in his grave, "I shop, therefore I am."

All too many people derive their self-images and judge others on the basis of the clothes they wear, the homes they live in, and the furniture and the automobiles they own. Too frequently we gauge our self-worth and that of others based upon material success or lack of it.

When we reflect on the decade of the 1980s, the operative word was greed. The insider-trading scandals involving Ivan Boesky, Michael Milken, and numerous others; the tax fraud schemes of Leona Helmsley, who lived and was tried by her motto of "Only the little people pay taxes"; the HUD scandals and the savings and loan debacles consumed headlines throughout much of the decade. The selfishness and greediness of these people has wreaked havoc on the American economy and social structure. And the attitudes from which their actions sprang will affect us for decades to come.

Enough is never enough. Human nature always wants more. No matter what circles we travel in, we will always encounter people who have more than we do. Ivana Trump is a quintessential example of this principle. When the Trumps first announced their separation, Ivana was offered a ten-million-dollar divorce settlement — which she summarily rejected as too paltry. Across the country, most Americans thought, "Hey, I could be quite content with ten million dollars." Yet, to Ivana, having only ten million dollars would cramp the style of living to which she has become accustomed.

Just as it is important to remind ourselves that clothes, homes, and automobiles do not make the individual, we must learn to distinguish between needs and wants, and we must teach our children to do the same. We must help our children develop strong, positive self-images so that they do not feel they have to have the latest in clothes, toys, and sports equipment in order to be liked and accepted by their peers. Children need to learn the value of money and the importance of saving for goals. If a child is desperate to own a hot item — such as roller-blades — the child will value the item more and will probably take better care of it if he or she earns the money to purchase it by doing jobs around the house, baby-sitting, and saving allowance money. Children need to realize that just as parents work to earn a living, children should work to earn the things they want. Children who learn to manage money at an early age will be better prepared to live within a budget when they are off at college, on missions, or as newlyweds. One of our great responsibilities as parents is rearing children to be independent and financially responsible.

In Saul Bellow's *Henderson the Rain King,* Henderson, the protagonist, experienced an insatiable little voice inside his head that continually cried, "I want. I want. I want." No matter what Henderson did or acquired, it wasn't sufficient. How many of us are like Henderson in this regard? Do we purchase things in order to feel good about ourselves? Do we spend hours shopping as a means to alleviate boredom and depression or as a means of recreation or entertainment? Do we use possessions to hide our inadequacies and insecurities? Or perhaps to bolster a weak self-image or to validate our lives: "If I live in a beautiful house, dress stylishly, and drive a nice car, then I must be OK."

It is sobering to note that in studies comparing the charitable contributions of different income groups, the percentage of gross income donated to charitable causes actually decreases as a person's gross income increases.

An annual Sub for Santa project carried out by a Salt Lake City law firm illustrates these studies. Each Christmas this firm acts as a Sub for Santa for three or four needy families. It is instructive, and perhaps disappointing, to analyze the generosity of different groups within the firm. The pattern of giving has remained the same year after year. The secretaries, who make the least money, are by far the most generous. They donate beautiful gifts and contribute substantial amounts of cash. The young associate lawyers, whose incomes are significantly higher than those of the secretaries, are considerably less generous. The most parsimonious and penurious group are the senior partners, whose annual incomes exceed $100,000.

Greed not only keeps us from giving of our economic resources but may also start corrupting our sense of honesty. We may come to value money to the exclusion of integrity. I am reminded of a New York attorney who was married to a Wall Street investment banker. Their combined annual income easily exceeded half a million dollars. This couple was at a store purchasing a case of baby formula in the days before electronic scanners, and the clerk inadvertently transposed the numbers on the price sticker, ringing up $29 on the cash register instead of the correct price of $92. The clerk then commented that it was amazing that people could buy all that formula for only $29. The wife looked at the husband and the husband looked at the wife. They both knew the correct price, but neither of them said anything. Later, in telling me this story, the wife claimed that she felt absolutely no obligation to call the mistake to the clerk's attention, rationalizing that store clerks often overcharge customers and concluding that her failure to tell the truth merely served to even the score.

Richard Johnson, a Brigham Young University sociology professor, has noted that those of his students who thought that "a 'high' standard of material comfort may, in fact, be a form of selfishness or oppression are quick to define 'high' as well beyond their own levels"[1]—whatever those levels might be. Because Scott and I have scaled down our standard of living to manage on one income, am I now safely out of the "high" income bracket? I lead a comfortable middle-class existence. I have to ask myself, how much is necessary for a happy life? Where do I draw the line between adequacy and excess?

In the October 1990 general conference, Elder Joseph Wirthlin said that one of the obstacles to achieving spiritual salvation is, "placing improper emphasis on the obtaining of material possessions. For example, we may build a beautiful, spacious home that is far larger than we need. We may spend far too much to decorate, furnish, and landscape it. And even if we are blessed enough to afford such luxury, we may be misdirecting resources that could be better used to build the kingdom of God or to feed and clothe our needy brothers and sisters."[2]

On March 26, 1991, the *Salt Lake Tribune* published a survey which indicated that 1 in 9 children under the age of 12 in Utah go to bed hungry each night and that nationally at least 1 in 8 children under the age of 12, or approximately 5.5 million children, are not adequately fed. The study found that poverty-stricken families spend so much of their income on housing that they can afford an average of just 68 cents per person per meal. If children are malnourished, they cannot achieve their full potential. It is a terrible indictment that a country as wealthy as ours is not willing to take care of innocent children.

The latest infant-mortality statistics available indicate that, in 1989, the United States's infant-mortality rate leveled off at 9.7 deaths per 1,000 births. It now stands at twice the rate of Japan and below that of 23 other countries, including such poor countries as Singapore and Spain. Also troubling is that in the United States twice as many black babies will die within the first year of life as will white babies.[3]

Our purpose in this panel discussion is perhaps to prick our individual and collective consciences so that each of us might analyze our attitudes towards obtaining material goods and achieving a comfortable life. There is a great danger for an individual who has done well materially to think that if another person is poor, it is because that person is lazy and therefore deserves to be poor. While that may be true in some instances, it does not hold true for most of the people who live in poverty. Most of the people who are poor were born to poor parents. With the recession and changes in a global economy, thousands of people have lost their jobs and, consequently, their homes. Many of these people are now living with their families in shelters for the homeless.

If we visit any poor section of any city or town in the United States, we will encounter people who are malnourished, ill-clothed, ill-housed or homeless, unemployed with no hope for the future, and some spaced out on drugs or alcohol to try to blot out their dreary existences. We will find teenage girls, who look no older than seventeen, who have a baby in their arms and a toddler in tow. People hang out in the streets, sitting on steps with nothing to do and nowhere to go. The enormity of the problem is overwhelming, and we feel helpless because we know that only a minute fraction of the children growing up in these environments will have the education or vocational opportunities and the role models that will help them break out of the pernicious cycle of poverty.

Neighborhoods are economically defined. If we are middle class or higher, it is easy to insulate ourselves from those people who are trying to eke out a subsistence level of life on the earth. We can go about our lives and avoid witnessing human suffering and poverty. We can pretend that it does not exist and not notice that it is getting worse.

With the ever-widening gap between the "haves" and the "have-nots," those of us in the middle need to be doing more. There are no comfortable, easy solutions to determining how much to give. I have a video camera; the divorcee down the street can scarcely afford a decent pair of shoes. It was intended that we struggle over these questions — that we struggle, think, and pray, asking for guidance in determining what we should do with our material means. Even a small increase, if all of us resolve to give a little more, can make a difference. It is said that if you are not in the habit of saving, you can establish that habit simply by saving a dollar a week. I think that this principle also applies to helping other people; if we stretch a little bit more than we think we can, somehow we will find the money and the time to help more people more often.

I have no doubt that each of us knows that ultimately God

will judge us on how well we have used our time and resources, including our economic resources, to help our fellowmen. I know that I need to become much more selfless and more generous with my time and money.

Greed can become an invasive cancer that will kill our souls if it is not checked. Greed is the antithesis of the gospel of Jesus Christ. If we will take the time to analyze our attitudes and the importance we place on obtaining the ephemeral things of this world, we can change our behavior so that our lives are more compatible with the teachings of Christ.

Notes

1. Richard E. Johnson, "Socioeconomic Inequality: The Haves and the Have-nots," *BYU Today,* Sept. 1990, p. 49.
2. Joseph B. Wirthlin, "The Straight and Narrow Way," *Ensign,* Nov. 1990, p. 65.
3. Priscilla Painton, "Mere Millions for Kids," *Time,* 8 Apr. 1991, p. 29.

No Poor among Us?

RICHARD E. JOHNSON

Every semester several students in my social problems
course at BYU propose that the extent or seriousness of certain
social problems represents a sign that the world is about to
end and the Millennium is near. Their common conclusion is
based on a set of three shared beliefs or perceptions. First,
they believe that the "last days" will be characterized by unprecedented displays of sin and evil. Second, they see the
traditional and highly publicized problems of crime, violence,
drug abuse, and sexual deviance as the primary indicators of
sin and evil. And third, they perceive America as now experiencing unprecedented levels of crime, violence, drug abuse,
and sexual deviance.

Two aspects of this line of thought strike me as rather
narrow-minded. First, it seems both narrow and presumptuous
for Americans to evaluate the condition of the entire human
race and the fate of the planet on the basis of their perceptions
of America's social problems and moral climate. It seems possible that events or morality in the rest of the world just might
also have something to do with the timing of the Millennium.
Second, the criteria for judging the "badness" of American
society (sex, drugs, crime, and violence) are rather narrow.

It seems to me that if we are serious about contemplating
the moral state of contemporary American society, we might
gain valuable insight by broadening the measure of morality
beyond the traditional sins to include such variables as poverty,
homelessness, and socioeconomic inequality. Perhaps the
central moral problem of our time is primarily economic or

*Richard E. Johnson is an associate professor of sociology at
Brigham Young University. He and his wife, Deborah, are the parents
of six children.*

materialistic, involving behavior that is more often than not perfectly legal and socially acceptable. It also seems that any speculation about "the signs of the last days" must be based on observation of conditions both within and beyond the borders of the United States.

Moral self-assessment, though often a difficult and ambiguous task, is absolutely vital to societal and individual integrity and well-being. I certainly claim no right to judge the moral quality of American society, but I feel an obligation to try. I freely admit to applying a very personal and biased "moral measuring rod" to American society. My measuring rod is based on my personal interpretation of LDS scriptures. In short, I cannot be objective, and I freely admit that I may be way off base.

It seems to me, however, that the most powerful and consistent scriptural warnings given to those who live in the "last days" (as found particularly in the Book of Mormon) center on a single set of interwoven evils—the evils of materialism, consumerism, worldly vanity, and socioeconomic inequality. These traits and conditions are unequivocally condemned throughout the Book of Mormon.[1] Moreover, they are generally described as the root from which other "sins" take nourishment and as the ultimate cause of both personal and social destruction. In short, the prevalence of selfish striving for the "lifestyles of the rich and famous" (by both those who succeed and those who fail), and the consequent inequality that results, appear to be appropriate criteria for assessing a society's moral climate.

Judging from the responses of my students (who are typically "active LDS" from relatively comfortable socioeconomic backgrounds), these are not common measures of immorality or evil. Many, in fact, are shocked by the suggestion that morality could have anything to do with either (a) the seeking or obtaining of a high standard of living, or (b) the presence of grossly unequal standards of living. Those who agree that a "high" standard of material comfort may, in fact, be a form of selfishness or oppression are quick to define "high" as well above their own level. My response is that I, too, am both confused and disquieted by the whole question, but that I cannot ignore it given my interpretation of the scriptures. Furthermore, I cannot have confidence that my "modest" American life-style is safely below a selfishly "high" level of comfort and convenience, given what I know about inequality and destitution in my own society or in the world.

It is certainly understandable that mainstream American Mormons (such as those who read this volume of essays, myself included) are more inclined to condemn the behavior of "traditional sinners" (thieves, addicts, abusers, etc.) than to condemn the behavior of materialistic consumers of legal goods obtained by legal means. Traditional sinners are clearly self-indulgent, satisfying their whims and appetites for comfort or pleasure through sexual, chemical, or violent means. It is also clear that innocent others often suffer because of the self-indulgence of these sinners. We law-abiding, high-living consumers, on the other hand, satisfy our self-indulgent whims and appetites for comfort or pleasure through clearly superior means—we buy goodies, ranging from mansions to microchips. In the process, we ignore King Benjamin and countless other prophets and tell ourselves that we "earn" or "deserve" the goodies that give us comfort and pleasure, and we fail to note any consequent suffering by anyone. I simply cannot shake off the nagging thought that our traditional definitions of morality—our division of the world into the "good guys" and the "bad guys"—is based on convenience and rationalization, as well as on some truth.

Whether or not materialism and inequality are key signs of the moral battles that are to mark the last days, or even whether or not they are evil at all, the fact is that poverty and inequality are flourishing in America today. There is general agreement that three clear trends have occurred in America during the 1980s.

First, inequality in both income and wealth has increased.

The rich have gotten richer and the poor have become poorer—not merely poorer relative to the increasing income of the rich, but literally and absolutely poorer: less able to sustain life. The Census Bureau reports that the richest one-fifth of American households now receive almost ten times the average income of the poorest one-fifth, which is the highest ratio of inequality since they began keeping records following World War II. America's inequality ratio is also the highest among Western industrial nations.

Income inequality represents more than mere differences in the sizes of the piles of goodies that families can afford. For millions of families at the bottom of the distribution (perhaps the 10 percent with total yearly family incomes averaging $3,157), we are talking about malnutrition, literal starvation, little or no access to health care or education, homelessness, and utter hopelessness.

Second, there have been significant increases and changes in the distribution of American poverty, which is rapidly becoming a more common condition for women and children. One-fourth of all American children are now in poverty, and if current trends continue, the number will be one-third by the end of the decade.

Third, we have experienced rising rates of homelessness, along with changes in the characteristics of the homeless. The homeless population today includes an increasing proportion of mentally disturbed people, of families (especially single-mother families), and of working people. The lack of low-cost housing is becoming so acute that even some full-time workers simply cannot find a place they can afford to buy or rent.

Let me repeat that the growing inequality and poverty are not simply a matter of some folks having fewer goodies than others. We are talking about basic shelter, malnutrition, and little or no access to health care or education. We are talking about millions of Americans, many of whom are children, who simply have no concept of what it means to have a "brightness of hope."

I think many of us are ignorant of what is going on and prefer to remain so. Few of us realize that infant mortality rates among America's poor exceed those in many Third World countries and greatly surpass the rates in other Western democracies. All of this occurs in the midst of wealth almost unimaginable to the vast majority of the planet's past or present inhabitants; all of this occurs while the rich get richer. I cannot divorce this reality from my concept of morality. I am ashamed to be a part of it.

There are numerous reasons for these conditions. I have listed nine in a related article on the subject.[2] Let me focus on the last, and most important, which is public stereotypes and attitudes about wealth, poverty, and welfare. Frankly, I am continually amazed at the strength and harshness of the antipoor attitudes exhibited by some of my students and at their unwillingness to reconsider their views on the basis of clear contradictory evidence. Antipoor attitudes come in a wide variety of hues, but the predominant theme is that the poor have earned their lot in life because they are lazy, stupid, and/or satisfied with their way of life — that they "deserve" to be poor.

Numerous studies show that the poor as a group have the same goals, desires, work ethic, and work habits of the nonpoor as a group. Obviously, you are going to find "slackers" in any group, but there doesn't seem to be a systematic correlation between poverty and work habits.

Consider the case of Eugene Lang, a millionaire who grew up in a now dilapidated area of New York. He was asked to come back and speak to his alma mater at a grade school graduation. He had planned to deliver a traditional "rah, rah, work hard, this is the land of opportunity" speech, but when he looked around, he saw that his originally working-class East Harlem neighborhood had changed. The audience consisted of poor minority kids, and he didn't think they actually had much of a chance. So, on the spur of the moment he promised them, "All of you who stay out of trouble — who stay in school and graduate from high school — I am going to fund your college education." The dropout rates of that school were normally 60 to 70 percent. Of the group to whom he offered a college education, the dropout rate fell to about 10 percent. That is called making a permanent difference in someone's life. It wasn't that he gave them money. They didn't see a penny for a long time. What he gave them was hope and respect and opportunity. To some people those words seem just jargon, empty clichés, but I believe that if we give people respect and hope—which may or may not cost money—we will see that the poor are no more lazy, stupid, or satisfied with remaining in poverty than the rest of us.

The missing ingredient in the lives of Mr. Lang's recipients had not been the desire or willingness to work. It was hope. Most college students I meet have long taken for granted that college was an expectation or at least a realistic option for them. Are they—we—to be particularly admired for simply following the most reasonable path to socioeconomic success, while others "fail" because they see no realistic hope of even getting on the path?

Today, more poor and minority high school seniors than ever before report that they want to and plan to go to college, yet fewer and fewer of them are enrolling. By far the leading reason for their "change of mind" is reported to be the high cost of school and the absence of financial assistance programs that were much more available in the 1970s.

Work ethic, hours worked, ambition, and IQ are very poor statistical predictors of adult socioeconomic attainment in the United States. By far the best predictor is the socioeconomic position of one's parents. In short, poor Americans of any age are poor primarily because they were born poor. And the second major reason of poverty is similarly unrelated to in-dividual character: The poor have often "landed" in an unfavorable macroeconomic setting. Not unlike victims of earthquakes or hurricanes, victims of structural economic depression often have little control over their fate.

It makes just as much sense to blame the current poverty

on individual laziness as it does to attribute the Great Depression of the 1930s to an outbreak of a "lazy-bum virus." Certainly, some poor folks should heed the traditional advice to "get a job." (As, by the way, should some rich folks.) However, well over 90 percent of all poverty-stricken Americans fall into one or more of the following categories: under 18 or over 65 years old, disabled, working (for poverty pay), or rearing infants or small children. Evidence is clear that when the disadvantaged are given real opportunities to succeed, the vast majority work hard and take advantage of those opportunities.

In spite of massive evidence to the contrary, many still cling to the notion that America is the land of equal opportunity. That belief, in turn, makes a convenient basis for the conclusion that the "haves" deserve their goodies and are not obligated to assist the "have-nots." My response to this conclusion is twofold. First, LDS scriptures state clearly that the obligation to assist the poor remains intact whether or not the poor are judged to be deserving. Second, how can one reasonably view the growing millions of poor children as blameworthy, no matter what one thinks of their parents?

The President's Commission on Children recently called the poverty and despair facing many American children "a staggering national tragedy." Happily, yet sadly, the resources needed to save America's children are readily available, at an affordable cost. The price tag would amount to relatively small sacrifices of time and slight reductions in our consumption of goods and services. How can anyone in a position to help, including Latter-day Saints, simply sit back and enjoy a life of ease? Is not the lack of social action in this regard an indictment of American society?

It matters not whether remedial action is private or public, Republican or Democrat. I have absolutely no particular partisan or political agenda in mind: I am simply advocating action. What matters is that inaction is both moral and social suicide. Because of our selfish and short-sighted desires for immediate materialistic self-indulgence, mainstream America

172

is nurturing the growth of a subpopulation within society that will have little or no ability or desire to participate in conventional social or economic life. The prospects for a productive economy in years to come are thereby reduced. The prospects for flourishing drug and crime problems are thereby increased. Everyone's quality of life will be affected by the current neglect of our children.

I would like to believe that my material living standard is not a moral issue as long as I am a "good person" in other ways. I really would like to believe that. I would be so much happier. Given the national picture, however — not to mention the world picture, which is much worse in deprivation and inequality — such a belief strikes me as wishful fantasy. The evidence is simply too clear that a great deal of the evil and suffering in our land can be traced to the individualistic and materialistic pursuit of happiness and to the tremendous socioeconomic inequality that follows. Unfortunately, I do not believe these attitudes are absent from the LDS subculture.

On the positive side, it is not impossible for the recipient of a high income to live a modest life-style and use the money to benefit others. In fact, the world needs many more of those kinds of people. But as the scriptures repeatedly remind us, a high income represents a temptation that very few can withstand. Moreover, the definition of modest can easily be stretched beyond all recognition. A major point from the parable of the widow's mite seems to be that moral judgment over the use of money is based not on how much we give but on how much we keep for ourselves.

Whether or not we are witnessing signs of the last days, we are certainly witnessing global trends and events unprecedented in world history. Never before have scientific and political developments allowed so many hundreds of millions of people to realistically seek the "good life" of physical ease and comfort already enjoyed by the American middle class. The materialistic "good life" is fast becoming a global aspiration. Recent events in Eastern Europe, for example, represent not only the unshackling of political and religious bonds but the unleashing of materialistic striving.

Could not the great and unprecedented battle between good and evil that seems to be predicted for the end of the world refer to the dual evils of insatiable materialism and unspeakable inequality? Certainly, opportunities for engaging in economic selfishness are expanding rapidly. There may be more people alive today exercising substantial political and economic agency — facing real choices between personal luxury and Christian charity — than there have been in all previous centuries combined. How will they handle their "opportunity" to engage in direct or indirect oppression, their choice to hoard or to share? How are we handling ours?

It is no longer possible even to pretend that material acquisitiveness can be morally neutral. Never before has it been so clear that the earth's capacity to sustain life is limited. Never before did humankind realize that a high standard of living must be purchased at the cost of depletion of finite resources and pollution of a fragile environment.

The inescapable conclusion is that when one person lives a life of luxury in a society or a world of limited and finite resources, others are forced to have less. Many, in fact, have so much less that they will suffer and die but only after watching their loved ones suffer and die. Increasingly, the dying — and the injustice — are becoming more difficult to ignore. Modern communications systems continue to shrink the world, bringing into greater light and clearer focus the juxtaposition of unprecedented abundance and unprecedented suffering. The rich have run out of excuses. What happens when the poor run out of patience?

Whether we become more willing to sacrifice and share out of fear, economic self-interest, or charity, it seems that the time has come to do so or face the consequences. How long can we ignore the scriptural description of socioeconomic inequality as evil? How long will we be guided by the "traditions of our fathers" instead of the Savior of humanity? How long

174

will Church members join mainstream America in not only condoning but promoting and admiring materialistic self-aggrandizement? Might not the great lesson for the last days be that in order for there to be a world of peace or a Zion with "no poor among [them]" (Moses 7:18) that there must also be no rich among them? (See 4 Nephi 1:3.)

Notes

1. 1. Jacob 2:13–19; Mosiah 4:16–18, 21–23; Alma 1:26–32; 4:6–15; 5:53–56; 16:16, 21; 31:24–30; 34:28–29, 40; Helaman 3:33–36; 4:11–12; 7:20–21; 13:21–22; 3 Nephi 6:10–15; 24:5; 26:19; 4 Nephi 1:3, 24–26, 43; D&C 6:7; 11:7; 49:19–20; 70:14; 105:3.
2. Richard E. Johnson, "Socioeconomic Inequality: The Haves and the Have-nots," *BYU Today*, Sept. 1990, pp. 46–58. (Excerpts reprinted with permission.)

"That Which Hath No Life"

SUSAN LILLYWHITE WARNER

"Mom, Mom, you've got to get up and help me make a treat for my class today." As I struggle to open my tired eyes, memory returns like neural static: Mitchell's third-grade class, the contest, losing team brings treats for winning team, Mitchell's turn, my turn. Mitchell is reminding me now—urgently, insistently—that it can't be just any treat: it has to be a bigger and better treat than the one provided last week. I can see how important it is to him to take not merely an acceptable treat but, if at all possible, a truly spectacular one.

We had barely begun making the treat when Jenny, who is eleven, announced that she needed two card tables and an easel to display her science fair project.

"Are you sure you need tables? What are the other children using for their displays?"

"Mom—nobody wins if they don't have tables and easels."

"Well, I'm certain every child is not bringing tables and easels."

"That's what I'm trying to explain to you—you can't win without them. Everybody doesn't win."

As I was directing Jenny to the possible location of the card tables, Carrie, who is a freshman in high school, reminded me to pick up the suckers she wanted to sell to earn money for her school choir tour. "Be sure to get them today, or I won't have time to earn my money," Carrie warned me.

Reared in California, Susan Lillywhite Warner has also lived in Connecticut and England. After graduating from Brigham Young University, she taught elementary school for two years. She and her husband, BYU professor Terry Warner, are the parents of ten children. She has served on PTA boards and as president of her ward Relief Society and Young Women organizations.

"Are all the kids in the choir earning two hundred dollars to go on tour?"

"You can't go unless you can come up with the money."

"Is *everybody* in the choir going to be able to go?" I asked.

"I think there will be a few who can't go."

"Is anything being done to help them?"

"Mom, everyone is having a hard enough time coming up with their *own* money."

One need not be a social scientist to observe and record attitudes that characterize our materialistic society. We are possessive, acquisitive, competitive, self-centered, opportunistic, and selfish. In the first forty-five minutes of a typical school day I found evidence of each of these attitudes in my own home.

I have been exceptionally sensitive to these attitudes lately because I have been reading and thinking about the plight of the hungry and homeless in this country and around the world, and the wide discrepancy between the "haves" and the "have-nots" has been very much on my mind. I seldom polish my furniture, but last week my son asked to film a scene in our living room for a movie he is making in his efforts to get started in that business. I decided I'd better give the furniture in that room a "once over lightly." As I polished the legs on the piano, I couldn't help reflecting on whether we really need a piano in our home. We love music — it is an important part of our family life — but I wondered how we could justify owning a lovely piano so that we can enjoy the luxury of making music, when children all over the world, including hundreds in our own state, go to school hungry every morning or to bed without dinner at night. After some thought about the piano, I expressed my concerns at the dinner table. My family thought I was slipping over the edge. "Mother's really losing it now!" "This is definitely the wrong topic for her to be speaking on." "Let's hope the conference is over soon."

Fourteen-year-old Carrie spoke up. "What are you proposing, Mother? Do you want to sell the piano and buy

177

McDonald's Happy Meals to drop from an airplane?" She didn't want to take me seriously, but I could tell that deep down all of them sensed it was an important issue.

As I thought about my family's response, I had to ask myself, What is my responsibility in this? As a parent, do I bear responsibility for the attitudes of my children? If so, I need to ask myself these questions:

As a result of living in my home, are my children more caring and compassionate or are they more selfish and competitive?

Is looking out for Number One an accepted attitude in our family?

Do we dismiss the misfortunes of others with unfeeling comments such as "That's how the ball bounces" and "You get what you deserve in this life"?

Do the people in our family learn from the atmosphere in our home that things are more important than people?

Is it evident to them that happiness comes from the kind of people we are and not what we have?

Are we making a conscious effort to live in such a way that we can share our abundance with those who have less?

Some of us think materialism can be a temporary expedient to a higher end. We think we need to compete, make our place in society, and watch out for ourselves, supposing that sometime in the future, when we "arrive" socially and economically and also at last have some free time, we will pay attention to spiritual matters, give to the poor, and devote more time to caring about other people. This is a terrible mistake. The means by which we live will, without our realizing it, become our ends. They will take over our affections. They become habits — our very way of life.

When my husband and I were in graduate school in the East, we belonged to a struggling branch of Saints. For the branch to operate, every member was needed. But many felt that while in school their main concern should be their formal education. For the time being, they would leave Church service

178

to others so that they could prepare for an eventual greater contribution to Church and society. Predictably, they never realized their plans. In later years, they continued to focus on career and worldly pursuits. On the other hand, those who served while going to school continued serving after completing their degrees.

Brigham Young said, "Why do the children of men set their hearts upon earthly things? ... [The] moment that men seek to build up themselves, in preference to the kingdom of God, and seek to hoard up riches, while the widow and the fatherless, the sick and afflicted, around them, are in poverty and want, it proves that their hearts are weaned from their God; *and their riches will perish in their fingers, and they with them.*"[1]

If we concentrate on "getting ahead" and are preoccupied with material goals, we may *say* that doing so is a means to a higher end, but we communicate to our children that material goals are the ends worth living for. I have been greatly disturbed to observe the attitudes of school children. They are often preoccupied, almost obsessed, with establishing a social identity, which includes maintaining a socially approved physical appearance and material possessions: Guess jeans, Polo shirts, Air-Jordan Nike basketball shoes. The impressive brand names are difficult to keep up with because they change from year to year. I can remember when an alligator emblem on a shirt was a must; now our children wouldn't be caught dead with a "crocodile" on their pocket. All too often we and our children are self-centered and alarmingly calloused towards the feelings of those who do not possess the material qualifications for social approval. We, the "haves," think only about how *we* feel, with little regard for the feelings we may be evoking in the hearts of the "have-nots."

Moroni speaks of our day when he says, "And I know that ye do walk in the pride of your hearts; and there are none save a few only who do not lift themselves up in the pride of their hearts, unto the wearing of very fine apparel. ... For behold, ye do love money, and your substance, and your fine apparel . . . more than ye love the poor and the needy, the sick and the afflicted. . . . Why do ye adorn yourselves with *that which hath no life,* and yet suffer the hungry, and the needy, and the naked, and the sick and the afflicted to pass by you, and notice them not?" (Mormon 8:36–37, 39; italics added.)

I fear that too often these attitudes in children reflect the values of the parents. Indeed, sometimes parents push their children to succeed, as if our worth and happiness were somehow predicated upon a favorable comparison with others. Some parents even believe their own value and happiness is closely linked to the social acceptability and achievements of their children. As I said before, though such parents think of material achievement as a *means* to happiness, the children will come to equate possessions and worldly success with happiness.

Rather than focus on the problem of materialism in our homes and society, let us press forward to seek some solutions. Let us raise these issues not to cast blame but to help one another combat this menacing trait in our society.

Clearly, to make changes in our homes and children, we must change ourselves. We change by trying right now to live the way of life which we hope will be ours forever. And when we change, we will teach our children the right values. Changing *oneself* is the most powerful way any individual can combat the menace of materialism in her daily walk.

My neighbor who was approached about making sandwiches for the homeless thought, "How do I have time to do this? I barely have time to make lunches for my own children." But she decided to try. She was amazed to find she was able, with the help of her family, to work out a system so that she could efficiently accomplish this task each week. And her good example has inspired others. Hearing of her efforts, the Young Women have begun making dinners for the homeless shelter. Service can be a fun family project—many of us have missed working together as families on the stake welfare farms. Another friend is active in Project Read, teaching adults who for some reason have not yet learned to read. A retired couple on our street are helping handicapped people learn skills so they can be productively employed.

Sometimes we need to help our families develop the habits that bring lasting joy rather than fleeting pleasure. Driving home from Salt Lake, I saw a billboard, "If saving money is your favorite sport—shop at University Mall." I had to chuckle. The ad was a clever twist on the fact that in our society we shop as often for recreation as for necessity. Shopping has become a sport.

How many children and teenagers do you know who love to "walk the mall" on Saturday and feel unfulfilled if they return home empty-handed? Perhaps such activities could be replaced with service projects involving friends. I know some boys who collect surplus papers on Saturday mornings for their Scout troop—they seem to be having a good time piling the papers in the back of an old trailer. I see many young people involved in service projects, socializing while also giving their time and energy for the good of someone else. These are habits worth our fostering in young people.

I asked one of these service-oriented teenagers how she got started. After thinking, she said, "I guess it started when I was very young. Our family used to sing carols at rest homes at Christmastime. I could see the light come into those lonely faces as we sang, and it made me happy." Very early in her life someone provided an experience that helped this young woman learn that she could make a difference.

Though important, it is not enough to talk about materialism, publish arguments, and work for legislation. We each must do something personally. We must decide to spend some of our own time and resources, to sacrifice some of our pleasures and perhaps even people's good opinion of us as we swim against the current. Otherwise, the way we spend our time, the subjects of our daily conversations, will become not just the style but the substance of our lives. Our means will become our ends. And to our disappointment, our children, learning from us by mimicking us, will grow up preoccupied with shallow values and selfish concerns. Not only will these children hurt others by their failure to share, but the children themselves will become petty and empty people. Materialism is pride, pride is sin, and sin destroys. Though all suffer, materialism destroys the souls of the "haves" more than the souls of the "have-nots."

The modern philosopher Emmanuel Levinas quotes a Jewish proverb: "The other's material needs are my spiritual needs."[2] Often when we feel unhappy or unfulfilled, we try to fill our own need in the world's way—by buying, acquiring, spending time and energy in indulgent activities. But Levinas is right: our spiritual need is satisfied when we lift the burdens of others. We live in a time when electronic media allow us to know of the lives and needs of our brothers and sisters all over the world. It is our spiritual need not only to know but to choose to help. The Savior has told us, "It is not given that one man should possess that which is above another, wherefore the world lieth in sin." (D&C 49:20.) If it is our desire to bless the lives of others, he will help us give up that which hath no life and open the way for us, in turn, to help those who need that which giveth life.

Notes

1. Brigham Young, 14 August 1853, *Journal of Discourses*, 26 vols. (Liverpool: F. D. Richards, 1855–86) 1:272–73; italics added.
2. Richard A. Cohen, *Face to Face with Levinas* (Albany: State University of New York Press, 1986), p. 24.

The Miracles of Service

MARY B. JOHNSTON

My interest in service began the summer of my junior year in college. I was a camp counselor in rural New Jersey for New York City kids from disadvantaged homes. During the two-week training session, I learned that many of the children were on welfare, came from single-parent homes, had been abused, and had certainly never spent much time in the outdoors. Once the children arrived, the other counselors and I dedicated ourselves to teaching and loving them. Among other things, we taught them how to build shelters, cook food outdoors, wash and sanitize their dishes, swim, and plan and go on hikes. Though ten and eleven years old, many still wet their beds at night. So we took turns waking them up in the middle of the night to take them to the latrine, often in the rain. I did not sleep much that summer and had no time to read and phi-losophize — two of my favorite pastimes in college. During the stressful and loving hours of that summer, I learned the joy of abandoning my concerns and dedicating myself to the welfare of others. But it was overwhelming to hear one sad story after another about neglect, abuse, and poverty. Dealing with in-numerable discipline problems and constantly attending to physical and emotional needs threw me down from my intel-lectual tower and brought me to a new place full of sorrow, struggle, and love.

In her short story "Marigolds," Eugenia Collier writes about

Mary B. Johnston received her bachelor's degree in English from Brigham Young University and her master's from Middlebury College in Vermont. She has taught junior high and high school English at several private schools. Interested in helping her students become aware of needs in their communities, she has spent the last five years building volunteer programs for high school students.

183

Lizabeth, a fourteen-year-old girl whose vision of the world is changed. At first she is aware only of her own feelings and thoughts; after an act of impulsive, destructive anger, she finally sees into another person's heart. Disheartened and angry about her own poverty and her father's recent humiliating layoff, Lizabeth runs off in the middle of the night to the only bright and hopeful spot in her neighborhood, Mrs. Lottie's "brilliant splash of sunny yellow marigolds." Unleashing her anger on Mrs. Lottie, an old, lonely, and impoverished woman, Lizabeth furiously uproots all the flowers. After the garden is ruined, the fourteen-year-old girl looks up to see Mrs. Lottie and regrets her act. "Whatever verve there was left in [Mrs. Lottie], whatever was of love and beauty and joy that had not been squeezed out by life, had been there in the marigolds which she had so tenderly cared for." The narrator continues, "I know that the moment [I realized this] marked the end of innocence. Innocence involves an unseeing acceptance of things at face value, an ignorance of the area below the surface. In that humiliating moment, I looked beyond myself and into the depths of another person. This was the beginning of compassion, and one cannot have both compassion and innocence."[1]

The innocence that the narrator describes clearly does not refer to sinlessness or purity but to a self-involved, naive view of the world that prevents her from understanding and caring about another person's experience. Losing my own innocence during those hot summer days of camp was the time I began to see into the depths of those children's hearts. Since then my desire has grown and taken me to shelters, hospitals, food banks, impoverished neighborhoods in America and in Eastern Europe—all to be closer to the mystery, pain, and beauty of the human heart. Inside these moments of compassion, magic happens. We discover the deep love we have for other people and that others have for us. But most importantly, we get a glimpse of Christ's and Heavenly Father's unfathomable love for mankind.

During his ministry, Christ lived inside of these moments

and as a result transformed people's lives. In the four Gospels, the apostles record that when the blind and the lepers came to Jesus to be helped, he had compassion on them and healed them. Matthew writes, "And Jesus stood still, and called them, and said, What will ye that I shall do unto you? They say unto him, Lord, that our eyes may be opened. So Jesus had compassion on them, and touched their eyes: and immediately their eyes received sight, and they followed him." (Matthew 20:32–34.)

Nephi, the son of Helaman, writes that during Christ's visit to the Americas, Christ said, "Behold, my bowels are filled with compassion towards you. Have ye any that are sick among you? Bring them hither. Have ye any that are lame, or blind, or halt, or maimed, or leprous, or that are withered, or that are deaf, or that are afflicted in any manner? Bring them hither and I will heal them, for I have compassion upon you; my bowels are filled with mercy." (3 Nephi 17:6–7.)

During his ministry, Christ showed his godly power and his love for humanity not only through teaching divine principles but also through performing physical and spiritual healings. Serving one another is a divine experience that fills us with the love of God and enables us, through heavenly powers, to accomplish miracles. My notion of miracles has changed since I began serving in the community. I have never seen any physical healing or heard people speak in tongues, but I have seen my high school students grow to love homeless people whom they once feared. I have seen them change their focus from caring primarily for themselves to sacrificing social opportunities on weekends and study time on school nights to run fund-raisers for our sponsor child, play cards at a shelter with a recovering drug addict, or take children who live in shelters to the Aquarium.

Compassion — a wind that blows down walls, whispers away prejudice, and cools anger. Compassion — a magic alloy that builds bridges and creates inseparable bonds. Think of all the forces that have had the power to separate us from each other:

religion, race, class, age, political persuasion, nationality. The list is painfully long. With compassion, these differences do not need to separate or threaten us but instead can provide an opportunity to feel the love of God fill our bowels.

Let me tell you a story. A few years ago eight high school girls and I were invited to be a part of an education project about abuse. After attending eight training sessions, the students were to give a presentation to high school students informing the audience what to do about current or potential abuse. For our first session, we visited a shelter where we spent two hours with four women who had been severely battered. Before we began talking, I was very nervous. On one side of the room sat a row of white, upper-middle class, well-educated girls, none of whom had been abused; opposite them sat one white and three black women, none of whom had graduated from high school or ever known any kind of plenty. They had been abused as children and as adults. I was worried that the students would not be sensitive and that the women would be angry about our intruding into their lives. How could these two groups possibly find a common ground? The experience that followed was one among many that have built the foundation of my spiritual faith. The Spirit of God was in that room. The students asked very personal questions in a caring manner, and these women — strangers to us only minutes before — freely told us their stories. And though we were discussing violence, there was no hatred in the room, not even towards the men who had so severely hurt the sheltered women. In addition, there was little sense of division among us because we all had a common goal: to eliminate abuse. Had we concentrated on what separated us, we all would have been convinced that people with disparate backgrounds should avoid each other and have reason to fear one another. Such decisions are unfortunate because they reinforce stereotypes and prevent social change.

Let me tell you about another miracle. Julie, a student of mine, had a series of very poor relationships with men and

186

had not been doing particularly well in school. She also had serious health problems and was not getting along with her parents. Despite her low confidence, she signed up to be a hospice volunteer. After attending six two-hour sessions, she began taking care of a ninety-year-old man who had terminal cancer. He had only three months to live. At first she visited him a few times a week and then every day. Spending time with this man in need blessed his last days with comfort and warmth and blessed her with a sense of personal worth. Their differences—his blindness and her sight, his age and her youth—united rather than separated them. They found the grace of compassion. Now a senior in college, Julie says her time with this man was among the most important experiences in her life.

Perhaps the most difficult and powerful moments of service come within our own families. A woman whose father had cancer tells of flying in to visit him, entering his room, and not recognizing her own father. This pale, hairless, thin man who breathed with great gasps could not be her father. She explains, "I had to look through him and find something besides this astonishing appearance of a father I could barely recognize physically. . . . Suddenly this thought came to me, words of Mother Teresa, describing lepers she cared for as 'Christ in all his distressing disguises.' I never had any real relationship to Christ at all, and I can't say that I did at that moment. But what came through to me was a feeling for my father's identity . . . as a child of God. That was who he was behind the 'distressing disguise.' And, it was my identity, too, I felt. I felt a great bond with him which wasn't anything like what I had felt as father and daughter."[2] When we see each person as a child of God and see that within each person is goodness or at least potential for goodness, we are empowered with a faith that can lift another person to see her or his own power. With this faith we are less likely to become a part of a helping relationship that initiates or perpetuates dependency. Ram Dass and Paul Gormon, the authors of the wonderful book on service *How*

Can I Serve? explain, "The more you think of yourself as a 'therapist,' the more pressure there is on someone to be a 'patient.' The more you identify yourself as a 'philanthropist,' the more compelled someone feels to be 'supplicant.' The more you see yourself as a 'helper,' the more need for people to play the passive 'helped.' You're buying into . . . what people who are suffering want to be rid of: limitation, dependency, helplessness, and separateness."[3]

The last two Christmases my ward in Boston learned a great deal about separateness. A Spanish branch and my ward meet in the same building. Once the service committee became aware that many of the Spanish branch families did not have enough money to buy their children presents, we decided to fill Santa's sack with gifts. The Spanish branch was thrilled and invited all of us to come to their Christmas party. Though the party was publicized, no one came except me. Yes, we had helped the Spanish kids, but we remained the distant donors, not fellow Christmas celebrators. This year Kristine, a woman on my ward's service committee, suggested that the two congregations have a party together. We still gave the presents, and the Spanish-speaking branch did what they had wanted to do the year before: treat us to their traditional Christmas meal of hot tamales. The Portuguese branch joined in with a Brazilian fruit drink and Primary children acted out the story of Christ's birth in their native Portuguese. The evening culminated in a dance that included Spanish, Portuguese, and American music. By sharing we found a way to bless each other rather than creating dependency and separation.

The most effective community service programs involve not only sharing but also taking responsibility. Habitat for Humanity volunteers work side by side with the people who will be living in the house that is being built.[4] The beneficiaries are required to help build. They lack the funds to have a home but gain a sense of pride and dignity as they help build the foundation and structure of a more stable and secure life. In my favorite New Testament story, Christ teaches us the importance not only of loving and serving people but also of helping them take responsibility. When the adulteress's accusers are eager to stone her, Christ challenges them, saying, "He that is without sin among you, let him first cast a stone at her." (John 8:7.) Christ finds a way to teach her neighbors not to judge and a way to protect her. But to empower her and help her find a better life, he admonishes her to sin no more. (John 8:10–11.) Christ believes that both He and she could change her life. May we find this delicate balance in our own efforts to help each other.

So far all of the stories I have told have mentioned little struggle or doubt about serving in our families and communities. From my experience, the ratio of confusion and doubt to miracles is high. Letting go of our own agenda and interests to extend ourselves to other people can be very difficult. It takes energy to enter someone else's world and imagine what they are experiencing, to figure out what might be helpful, and to suspend judgement. We might be unable to do these things if we are confronting an unfamiliar situation.

When students of mine return from their first visit to the homeless shelter, many of them are deeply disturbed by what they have seen and are paralyzed by their questions. "How do these people become homeless? Where are their families? Are they in the shelter because of low motivation, mental illness, or drug addiction? Will they ever be able to start another life? Am I doing any good by serving a meal and playing cards with them, or am I somehow perpetuating the problem?" The questions go on and on.

Anytime we enter an unfamiliar situation, we will have questions, and unless we find a way to sort through them, our doubts and confusion could very well prevent us from being effective or even continuing our work. We need to have people with whom we can confer. Volunteering with a friend or family member helps. Relying on people within the Church who may be more familiar with the difficulties you see could be useful. Perhaps your visiting teaching supervisor or a member of the

Relief Society presidency may be able to help you sort through your questions. In addition, speaking with professionals in the field can help put the situation in context.

I remember a time last year when I had real difficulty going to the shelter with my students every Thursday night. I was so troubled by what I saw there that I could not answer my student's questions. I had so many misgivings that I felt hypocritical even sponsoring the activity. I was especially troubled when one evening I brought a sweater to a Romanian friend, and she yelled at me about presuming that I could understand what she was going through. She said the sweater that I had brought was ugly and insisted I take it back and leave. This, among other experiences made me wonder what I was doing there and think about other, perhaps more effective, ways or places I might choose to serve. Finally, I called the shelter's volunteer coordinator, a woman who had worked with the homeless for five years, and told her what was bothering me. She helped me understand the embittering experiences those people have before they talk to me. And, really, my purpose there is not for me to be comforted, but to show them a kind of patience and unconditional love that they don't experience during the day on the street. After I spoke with her and attended several different workshops about mental health and homelessness, and spent many hours with my students sorting through our experiences, I returned to the shelters and soup kitchens with a more realistic perspective about what I was looking at, and with more patience and love.

As we enter unfamiliar situations, it is important to get training. Programs such as Hospice will include training sessions which are informative and reassuring. It is also important to choose mentors in the community who have blazed trails that we want to blaze ourselves someday. We can ask them about how they endured because anyone who has entered this kind of work has gone through struggles and has stayed in it for very good and powerful reasons.

Equally important to understanding the dynamics of a prob-

190

lem is assessing our own interests and talents. A few years ago, several of my students volunteered in a local public library. Most of them found the work tedious and often did not fulfill their commitment. However, one intellectual senior, who had always found difficulty fitting in socially, made dramatic contributions and won the hearts of all the librarians. For the first time in his life, he felt accepted and valued for who he was. In order for our service to become part of our spiritual and intellectual growth, we should — whenever possible — try to get involved in ways that will allow us to use our talents and training and to develop our interests.

I have left the very most important counsel for last. As we serve our families, communities, and fellow Church members, we will need wisdom, patience, and insight. Nothing brings all of these gifts in greater abundance than a prayerful relationship with God. We are letting the Lord teach us how to see divine potential not only in those whom we serve but also in ourselves. When we extend ourselves to others, we are inviting Christ to teach us about the principles of service and compassion that were the heartbeat of his ministry and the power of his atonement. That can only happen if we regularly consecrate our lives to the welfare of others and believe in God's power to act through us. If we do, miracles *will* happen.

Notes

1. Eugenia Collier, "Marigolds," *Negro Digest* (n.p.: Johnson Publishing Co., 1969), pp. 166–67.
2. Ram Dass and Paul Gorman, *How Can I Help?* (New York: Alfred A. Knopf, 1985), pp. 18–19.
3. Ibid., p. 28.
4. Habitat for Humanity is an international volunteer organization that helps build houses for the poor.

SEASONS OF FAITH

I came to believe that ... faith too has different seasons. It has its warm, sun-filled days of spring and summer, and its long, dark, bitter winters. ... God will not remove our winters, for through winter comes spring.

—Lisa Johnson Boswell

A Fertile Faith

LISA JOHNSON BOSWELL

In the scriptures, faith is often referred to as a plant; for instance, we speak of planting the seed of testimony and watching it grow, we speak of the fruits of faith, and we speak of faith like a grain of mustard seed. I have come to believe that faith is spoken of in these terms because like plants, faith too has different seasons. It has its warm, sun-filled days of spring and summer, and its long, dark, bitter winters. I first heard this idea from a woman who talked with me after a Relief Society lesson I gave on personal testimony several years ago. She told me that she had recently entered a winter of faith, a time when her own faith seemed as dead and without the chance of re-generation as barren trees seem in December, but she looked forward steadfastly to spring, believing that like plants, her faith too would be regenerated.

I have often thought of this woman as I have faced my own adversities. Through years of infertility tests, I have at times experienced my own Alaskan winter of faith. In fact, when asked to speak on the subject of faith through adversity, I replied that I might more honestly label my remarks "Faithless through Adversity." I certainly do not purport to have had unwavering faith during my infertility. It is not easy to be infertile in the Mormon community, as I discovered not only from my own experience but from interviewing other infertile LDS women and men for a book on that topic.

Infertility, like many other adversities, is at the core a dream killer. The dream of having children is one of the most basic

Lisa Johnson Boswell is a convert to the Church. She received her master's degree in English from Brigham Young University and has taught part-time for the BYU English Department. She and her husband, Grant Boswell, are the parents of two children.

human desires. Yet for approximately 15 percent of married couples, this dream is either never realized or bought with great pain.

Having no control over one's ability to procreate can have a devastating impact on self-image. One woman I interviewed mentioned that she had come to view herself as a third gender. There were males, females, and then her. In some instances infertile wives and husbands have suggested divorce so that their spouses could remarry and have children.

Infertility affects the entire family. It affects the parents of infertile couples who long for grandchildren. It affects the children who are finally conceived by couples with infertility problems. My daughter used to come home from kindergarten and implore me, "Mom, I'm the only kid in my class who doesn't have a brother or a sister. Can't you get me one? I don't want to be an only child." Hence infertility can mean feeling that besides losing your own dream, you have prevented loved ones from realizing their dreams as well.

The problem goes far beyond not being called Mom or Dad. Infertility colors many aspects of our lives. Being infertile means not having any good reason to buy a minivan, even if it is on sale. It means being able to buy a house with a small backyard because there won't be children to play in it. It means trying hard to act pleased when one's old college roommate happily announces her third pregnancy.

Infertility not only colors the present but it also clouds the future. A twenty-eight-year-old woman I interviewed confessed that she had already worried about becoming a burden to her brothers and sisters, nieces and nephews, in her old age. Another couple wondered who they would pass their photo albums on to. They wondered if anyone would want them or value them.

Infertility, then, would be hard for anyone, but for infertile Mormons, the pain of this adversity is often even more acute. Ideally, church is where our trials melt away for awhile, where we can come for renewal and leave better able to face life's difficulties. But sadly, church meetings are where many infertile Mormons are most reminded of their loss.

Being an infertile Mormon can mean hearing in a Relief Society lesson that a woman's crowning glory is to bear children. Being infertile may mean listening to someone in testimony meeting testify she knows there is a God because her prayers have been answered and then wondering, "So what does it mean if my prayers are not answered? Does that mean there is no God?" Being infertile often means coming in late to fast and testimony meeting so you miss the blessing of the babies and then leaving early during an earnest man's testimony that he knows that in the premortal existence his eight children all individually chose to come to his earthly home.

Being an infertile Mormon woman means going to a Relief Society dinner and trying to find a table where the discussion won't be centered on pregnancy, childbirth, or the PTA. It means accepting a call in the Primary because, as the bishop assures you, there are many ways to mother. Sooner or later it will mean a day when you go home and cry because your heart grieves for children of your own. You want to mother your own children, not everyone else's.

Unfortunately, being an infertile Mormon can also mean coping with unfair judgments from members who assume that your childlessness is by choice rather than necessity. Infertility in the Mormon community can be unusually difficult. Yet within the gospel are the truths that make adversities easier to bear. Many infertile couples worked through their winters of faith as they came to understand these gospel truths.

Young infertile couples question whether their adversity has been brought on because of unworthiness. They acknowledge scriptures that remind us that rain falls on both "the just and on the unjust," or "whom the Lord loveth he chasteneth." (Matthew 5:45; Hebrews 12:6.) So they recognize that adversity comes to good people, but they also remember Doctrine and Covenants 130:20–21: "There is a law, irrevocably decreed in heaven before the foundations of this world, upon which all blessings are predicated — and when we obtain any blessing from God, it is by obedience to that law upon which it is predicated." When their prayers seem to go unanswered, they can't help wondering if their infertility is a punishment for having disobeyed a law.

Such feelings can be exacerbated by the misguided comments of others. One woman's mother-in-law, for instance, called her monthly to ask if she had yet found the sin in her life that was keeping her from being able to conceive. Another woman told me of a visiting teacher who urged, "If you will just put your house in order, you will surely conceive."

Fortunately, as the months and years pass, most couples recognize that their adversity is not a God-given punishment but simply a natural consequence of physical limitations. They are not infertile because they have displeased God, but because their ability to conceive is affected by endometriosis, or a low sperm count, or difficulty ovulating.

Despite this reconciliation to the physical causes of infertility, many still experience spiritual struggles, especially with their understanding of faith. Believing wholeheartedly in the power of faith and in the scriptural promise that those who pray with true faith can work miracles and move mountains, they reason: "Why should a moment of fertility be out of reach?" But when their inability to bear children is not removed, some wonder if it is a sign that their faith is weak — even though their life histories often show remarkable faith. For example, one woman I interviewed had endured fourteen miscarriages, losing the babies between the fourth and the fifth month. Another woman had given birth twice and then suffered eight miscarriages, during two of which she almost hemorrhaged to death. Certainly these women had exercised great faith as they continually placed their lives and emotions in jeopardy to bring about the miracle they so desperately wanted. Similarly, I have interviewed couples who have gone to various infertility experts for well over ten years, subjecting themselves to extremely intrusive, expensive, and sometimes painful infertility

198

tests, having the faith that eventually someone could help them conceive. Without strong faith, these couples would not have struggled so many years.

Ultimately the question for many couples becomes, "If faith doesn't mean being able to get what I want, what does faith mean?" The answer to that question is not the same for everyone. One infertile woman said that her crisis of faith had been healed by the example of the Savior. She had wanted her faithful prayers to heal her infertility. She had tried not to doubt God or his power to heal, and she sought to live the kind of life that she felt merited her Heavenly Father's help. She believed that her faith could remove this mountain of frustrated dreams. Yet her infertility persisted. Finally she realized that Christ, whose perfect faith had healed lepers, given vision to the blind, and raised the dead — and who had pleaded that his bitter cup be removed if possible — had finally been spared neither the agony of Gethsemane nor the pain of the Crucifixion. Christ's perfect faith had not altered Gethsemane but rather helped him to endure it. This woman came to see her faith in a different light — not as an imperfect faith that had been insufficient to remove her trials but as a vibrant faith that could help her endure them. Not faith to remove mountains but faith to climb them.

It is common for people to experience a variety of spiritual doubts during different phases of their infertility. Yet most individuals confide these doubts very apologetically, as if convinced it is morally wrong to doubt God's goodness or question God's existence. They are ashamed of their doubts. One notable exception was a paralyzed man who told me very honestly that doubts were good. In fact, he said, the deeper the doubt, the better. I was surprised by his comments, for I too had doubted and felt ashamed of my doubts. I felt they were a sign of my weakness. He, however, saw doubts differently. He claimed that only through questioning his views of God, only through crying out at midnight from the depths of his soul, had he come to a more profound understanding and love for God than he had known before his trials. His conviction that God was loving, merciful, and just had come about not despite his doubts but because of them. He saw his doubts as catalysts for understanding rather than obstacles. The winter of his faith was a natural predecessor to the spring. He knew God better, he explained, from having grappled with questions not easily resolved.

During my interviews, I have marveled at the fruits of faith that I have seen in this man and in the lives of other infertile Mormons. Ultimately, everyone I interviewed wanted the opportunity to bear and love children. Some received that opportunity. Others did not. Yet their faith had also borne fruit.

One infertile woman was, ironically, a social worker who worked with pregnant teens. As she sat in her office watching these young unmarried girls come and go, she found it impossible not to feel bitter towards them. She thought, "Why in the world are they pregnant and not me? It just isn't fair." But, she endured. And slowly, faithfully, she worked through her bitter feelings. She came to view infertility as her handicap. She could see, she could hear, she could walk, but she could not bear children. And she asked herself, if I were blind, would I hate everyone who could see a sunset? Would it help to hate everyone who could hear a symphony, if I could not? She realized that bitter feelings would not produce the quality of life she wanted. The struggle of faith produced an insight, and this insight helped her to be more loving and accepting. She later had great need for those qualities when she became a mother to five older, adopted children.

Another infertile woman told me that instead of letting her infertility distance her from other women, she let it form a common bond between them. She explained that her infertility had been the loss of a dream. Losing her dream helped her empathize with all women who had experienced loss — whether visible losses, such as the loss of a loved one or of health, or less obvious losses, such as the loss of self-esteem or the loss of hope. The fruit of this woman's faith was not fertility but compassion. Her life would not be filled with many children, but it would be a life filled with love.

One woman who had felt very marginalized in the Church told me that she felt like a blind person who was a member of a church that worshipped sight. She often left church meetings feeling that without children her life was less meaningful. At one point she was considering leaving the Church because its emphasis on families caused her such pain. It took years for this woman to work through her feelings about being an infertile Mormon woman. Finally she told me that in the intervening time she had come to realize that this was *her* church and that she didn't want to leave it. Although she might not *find* a place for herself within the Church, she determined that she could *make* a place for herself. She explained that when members always speak of love in terms of either maternal or married love, they don't realize that unmarried, divorced, or infertile women often feel left out. So she had decided that her place would be to remind others of Mormons who do not fit standard patterns. She would seek occasions to encourage understanding and sensitivity to the needs of Church members struggling with unfamiliar problems. This woman's faith did not cure her infertility nor take away all her pain, but it enabled her to endure until she had learned the lesson that Christ's inn has room for all.

From one couple who experienced unusual hardship in their struggles for a family, I learned one final lesson about the spring that can follow long, hard winters. Six times their hopes for a baby ended in miscarriage. The seventh time the woman carried the baby into the sixth month. The child was born, lived eleven days, and then died. After that, the couple decided to try adoption through LDS Social Services. After filling out the paperwork, writing their autobiographies, and obtaining an evaluation of health from their family physician, they were disheartened. The wife had recently been diagnosed with lupus, an autoimmune disease that can be disabling or in extreme cases even fatal. Knowing that birthparents participate in the selection of adoptive parents from nonidentifying files, they feared that the wife's health problems would probably discourage a birthparent from choosing to place a child with them. Yet after waiting a few years (not an unusually long period to wait for adoption through LDS Social Services), this family received a phone call informing them that they could come and pick up a beautiful baby boy.

Then they learned how their child's birthmother had arrived at her decision to choose their file. First, the birthmother had grown up in a family sensitive to the needs of those with health disabilities, for her own mother was legally blind. Second, when she did at one point waver—after her social worker conscientiously pointed out that a health condition such as lupus might limit the adoptive mother's ability to care for the child—the birthmother called a close friend for advice. When she asked her friend if she knew anything about the disease lupus, her friend replied, "I *have* lupus." Reassured, the birthmother decided to place her child with the family. Despite all odds, this family received a child, and now, although they still struggle with infertility and with health problems, they see the love of God in the eyes of a son.

While faith doesn't guarantee us the realization of dreams, a fertile faith can give us the ability to build new dreams, quite literally from the ashes of the old. For this couple the death of one dream—biological children—allowed the birth of another dream—sharing their lives with an adopted child.

Yet, the process of spiritual regeneration will bear many different types of fruit. The hoped-for conception or the long-awaited adoption is not the only sign of God's love. For some couples, spring brings new dreams of sharing their time, talents, and love with their fellow men and women through fulfilling careers or compassionate service. That is the wonderful thing about faith. It helps us to find peace in a myriad of different circumstances according to the individual needs of each daughter or son of God.

During my interviews I have seen the hand of God moving

quietly in the lives of sorely tried individuals. This hand does not remove all pain or trial, for the seed of faith needs both rain and sun to grow. But I have learned that as our Father heeds even the fall of a sparrow, he also knows what we need to bear our trials—and faith can eventually lead us to God's answers. (Matthew 10:29–31.)

God will not remove our winters, for through winter comes spring. And through adversity and doubt can come a stronger and more meaningful faith.

Finding Lightness in Our Burdens

CHIEKO N. OKAZAKI

In Matthew 11:29 is one of the loveliest promises in the New Testament, the promise that those who take upon them the yoke of Christ "shall find rest unto [their] souls." This promise is embedded in a chapter of questions, warnings, and chastisements; and I think that context is important. Some of John the Baptist's disciples had come to Jesus, questioning whether he could be, in fact, the promised Messiah. Jesus did not answer them directly but instead told them to observe his works.

After they departed satisfied, Jesus spoke to the multitude through indirection and paradox. Once he warned, significantly, "He that hath ears to hear, let him hear." Once he prayed, thanking the Father "because thou hast hid these things from the wise and prudent, and hast revealed them unto babes." (Matthew 11:15, 25.) He "upbraid[ed]" the cities that had not believed his "mighty works" and "repented." (Vv. 20, 21.) In other words, Jesus dealt with three or four different kinds of disbelief or lack of understanding, teaching with chastisement, paradox, and riddles. Then he gave this promise:

"Come unto me, all ye that labour and are heavy laden, and I will give you rest. Take my yoke upon you, and learn of me; for I am meek and lowly in heart: and ye shall find rest

Chieko N. Okazaki was born in Hawaii, where she joined the Church at age fifteen. She has served as a member of general boards of the Young Women and the Primary and as first counselor in the Relief Society general presidency. She taught for twenty-three years in the public schools of Hawaii, Utah, and Colorado and served for ten years as a school principal. Sister Okazaki and her husband, Edward Y. Okazaki, are the parents of two sons.

unto your souls. For my yoke is easy, and my burden is light."
(Matthew 11:28–30.)

This promise also appears paradoxical. If we are already
burdened, how will taking yet another burden—a heavy yoke
upon us—give us rest? And how can his burden be "light"?

These are important questions. Sometimes we feel that we
should not have burdens—that there is something wrong with
us if we have problems in our lives. That is not the case. Burdens
are a part of life, and we all struggle with burdens that are
grievous to be borne. There is nothing reproachful about having burdens, and there is nothing wicked in the struggle.

In fact, I am so sure burdens are part of life that just before
this meeting started, I asked the ushers to hand a note to four
sisters asking them to share with us a burden they are struggling
with and tell us what, if anything, seems to lighten that burden
and give them moments of rest. Each of the four agreed, and
I am very grateful to these sisters for their willingness to speak
to us.

SISTER 1: "One burden that has been troubling me lately
is loneliness. I was married a year ago, and my husband is still
going to school plus working full time. We moved into a new
ward and new neighborhood, and I am at home in a very lonely
house a lot of the time. I don't like being alone. Being alone
is especially hard for me because I get very depressed. Sometimes at night when I am starting to feel lonely and depressed,
prayer helps. If I can get on my knees and talk to Heavenly
Father, he assures me that I am not alone but that he is there
with me. I also like to read, but unless I have a prayer I remain
lonely."

SISTER 2: "My husband and I have been married for about
fifteen years, but we have no children. About two years ago
we started the process of adoption from Mexico, but we are
still waiting. My burden is not knowing if all these delays mean
that what we are attempting to do is not what Heavenly Father
wants us to do or if recurring bureaucratic problems are typical.
We have spent many hours in prayer and can't seem to get a

definitive answer to this question. The doors keep closing, leading us over and over again to wonder, 'If the doors keep closing, then maybe that is our answer.' Yet we really want children, so we persevere. I feel that Heavenly Father loves me and wants me to be happy and I feel that being a parent will make me happy. So we persevere, even though we don't seem to get answers to our prayers — at least not the answers we are looking for. Ward members and family comfort me, but the greatest comfort is from my husband, because he shares and understands the whole situation."

SISTER 3: "I am ashamed to confess I have sometimes wished I didn't have any children. I have been blessed with four daughters. Through them I have learned that my burdens are in fact painful blessings. I have three daughters who please me and make me happy. I have one daughter who keeps me humble. She has chosen on her own to scorn Church values, leave us, and leave the Church. It is painful to raise four daughters, teaching them all the same principles, sharing together all the same family and Church traditions — and have one choose a different road. But because of her I have learned humility. I have learned to love my Father in Heaven and daily to ask on my knees for his help. How can I consistently ask him for help and protection of this girl who has removed herself from us if I don't do all he has asked of me?

"What am I doing to relieve my burden? Temple attendance, tithing, church service: I am trying to live the commandments because I am asking for a blessing in hope. And I am able to 'press forward with a steadfastness in Christ, having a perfect brightness of hope' (2 Nephi 31:20) because of something I have learned through this hard lesson. One day, weighted with the heavy burden of care and worry over this child, I was bending down picking up clothes, and the Spirit — it must have been the Holy Spirit because it spoke from my heart — said to me, 'She is your daughter, but she is my daughter, too, and you are to love her regardless of what she does.' Thereafter my heart took hope and my burden was lighter."

SISTER 4: "In January of 1990, I was diagnosed with a seven-centimeter tumor in the center of my brain. A human brain is only about fourteen centimeters by fourteen, so this tumor took up almost half of my brain. Last January—even before I knew of the tumor—I was so depressed and discouraged about other trials and marital problems I was facing in my life that I actually prayed either to die or to have my life miraculously healed in some way. The Lord answers our prayers not always as we expect: I did not find myself dead; instead I found myself with a brain tumor, no husband, and four little children to continue rearing. I was in despair until I received a blessing from a very spiritual man who told me it was the Lord's will for me to live. That was confusing because only hours before the doctors had insisted my tumor was probably inoperable because of its location in the center of my brain. Yet in the blessing I was assured that I would learn many things that would help me carry out my purpose on earth.

"The first thing I learned was that I need the will to live. No matter what storms we face, we need to have the *will* to live. The tumor is now in remission. I have had radiation therapy, and we are waiting to see what will happen. The second essential lesson I learned through this ordeal came to me while I was on my knees in prayer looking at a picture of the Savior. In anguish I asked, 'How can you let me go through this? I am a good daughter. I am faithful. I strive to be righteous. I take care of my children. I attend church. Why is this happening to me?' Then I suddenly remembered a day a few years ago, when I had prepared a lunch for my children who were playing outside in the sprinklers. I had made a very healthful lunch: carrot and celery sticks and tuna on whole wheat bread. I called the children in from playing, putting my all into being a wonderful mother. But they looked at this lunch in disgust and said, 'Mom, you are the worst mother in the world. This is gross. I can't believe you make us eat this junk. Aunt Becky up the street gives her kids Oreo cookies and Kool-aid for lunch every day. In fact, they have Oreo cookies and Kool-aid picnics every Sunday.' I wanted to boot them outside, and say, 'All right, go hungry. Go over to Aunt Becky's and play. I'll eat it.' But instead I crouched down before them on my knees and tried to explain, 'I give you this kind of food and these vegetables because I love you. These are the foods you need to grow big and strong, and you will need strong bodies to get you through this life.' With this memory, a peace and a calmness came over me as I realized that the storms and burdens that come to us are burdens that make us healthy and strong. They will prepare us for the steps that still remain as we become what we want to become."

Thank you, sisters, for your courage in sharing your burdens with us.

These sisters' situations remind us that all of us have burdens and that what might be easy for one person is an ultimate test for another. We cannot judge the heaviness of another's burden until we have borne it ourselves, nor can we easily prescribe what will work to ease another's burdens. Yet our challenges and burdens are not meant to crush us but to strengthen us. Note the double promise: "I will give you rest" (Matthew 11:28), says the Savior, and also "ye shall find rest unto your souls" (Matthew 11:29). In some cases, the promised rest will be his gift; in others, it will be something he helps us find ourselves.

I would like to explore now three ideas drawn from my own experience about how we can receive the promised rest: first, the resources of survivorship in each of us; second, the ability to identify blessings in disguise; and third, the power to choose our response to adversity.

Being a Survivor

I am convinced that we are all survivors. In all of us, there is a toughness that we can capitalize on. Our hope in Christ and our faith in his gospel provide us with an enormous resource of resilience and courage to call upon. Think of the Apostle Paul, cheering the Roman Saints by acknowledging the genuine afflictions and persecutions they were suffering and then triumphantly asserting, "We are more than conquerors through him that loved us." (Romans 8:37.)

I am a survivor of cancer. On Tuesday morning, 3 March 1973, when I was a teacher in a school near Denver, I woke up with a pain in my side and found a lump in my breast. I called my doctor. He had a specialist waiting, and we made the surgical appointment for Friday. My husband and I signed the consent forms for the biopsy to be performed and analyzed on the spot; if it proved malignant, a mastectomy would be performed as part of the same operation. After Ed's priesthood blessing and with him beside me, I lay quietly and let the anesthetic take effect, falling asleep, as it were, with a question. When I woke up, with Ed still beside me, I knew what the answer had been.

Counseling was available at the hospital plus a support group in the community for women who had had similar operations. My doctor was also very helpful and encouraging as I went through the prescribed course of radiation, which seems to have been successful. I am in remission. But I also know that this cancer could recur at any time or that another cancer could develop. The operation was an event to be dealt with and to be put behind me. The cause of the operation—cancer—is something that I have to live with every day as a possibility; and of course, I live with the effects of the operation as well.

I do not feel frightened or discouraged. Ed and I are both cheerful, optimistic people; and he was a great strength to me while I was recuperating from the operation and the radiation therapy. Since the exact cause of breast cancer is unknown, I cannot take specific steps to avoid a recurrence. I can take general precautions—such as eating a healthy diet, exercising, getting enough sleep, and watching for the danger signals of cancer. But the rest of it is simply out of my hands.

Making that clear—what I could and could not do—was an important step. It was as if a great weight rolled away. I have never mistaken worry for action, and I did not fool myself now that worrying about this condition was the same as doing something about it. So I just laughed and said, "I have survived cancer! What's next?" You see, I'm sure there will be something else, but my best prevention and also my best preparation is to lead a life that, besides being physically healthy, is spiritually and emotionally healthy as well.

I remember seeing a television special about women who had been sexually abused as children. The therapists and others who worked with them referred to them as "incest survivors," or "abuse survivors" rather than "incest victims" or "victims of sexual abuse." To me, there is a world of difference between these terms. One leaves you passive, helpless, dependent. The other communicates toughness, resilience, and self-reliance. We are all here today, and we have arrived by many paths. Not one of those paths has been free from chuckholes, washouts, and even avalanches — but we have survived the journey up till now. Let's give ourselves credit for that. We can call ourselves not victims but survivors. And Paul gives us the right to call ourselves not just survivors but conquerors. That should lift our hearts!

I love Mother Lucy Mack Smith for this very quality. What a great lady she was! She had a tender and loving heart — and a tough backbone. She suffered under repeated blows of fate, but she did not give up despite losing their farm, Alvin's unnecessary death, their repeated financial reverses, the scorn and contempt of neighbors who mocked Joseph's vision, relentless persecution, and the Church's moves from one community to another. All of these adversities could have broken a woman of less resilient spirit, but she did not give up. When her cherished companion, Joseph Smith, Sr., died soon after the Saints were driven out of Missouri, she wrote: "I returned to my desolate home; and I then thought that the greatest grief which it was possible for me to feel had fallen upon me in the death of my beloved husband. Although that portion of my life which lay before me, seemed to be a lonesome, trackless waste, yet I did not think that I could possibly find, in traveling over it, a sorrow more searching, or a calamity more dreadful, than the present."[1]

What awaited her still, of course, were the deaths of four of her sons: the fatal illness of Don Carlos in Nauvoo, the assassinations of her two noble sons Joseph and Hyrum in Carthage, and the almost immediate death of Samuel as a result of being pursued by a mob. When Joseph's and Hyrum's bodies were brought home, washed, and dressed, she wrote this moving account:

"I had for a long time braced every nerve, roused every energy of my soul and called upon God to strengthen me, but when I entered the room and saw my murdered sons extended both at once before my eyes . . . it was too much; I sank back, crying to the Lord in the agony of my soul, 'My God, my God, why hast thou forsaken this family!' A voice replied, 'I have taken them to myself, that they might have rest.' "[2]

This promise of rest is the promise that the Savior made, as we have seen, coupled with warnings that we would have to have eyes to see and ears to hear before we could understand his meaning and also that these things were hidden from the wise.

Surely Mother Smith must have wondered if there were no other way and whether this "rest" could not have been purchased in a less grievously burdensome way. She continues: "I was swallowed up in the depths of my afflictions. . . . As I looked upon their peaceful, smiling countenances, I seemed almost to hear them say, 'Mother, weep not for us, we have overcome the world by love; we carried to them the gospel, that their souls might be saved; they slew us for our testimony, and thus placed us beyond their power; their ascendancy is for a moment, ours is an eternal triumph.' "[3]

After Samuel's death, William, her sole surviving son, brought his dying wife to Nauvoo early in 1845. Her fatal condition was a result of the persecutions in Missouri, "which makes the sum of martyrs in our family no less than six in number," wrote Mother Smith in great sorrow. But she ends her narrative, not with grief but with gratitude and with her ringing testimony: "The testimony which I have given is true, and will stand forever; and the same will be my testimony in the day of God Almighty, when I shall meet them, concerning whom I have testified, before angels, and the spirits of the just made perfect."[4]

Mother Smith lived for many more years. In those years, she did not find it necessary to revise a syllable of the testimony she had uttered with such firmness and conviction. Old age bowed her down, but not bitterness. Death finally conquered her, but not despair. She was a survivor, and we can all manifest the same kind of courage through our pains and losses.

I also think of a wonderful Hawaiian woman I know, Winifred Watanabe Chinen. Her husband is not a member of the Church and has poor health. He allows her to attend her meetings but insists that she not accept any callings. Knowing his feelings, the bishop does not ask Sister Chinen to accept any callings. Sister Chinen might well feel downcast and discouraged by her situation, but instead, she says: "I've decided that I do not need any calling. I volunteer for whatever I can do, in whatever capacity I can be of use in our Relief Society to relieve the president of any mundane responsibilities." Happily she cares for the sacrament cloths, brings flowers for the chapel, does visiting teaching, and renders compassionate service. "Being there and helping" at any Relief Society function is her calling. Her very countenance radiates a "brightness of hope." Instead of dwelling on the things she cannot do, she focuses on what she *can* do, attends her meetings with real gratitude, and constantly seeks out others in her neighborhood to help them. I would wager that she does as much good as any so-called fully active Latter-day Saint in Hawaii.

Recognizing Blessings in Disguise

The second gospel principle that helps us lighten our burdens and find the rest promised by Christ is the ability to recognize blessings in disguise. I have always loved the scripture in Hebrews that tells us to "entertain strangers: for thereby some have entertained angels unawares." (Hebrew 13:2.) Many times, experiences that we would not seek voluntarily and that come to us in bitter guises turn out to be blessings in disguise.

Ed was called to preside over the Japan Okinawa Mission in 1968, and one of the first things we did when we reached Japan was to visit all of the cities in our mission. We had never been there before, and we knew that it was important for us to understand as much about Japan, the Japanese people, and their culture as we could. When we went to a city for the first time, we would try to take a quick tour so that we would understand its physical layout and some of its important public areas, and we did that also in Hiroshima. We went to the Memorial Shrine, built at ground zero, and then visited the Atomic Age Museum, which documented the damage and preserved relics from that strange and destructive energy. The photographs helped us understand what the statistics meant. The bomb, which exploded about 1800 feet in the air, destroyed 4.7 square miles of the city. More than 92,000 people were dead or missing. We were filled with the sorrow of that event — the enormous destruction, the tragic loss of lives, the terrifying vision of what could happen to our planet if nuclear weapons were used again. It was very sobering for Ed and me, for we stood on both sides of that long-ago deed. It was our country, the United States of America, that had made the decision to use that bomb against Japan, the homeland of our ancestors. We grieved equally for those who had done the deed and for those who had suffered from it.

Our burden was lifted by the Saints in Hiroshima when we falteringly tried to express our confused and sorrowful feelings. "Yes, it was a terrible thing," they said, "but it was a blessing in disguise. You must not dwell on anything but the blessing." Brother and Sister Nishihara, whose son is now president of the Japan Osaka Mission in which they serve as a

213

missionary couple, said, "How could we have accepted the gospel if we had still been trying to believe in the divinity of the emperor? Or how could our country have moved forward economically if all of our energies and ambitions were being channeled into military purposes? It took this terrible blow to free us from the paths of the past and let us choose a new direction."

Thanks to them and to the other Saints of Hiroshima, we gained a new perspective on what had happened. We came out of the museum with our minds filled with images of devastation and destruction; but the reality of Hiroshima is that it is a thriving, lively city. There are no ruins, no shattered buildings. The city has been rebuilt. The many survivors of the bomb have gone on with their lives, just as Ed, who was wounded in Italy fighting with the 442nd Infantry in the U.S. Army, went on with his life. No one would have chosen such a devastating thing—and whether the decision to drop the bomb was right or not is something that lies beyond my wisdom—but I do know that in choosing to interpret it as a blessing, the Saints and the other residents of Hiroshima made the right decision.

I feel very strongly that we must never allow ourselves to linger in "what if's" or "if only's." Possibilities that seem more desirable to us but that are not possible sap the strength from our hands and the courage from our hearts. They become a snare to our feet so that we stumble and lose our way. All we can do is our best. We cannot control how things turn out. We cannot control the circumstances that life hands us.

In 1987, I retired from my job as principal, and Ed and I decided to move to Salt Lake City. In August 1988, Ed and I were invited to an interview with the Missionary Committee, and we suspected that it might be a mission call. Ed had an appointment for a physical already scheduled with his doctor, so at the end of the examination, he mentioned that we might like to think about going on another mission.

The doctor shook his head firmly. "You should be very careful about any strenuous activity, and you absolutely must not leave the country. Any other questions?" It turned out that Ed had a rare heart condition in which the muscle in one part of his heart had atrophied and was not working. The doctor told us later that he had not expected Ed to live out the year.

The Missionary Committee asked us if we would accept a calling to head the Missionary Training Center in Tokyo, and Ed had to tell them what the doctor had said. We were both bitterly disappointed that the calling could not be extended to us; but now, two years later, we see that it also was a blessing in disguise. I know my husband. He would not have spared himself, even if he had felt ill. He would have pushed himself beyond his strength in working with the missionaries and staff, interviewing missionaries until late at night, and working with the members. I think it is literally true that he would not have survived the year.

Instead, by following his medical plan consistently and working with the doctors, he has experienced a remarkable regeneration and renewed strength. Furthermore, I was here to accept a calling to the Primary general board and then, in March 1990, my current calling to the Relief Society general presidency. It has been a great blessing to both of us. I rely on Ed's constant support, his cheerfulness, his lively interest, and his intelligent analysis of my assignments. He truly companions me and is my partner as I have been his companion and partner in his callings. How foolish we would have been to think of the calling that could not be extended to us with disappointment or to feel that we had somehow been inadequate!

Choosing to Choose

In choosing to call ourselves survivors, not victims, and seeing the blessing behind the disquise, we exercise our precious gift of moral agency. Choosing to choose lightens our burdens and helps us find rest. One of the most powerful promises in the scriptures is in 2 Nephi 10:23: "Therefore, cheer up your hearts, and remember that ye are free to act for yourselves — to choose the way of everlasting death or the way of eternal life." That *is* a message of cheer and bright hope!

While I was going to high school, I had to live away from home and put myself through school by working as a maid. I was only fourteen, and I spent many nights feeling weepy, anxious, and frightened. What I had to do seemed so hard, and three years seemed so long. Then I discovered a wonderful fact. If I concentrated on how I was feeling, I only felt worse. But if I chose to behave cheerfully, resourcefully, and calmly, my mood changed. In other words, if I concentrated on how I wanted to behave, my feelings changed to match my behavior. The wonderful thing about choosing, for me, was that I didn't have to believe it would work. I just had to choose.

For example, when I would get up at 5:30 in the morning with a long list of household tasks to be accomplished before leaving for school and a long list afterwards, it was easy to feel overwhelmed, alone, and discouraged. Where could I find time to be happy? Where was there time to cheer myself up? But I was making it too hard. If I simply came into the school with a smile on my face and said, "Oh, good morning, Mr. Chuck," to my vice principal, he would look up, smile warmly back, and say, "Oh, Chieko, it's good to see you. How are things going? Are you doing all right with your schoolwork? Have you heard from your family?" In the ten minutes before the bell rang, my spirits would lift as if by a miracle. I felt consoled by Harry Chuck's concern and bolstered by his obvious confidence in my ability to handle both schoolwork and a demanding job. My teachers were equally supportive and kind. If I had decided instead that I felt too sad to talk to Mr. Chuck and had skulked past with my head down, I would have paralyzed myself with my own bad mood.

The important point is that I did not wait until I felt like smiling and saying hello. I *chose* to smile and say hello, and *then* my mood changed. I'm not saying that we should cover up serious emotional problems or try to deal with severe depression by pretending that everything is all right. Mental and physical problems need professional help and appropriate medical care. But where we can choose, I think it is incumbent upon us to exercise our agency.

What motivated me all through high school and college was an overwhelming desire to be a teacher. I was greatly inspired by my sixth-grade teacher, Mrs. Yuriko Nishimoto, who truly loved children and was the kind of person I wanted to be. I chose not only to get an education, which was what my parents also wanted for me, but to be an educator as my life's work. I carried that vision in my heart and in my mind. I measured my daily decisions against that vision. Was this what a teacher did? How she spoke? What she knew? How she behaved? What did I need to do to reach my goal? Would this activity help me reach that goal? If not, then what should I do instead?

I had not realized how powerful those cumulative choices had become; but when I was a senior in high school, Benjamin Wist, the dean of the Teachers College at the University of Hawaii came to visit our school. In the afternoon, the teachers held a tea for him, and I was invited to attend and help serve. In mingling and conversing with the teachers in the room, he at one point noticed me. "And what grade do you teach?" he asked, inviting conversation.

I stared back at him in astonished delight. "Do I look like a teacher?" I remember exclaiming.

"Yes, you do," he responded.

I felt as if I had just been crowned queen. "Thank you very much," I said proudly. "I want to be a teacher, and next year I hope to be entering your college."

He looked at me keenly and smiled kindly. "I will remember you," he said.

And he did. How I cherished that compliment! I realize now that he was seeing, manifested on the outside, the inner vision of myself that I had nurtured and labored for. It was the sum total of my choices up to that point, and those cumulative choices carried me through my college education and through the many challenges and opportunities that came to me later.

Another story from later in my life illustrates the power of our choices to alter adverse circumstances. When we moved to Utah, I was the first exchange teacher from Hawaii to teach at Uintah Elementary School in Salt Lake City. Ed was going to the University of Utah, working on his master's degree in social work. I had taught elementary school for three years in Hawaii and loved it thoroughly. I knew I could be a successful teacher. But still, I felt twinges of apprehension. Utah was a new place, new people, new customs. It had not been all that long since the end of World War II, and we were braced for some racism.

So I was not really surprised when Edith Ryberg, my principal, called me into the office a few days before school started. I could tell instantly that something was wrong. Hesitantly, she said, "I'm very sorry to say that three of the mothers of students assigned to your second grade have requested transfers to a different room. They don't want their children to have a Japanese teacher."

Her face was so sad; I hastened to lift her burden. "Oh, no problem!" I said cheerfully. "Don't worry about it. It's fine with me to make the switch. I came here to serve the children; and if the parents feel that way, I wouldn't be able to teach their children very successfully, even if they stayed in the classroom. I will love whoever comes into my class, so assign whoever will feel comfortable."

She looked at me in amazement, then breathed "Ooof!" in great relief. "This was so hard for me to do." When I told Ed about the incident that night, I still was not tempted to feel hurt and rejected. I threw back my shoulders, laughed, and said, "Well, three out of thirty-five isn't bad! I have thirty-two students who want me, and three more who are going to have that chance. And they're going to be *lucky* students to get me for their teacher! In fact, I feel sorry for those three whose parents want them in a different class."

Then I poured all my efforts into making that first day a

great success. In those days of limited and expensive travel, Hawaii was pretty exotic; and I was Japanese-American from Hawaii. That made *me* pretty exotic, too, so I resolved to *be* exotic! I sewed a fuschia-colored dress that showed off my skin and black hair and tucked a fuschia flower behind my ear. I was the most vivid thing in the whole school that first day!

The custom at that time was for each teacher to meet her children on the playground, call the roll so that each child would know where to line up, and then lead her children into their new classroom. The other two second-grade teachers, as a courtesy to me, the new teacher, said, "Would you like to assemble your class first?" I was absolutely delighted. It was exactly what I had hoped for.

I knew there was a lot of curiosity about me because many second-grade mothers were there with their children. In a neighborhood school, mothers would bring a kindergarten child for the first day, and maybe even a first-grader, but not a second-grader unless there was some special situation. Well, I was that special situation, and there they all were — including mothers of second-graders assigned to the other rooms. It could have been a threatening situation. I could have chosen to feel frightened and let the children and parents register that fear. Or I could have chosen to be ultra stern and rigidly professional to cover my anxiety. But what I wanted the children to feel was my own joy and excitement.

I still remember opening the roll book, calling each child's name clearly, looking directly at each child as he or she came into line, smiling, and making some comment. "James Backman — what a nice name!" (He came and stood before me and said, "My dad is the president of the Salt Lake Board of Education.") "Beth Benson — how carefully you've tied your hair ribbons!" (And she said, "My dad is an apostle in the Church!") I could have felt just a *little* intimidated. But when I led them off, I could feel their anticipation.

That very afternoon, the principal took me aside, smiling a little. "Chieko," she said, "I just wanted you to know that

219

those three mothers—you know, the ones who wanted their children in the other classrooms?—have come and asked if their children can be transferred back to you. I told them opportunity knocks only once." She laughed, "Can you imagine how furious the other mothers would be if I tried to talk them into transferring their children *out* of your room?"

I was smiling a little myself. That was one of many experiences I had in choosing my attitude and my mood, choosing how I would respond instead of letting circumstances respond for me.

These three principles of the gospel have been great resources to me in dealing with adversity: first, seeing myself as a survivor, as one of those who are "more than conquerors through him that loved us" (Romans 8:37); second, recognizing blessings, even when they come in disguise, so that we can entertain "angels unawares" (Hebrews 13:2); and third, deliberately exercising the power to choose and consistently choosing "the way of eternal life" rather than "the way of everlasting death." (2 Nephi 10:23.)

When our burdens are grievous to be borne, when we face a world in which it seems that there is only struggle and no rest, I hope we can remember the immense strength of our sisterhood, the reservoirs that we have within us, and the unfailing wellspring of the Savior's love for us, even in the midst of adversity.

For me, choosing to view burdens "lightly," so to speak, and exercising the divine gift of our free agency in this way is what brings us from hope to faith. I love Nephi's words, "Wherefore, ye must press forward with a steadfastness in Christ, having a *perfect brightness of hope,* and a love of God and of all [people]. Wherefore, if ye shall press forward, feasting upon the word of Christ, and endure to the end, behold, thus saith the Father: Ye shall have eternal life." (2 Nephi 31:20; italics added.) What I love about this scripture is that nearly every element in it lies within our choice: whether we feel like it or not, we can choose to "press forward"; we can choose to be "steadfast in

Christ"; we can choose to "feast upon the word of Christ"; and we can choose to "endure to the end." It is my testimony, proved through many experiences, that when we make choices like these, we are choosing to act in hope, and when we do, I believe that the Lord supplies the "brightness" for us.

We have, as well, a remarkable degree of choice about "having . . . a love of God and of all [people]," also a part of this scripture. Yet we also know that the pure love of God, or charity, is the gift of the Father, for Moroni urges us: "Wherefore, my beloved brethren [and sisters], pray unto the Father with all the energy of heart, that ye may be filled with this love, which he hath bestowed upon all who are true followers of his Son, Jesus Christ." (Moroni 7:48.) So again the reciprocal dynamic holds: if we *choose* to act in love, the gift of pure love will be given us.

There are many scriptures of comfort and consolation. This one from the Old Testament possibly refers to the Millennium, but it can also be seen as true for us in this life whenever we turn to the Savior with our burdens: "Do not fear, O Zion. . . . The Lord your God is with you, he is mighty to save. He will take great delight in you, he will quiet you with his love, he will rejoice over you with singing." (New International Version Zephaniah 3:16–17; see also KJV.) May we feel the stillness of that love and hear the rejoicing in that song and remember his promise: "Come unto me, all ye that labour and are heavy laden, and I will give you rest." (Matthew 11:28.)

Notes

1. Lucy Mack Smith, *History of Joseph Smith by His Mother,* ed. Preston Nibley (Salt Lake City: Bookcraft, 1979), p. 314.
2. Ibid., p. 324.
3. Ibid., p. 325.
4. Ibid., p. 327.

Getting Somewhere

SUSAN ELIZABETH HOWE

As I stop to think about where my life's journey has brought me, I am astonished, stunned. These are some of the labels that identify me: I am a single woman, forty-one years old; I am an assistant professor of English and a doctor of philosophy; I am a poet and playwright and the author of a few stories; I am a daughter, sister, aunt, and Merrie Miss teacher; I am also a tennis player, skier, traveler, and theatergoer. My labels show that I participate in many interesting and rewarding activities, but this is not the life I would have chosen for myself.

I remember, as a teenager, being on a seminary panel that considered marriage. When all the other panel members said they would probably marry quite soon after graduating from high school, I countered, "Well, I think I'll be older when I marry." But by older, I meant nineteen! The life I had planned for myself included marriage at the end of my junior year of college. (I would have been nineteen; I started at BYU just after I turned seventeen.) Then I thought I would graduate the following year, have a baby almost immediately, and spend the rest of my life as a wife and mother. That was the ideal life for good Mormon girls, and because I was a good Mormon girl, that was the life plan I wanted.

The years passed; I became a junior at BYU, and I wasn't even dating. I had senior panic that year, so you can imagine my emotional state when I was a senior. And then it happened — the worst possible fate: I graduated from college, and I wasn't

Susan Elizabeth Howe, assistant professor of English at Brigham Young University, has been the editor of Exponent II *and managing editor of* The Denver Quarterly. *Her play* Burdens of Earth *has been performed at BYU, and her poems have appeared in* The New Yorker, Shenandoah, Tar River Poetry, Prairie Schooner, *and other journals.*

married. And because marriage after college was the only plan I had considered, I had no idea what to do with my life. I was plumb out of goals.

So after BYU I didn't make any major life decisions for a long time — four years, actually. I stayed in Provo. I continued attending BYU student wards, hoping to run into the man of my dreams. I was hired by Provo School District, so I taught junior high for two years. (I had not taken seriously the possibility of a career, so I hadn't really considered what work I might enjoy for all the years of my life.) I next considered a mission, but my bishop advised me not to go. Because I had already resigned from my job, I had to find other employment; I worked as an assistant in the BYU law library. All around me were young men — and several young women — studying hard, working towards interesting, financially rewarding careers while I was making $3.25 an hour and marking time.

I coasted for several reasons. For one, I did not know there were any fulfilling, interesting roles a Mormon woman could play except the supposedly all-encompassing role of wife and mother. Marriage was the only life plan the culture — including my church leaders, my peers, and my family — presented to me as acceptable and worthy. And I can't express how much pain I have suffered between then and now because I did not marry. I wish that someone had taught me that my marital status had nothing to do with my value as a person or my potential to be a worthwhile human being. I wish I had been open to more possibilities for my future, so I could have felt that, even as I longed for a happy marriage, my life could always be interesting and exciting. But I was taught that only one option was desirable, that without it I would be a failure. So after college, my life essentially stopped as I waited to get married.

Another reason I didn't formulate new goals was the strong disapproval I felt from those around me for women who pursued professional degrees. I was warned by bishops, by friends, by intelligent, interesting young Mormon men I wanted to date,

223

and by *Fascinating Womanhood* that if I became too educated, too smart, I would be threatening and no one would want to marry me. Marriage or a career was presented to me as an either/or dilemma. The only thing I wanted in life was to get married, so I wasn't about to pursue any goals that might ruin my chances. For years, I hid my intellectual interests and capacities, as if they were a shameful secret.

Besides, there was a voice in my head telling me I couldn't succeed. Academic options seemed out of reach. Camille DeLong, a wonderful family therapist, helped me to understand how my own fears limited me. She said that we each have a voice in our head censoring us, stopping us. This voice comes as we internalize the criticism of parents, teachers, peers — anyone who is a severe and harsh judge. After hearing ourselves berated again and again, we eventually begin to criticize ourselves in the same way, with the same harshness. Camille asked me to consider how I felt about my body, my intelligence. She said, "Think of the things in your life you have told yourself you can't do because of your body or your mind."

Her challenge took me back to college. I wanted to be on the ballroom dance team because I am a very good dancer, and I wanted to act because I felt I had — at the time — a talent that could have been developed. But I didn't try either activity because I thought I was too tall. I thought I was too tall for any part in any play, even though — I've since learned — both Vanessa Redgrave and Sigourney Weaver are as tall as I am. And I thought I was too tall to have a partner on the ballroom dance team, so I didn't even try out. I'll never know if I could have "made it" in acting or as a ballroom dancer because I didn't even try. So I missed two enriching and satisfying experiences.

Even more serious for me, I have always had a voice in my head telling me, "You aren't very intelligent. You really shouldn't go back to school because you aren't smart enough to do well. You're just not an academician." Well, I now have two advanced degrees, so I guess I have been able to get over at least some of the obstacles that were before me. The journey to where I am now has not been direct, because it was not carefully planned. I lived in Washington, D.C., Salt Lake City, Cambridge, Denver, and San Francisco before returning to Provo to teach at BYU. In addition to teaching junior high and working as a library assistant, I have been a secretary, legislative aide, technical writer, editor, consultant, and college instructor. Often I have moved to a new place, accepted a different job, or started a graduate program simply because it felt like the right thing to do at the moment, not because I understood where I was going and could fit this next move into my life plan. After graduating from college unmarried, I no longer had a life plan.

But I have to say that, as I look over my life, I'm pretty happy with it. If I consider it as an offering to the Lord, I've done the best I could with the circumstances I have been given. I've tried to grow. I've tried to be a whole person. I've tried to use my talents to serve. I have made some mistakes, but I've also made some significant contributions. And so I ask myself what things helped me to achieve despite my own fears and the limitations the culture set for me.

First, I eventually realized that I had to do something, that marking time and waiting to get married were *not* healthy. My life was going on whether I did or not. When I finally decided to get a master's degree, I remember thinking, "In the next two years, I may or may not marry—I don't have much control over that. But in those two years, I *can* get a master's degree. At the end of that time, I can either look back and say, 'Two more years have gone,' or I can say, 'In this time, I've earned a degree.' Which would I rather say?" I've always thought that since I have only one life, I want to do the best with it I can, so I went after the degree.

What helped me ignore my self-doubts was that I have always valued learning. When I got out of college, I made a list of twenty books I had wanted to read but hadn't had time for. I had always wanted to study art, so I bought some art

225

books and began visiting museums. Learning became important enough to me that I looked for opportunities, which eventually led me to graduate school. Had I been in other circumstances, I could have used libraries, evening courses, and community classes as avenues for education. The important thing to me has always been the chance to learn, not necessarily the desire to get another degree. But my circumstances made graduate programs a good choice for me.

In the process of learning, I came to understand what work I really love, what fields of study are intellectually exciting to me. I have always been moved very deeply by literature. Certain novels—*Dandelion Wine, East of Eden,* and *All the King's Men,* for example—have opened whole worlds to me and helped me to understand life much more deeply. I soon realized that literature is incredibly important to me. I love reading it, teaching it, writing it. Literature became a focus; as often as I could in my very random life experience, I have directed myself towards the study and writing of literature. My route toward a doctorate and a university teaching job was circuitous, but since I always involved myself with reading and writing literature, when opportunities for in-depth study came up, I was ready to take advantage of them. For example, I did quite well on the advanced literature test of the Graduate Records Examination, even though I had been out of school for six years because I had been reading literature during all that time.

The next thing I had to do was learn to take risks. I remember swimming lessons at the Scera pool in Orem when I was about seven. Through each of the nine lessons, I dreaded the last week, the tenth, because that was when we would have to jump into the deep end of the pool. That awful day finally came. Before I knew it, I was the child at the front of the line, standing skinny and terrified with my toes on the concrete rim. As I looked into the sparkly blue water, I thought that if I jumped in I would die. I could vividly imagine myself sinking to the bottom of the pool, choking and panicking and thrashing around until I went unconscious. I thought that if I jumped, I would drown—and I jumped.

Adults, having developed areas of expertise within which they are relatively proficient, make the world comfortable by staying away from really difficult challenges in new areas where they might—to continue my swimming metaphor—drown. But that kind of terror is the cost, I think, of almost any significant learning experience, because learning that matters comes only when you push yourself beyond your known limits, when you risk a great deal.

I remember the first time I had the chance of having a public audience for my own play. I lived in Boston, and the Association for Mormon Letters was sponsoring a symposium in Charlottesville, Virginia, for Mormon scholars interested in presenting their works to other Mormon scholars. The conference chair asked me to participate. I didn't immediately refuse his invitation, but I didn't accept, either. I told him I'd think about it. What I thought was that maybe my play was awful and I was just too close to it to tell. Maybe a reading would bore the audience, and they'd all go away thinking to themselves that I was stupid to imagine I had any talent.

Then in a conversation one evening, a friend—a woman I had always considered articulate and intelligent and self-assured—said, "Whatever I've tried to do, I've always doubted that I could succeed. Some of us will never have confidence. We'll just have to go on guts." Her attitude helped me to learn that I could be courageous even if I couldn't be confident. She gave me the courage and spunk to try: to call up the chair and accept his invitation, to ask friends to read the parts, to travel to the symposium and present a reading of my play. And actually, everyone who spoke to me after the reading was gracious and supportive. I learned that the play had some problems but that people found it interesting. It had a great deal of potential for improvement, and so did I. Because I risked, I discovered that I did have talent as a writer, and that knowledge gave me tremendous excitement and enthusiasm to continue writing.

The more I have worked, the more I have improved, so the risks I have taken have definitely been worthwhile.

Not that I've always experienced success. I remember one nationally renowned poet saying, after he read my poem aloud in class, "This doesn't sound like it was written during this century. It's a throwback to the 1800s." And I also remember him saying of the next student's poem, "Much better. We've really upped the ante with this poem." His comments almost made me give up poetry altogether, thinking I just didn't have any talent.

But years later, in another poetry writing class, another well-known poet (and, incidentally, a former student of the first), said something that helped me continue writing poems, despite my perceived limitations: "Anything worth doing is worth doing poorly." Of course my early poems weren't very good. I was learning to write; I didn't just emerge from some cocoon as a full-blown poet. But I never would have become better if I hadn't written those first poems. And I never would have become better if I had let myself be discouraged and quit because my first poems were awful. I have had to work very hard for years and years, writing poem after poem after poem, to become a poet. But because I have written poems again and again and again, I have finally developed some expertise. And now I have confidence that I can, on occasion, write a good poem. And I know that if I keep working, I will get better.

Along with confidence in my abilities, I have had to learn that I am a valuable person, as valuable as anyone else. For a long time I felt that the Lord didn't want me to have anything that I wanted. I felt that I was being punished—or ignored—for something I didn't understand. But over the years I have come to realize that what I desire has to do with my unique, individual talents and that discovering what those talents are and developing them are probably the best gift I can give. In many ways our culture teaches women they must take care of everyone else's needs before their own. But I don't think God would put the constraints on me that the culture has. God

228

would not say, "Stop. Don't develop your mind. Limit yourself and ignore your potential. There's only one thing a woman can do, and if you can't do that, you're worthless. Give up your own joys and devote yourself to others. They are more important than you."

Married women with families often feel they have to accommodate their family's and their husband's schedule, carving out a space for themselves only after having provided what family members want and getting them where they need to be. Too often there is almost no time left to do anything for themselves. And because everyone else's needs take priority over her own, the mother often feels of less worth than everyone else — feels worthless. But a mother is as valuable as any member of her family. So if she is not in at least some ways getting to discover and work toward her dreams, then some adjustments within the family need to be made.

I myself have felt and acted as if everyone else's needs are more important than my own. Particularly as I have begun working as a professor, I have had trouble balancing my professional responsibilities with my own goals. I want to please everyone; I want both my colleagues and my students to like me; I want to do well. So I have felt considerable pressure to accept every assignment, and several tasks I accepted this past year fell through the cracks. Furthermore, I find that I am finishing everything in a haphazard fashion at the last minute and that I am very unhappy, both because I'm not doing well and because I have no time for myself. These failures have taught me to be more cautious about accepting assignments. And I am trying to learn — and this is still excruciating for me — to say no when I have to.

I am also learning to value my own work and personal needs as much as I value those of others. No one else can do my writing. If I don't give myself the time to write, the gift I might have given will be lost. So I must make a commitment to myself to write at least an hour every day, and I must take that commitment seriously. I see this as a step in learning to respect myself as much as I respect others. To break promises is a sign of very slight regard — for oneself as surely as for others.

My life has certainly not resolved itself into the neat, orderly plan I had originally set forth. And while I have not traveled the path I had intended and I'm not at all sure where the rest of my journey will take me, I believe I am getting somewhere. I imagine that my future will be as challenging, difficult, and rewarding as my past has been, but I would not even venture to guess where it might lead. Wherever that is, I'm sure it will be interesting.

And actually, I don't think my life is so different from most women's. Women have always had to be flexible about their plans, their goals, their aspirations, because women care so deeply about relationships and are sensitive to the ways in which their lives affect those close to them. Sometimes a woman will defer her own dreams or move toward them more slowly than she might otherwise, but she should feel that those dreams are important.

In the television documentary series *The Power of Myth*, Joseph Campbell said that if you "follow your bliss," opportunities will open for you in ways you can't believe. Each of us needs to discover her own value, her unique gifts. It is essential to be in contact with God about the direction of our lives, to change that direction from time to time as we grow and our situations change. Within the circumference of our lives, each of us has obligations we have agreed to perform and people we love and are responsible to. But we must place ourselves at the center: each woman needs to know that she is unique and that she is of immense worth. And that what she is working towards at any time of her life is of great worth to her and to God.

Finding Peace and Purpose in the Valley

CLAUDIA W. HARRIS

This past summer I thoroughly surprised myself by leaving a comfortable existence in Atlanta, Georgia, and moving twenty-six thousand pounds of household goods across the country to Provo, Utah. As I drove by myself across Wyoming in a car filled with what I had believed might not survive the moving van, I thought of my ancestors crossing the same terrain in handcart companies and yearned for the simplicity of their lives. Ostensibly, the reason for my difficult move was to accept a position in the English Department at Brigham Young University, but I know the actual reasons are not so easily stated. Perhaps my natural curiosity about my varied life and my discussion here of my own particular decisions will lead to a better understanding of life choices in general.

I was not aware of it at the time, but my move to Utah began one Friday afternoon, two years after my husband's death, as I stood by the side of a freeway in south Georgia looking down a steep hill at a clump of flattened weeds growing in a small stream. I had stopped on my way back to Atlanta after teaching all week at the Marine Corps Logistics Base in Albany, Georgia. I'd stopped that afternoon to see where I'd gone off the road the previous Monday morning, nearly killing myself. On Monday, 14 November 1988, I'd caught myself falling asleep as I drove south about 6 A.M. I awoke with a start just as I was about to go off a bridge, but then over corrected,

Claudia W. Harris received her doctorate in Irish studies and dramatic literature from Emory University in Atlanta, Georgia, where she lived until joining the English faculty at Brigham Young University in 1990. As a freelance journalist and theater critic, she has developed an abiding interest in Ireland, which takes her there nearly every year. She is a widow and the mother of three.

231

spun once and a half around, went backward across the grassy median, backward across the opposite two lanes of the highway, and backward down the steep embankment on the other side. I finally remembered to brake, disengaging the cruise control, which had been set at 60 mph.

Sitting in the stalled car at the bottom of the hill, I laughed and started the engine and drove up the hill—all the time marveling at how well my sports car was responding. When I got to the top, I began to turn right so I would be going the appropriate direction on the freeway but then shrugged and drove straight across both lanes and the median and then south again. After all, I'd traveled this odd route *backwards* just moments before. Twenty minutes later, I stopped the car and walked around it; as I stood there looking at my grassy but undamaged car, I wondered why it had all been such a ho-hum experience. I certainly felt no fear and wasn't even shaky; I felt nothing. I realized then that I didn't care if I lived or died. Telling people that week about my near mishap, I laughed and treated it like a lark—like a funny thing that had happened to me on the way to work. My response was completely inappropriate.

But that Friday afternoon as I stood in my depressed state looking down the hill for the first time, I saw from the tire tracks and the flattened weeds that my car had been sitting in a stream; I felt a chill as I realized that if I had gotten out of my car that Monday morning I would have been standing knee-deep in water. I did not know how I had been able to drive out of that stream and up the steep hill. The thought then came strongly into my mind—"You may not think there is purpose to your life anymore, but apparently there is, and you must discover what it is for yourself." What turned out to be almost an inevitable move to BYU began with that thought.

In a strange way, this near accident emphasized my lack of purpose. My husband of thirty years was dead; my three children were married, living good, productive lives, and nurturing their own children well. So all of my previous reasons for finding joy in living were either gone or fulfilled. And I cried to myself over and over — "Is this all there is?" My children now tell me that I worried unnecessarily about becoming a burden. But then life weighed heavily. I should count someday all of the times I wrote in my journal — "Life is too hard." Throughout this period, misleadingly, I appeared to be almost upbeat; however, when friends would comment admiringly about my life — my annual trips to Ireland for fun and research, my glitzy condo — when friends seemed to covet my freedom, I would usually say, "My life may look good on paper, but living it isn't much fun." The meaning, the heart, the vitality, the passion had disappeared.

So standing there by the side of the freeway, looking down into that stream, I took charge of my life again. I decided right then that I wanted to feel better. If I was going to live — and I knew I was not going to do anything deliberately to end my life — I wanted to be happier, to enjoy life again. *So I prayed.* It seems like such a simple solution. But considering that I had been angry at God for two years by then, my decision to pray for help was an extremely important step up out of that deep ravine I'd slid into. After all, God had not saved my good husband; God had not answered my fervent prayers on his behalf the way I had wanted; God had not taken me up on any of my pleas or desperate bargaining. So to repent of my irrational anger and to thank God sincerely for my blessings, blessings I knew I was receiving whether I asked for them or not, and then to ask humbly to feel better — this for me was a giant step forward.

Immediately, old and new friends began to reach out to me in unique and surprising ways. For instance, several ward members spontaneously offered to help me decorate for Christmas, and I was asked to speak in church for the first time since my husband's death. I'm sure my demeanor changed dramatically, but every special kindness that I received during this time cannot be accounted for only by my increased approachability. I started writing steadily on my dissertation for the first time since my husband's cancer had been diagnosed four years before. Miraculously, I did feel better—stronger and more confident. But it was my attitude that changed, not life events.

I had foolishly hoped that maybe my children and I would be free of further pain, but the world doesn't work that way. The fall of 1989 I went to Ireland again and to London to visit my son Mitch, my daughter-in-law Lorelei, and my sweet little granddaughter Fiona, who at nine months old had just suffered a stroke. Every bit of news about Fiona seems worse than the last. When I'm here away from her and unable to enjoy her smiles and hold her sturdy little body, I despair that we'll be able to keep her with us for very long. We've been worried about her ever since she was born with hemangeomas covering the right side of her face and her vocal cords. She has had great difficulty breathing, especially when she tries to sleep. There was also at the beginning the threat that she might have Sturg-Webber Syndrome, which could cause blindness in the affected eye, epilepsy, and progressive retardation. But with the stroke we learned that she has fibromuscular dysplasia which means, in her case, that all of the arteries to her brain are severely malformed. She would not be alive at all if her body had not developed an alternative blood supply, a supply which apparently failed her in July 1989, thus causing the massive stroke that destroyed a large part of the left hemisphere of her brain, in particular the speech center, and has left her with a partially paralyzed right hand. Pretty grim, isn't it. But I have never known a happier child. I was there for her first birthday and could enjoy her laughter and the zest with which she approaches everything. I thought then that when we are told to be as little children, it must mean that we should approach life with a Fiona-like joy. Watching her, I decided to do better at appreciating my own chance to live, to stop acting as if I were serving a life sentence, and to recognize instead my opportunities for joy.

But along with my desire to live more fully, not just to survive, came the growing realization that I needed to change my lonely life. My work caused me to be alone on the road much of the time. And although I was paid well, my consulting didn't gratify my other, more altruistic needs. I also questioned whether I was fulfilling my potential. Then, amazingly, on 14 November 1989 I was nearly killed on the freeway driving to Birmingham, Alabama. It was 6 A.M. and very dark and rainy. I was singing along with my tape player when a truck jackknifed right in front of me. I moved instantly to the right across three lanes, dodging other cars, and out onto the shoulder around the back of the truck. I was still going 45 mph at that point because whenever I'd tried to slow, I'd skidded. If anyone questions whether or not I can drive, that miraculous morning should provide the conclusive answer. But what was truly wonderful was that I felt weak-kneed, sick to my stomach, and very happy to be alive — all the appropriate emotions. I was euphoric all day and that feeling, in part, has stayed with me.

Later, when I was writing to my friend Lavina about the experience, I looked in my journal and realized that these two mishaps took place at exactly the same time of day just one year apart. Certainly, these near accidents may have been entirely my own doing, but the eerie coincidence makes me wonder. Even though I admit that I have the usual human need to divine some larger meaning in the events of my life — to create a novelization of my life — I cannot deny the dramatic change in my feelings. My reaction to the second incident was completely the opposite of my bizarre reaction to the first. In that year, I had been given back my life, and I continue to express gratitude to God for the lesson I relearned those early mornings on lonely southern roads: God does love me, bless me, care about me — personally.

Now, lest you misunderstand what I'm saying, let me reassure you that all during this three-year period after the death of my husband I was actively keeping the commandments, serving others, praying regularly, studying the scriptures, teaching the Gospel Doctrine class and the Primary inservice lessons, and working in the Atlanta Temple each Saturday. I don't believe anyone who knew me would have called me to repentance. And I never questioned the reality or power of God or of Jesus Christ. I could never deny what had been manifested to me so clearly.

On 30 June 1985, just two days after my husband learned he had cancer, I was looking into his face during the sacrament as he sat next to me in fast meeting, and I was feeling a level of anxiety I had never before experienced, when suddenly a sure knowledge of Christ's overwhelming love for my husband permeated my entire being. It was not *my* love for Chet that filled me, but *Christ's*. This was an outside force unlike anything I had ever felt before. Following immediately, Christ's deep sadness for what we were about to suffer washed over me; then instantly, Christ's strength lifted me above my anxiety. So you see, from that three-fold experience that helped sustain me throughout the difficult time that followed, I had personal knowledge of the power that was at my disposal, and I called upon it often. But nonetheless, I later felt deserted. And I deeply mourned the loss both of my husband and of the spiritual support.

About a month after my second near accident, I ran into Susan Howe at the Modern Language Association meeting in Washington, D.C.; neither of us expected to see the other there. Susan pulled me out of a crowd of twelve thousand English teachers in the huge Sheraton Hotel; she told me she was in Washington helping to interview candidates for openings in the English Department at BYU. I asked her why BYU was not interviewing me, verbalizing for the first time the change I wanted to make in my life. Later that evening at dinner, I told a non-Mormon friend the reasons why teaching at BYU would be good for me. Months later when Elder de Jager interviewed me for the job here, he told me I should come and, to support his opinion, he amazingly listed all of my own reasons, those I'd given my friend in Washington. Elder de Jager, of course, also assured me that I'd have to decide for myself, but when I walked out of his office and down onto the parking ramp, I started to cry because I knew I should come but didn't want to. It was too risky, too hard, too much to ask of myself—no, no, I couldn't do it. Leave a city like Atlanta where I'd lived for twenty years, where I'd raised my children, where I'd buried my husband. No, I couldn't; it would cost too much—move away from my children and grandchildren, take a cut in pay, lose my new house. No, it was too much to ask of anyone.

Choice is hard—unlimited choice is even harder. So we limit ourselves; we tell ourselves not to cross the line we draw; we place rigid parameters. Reasonable parameters are helpful, but those we place out of fear limit our progression. When I am depressed and monitor what I'm saying to myself, I find, inevitably, that I'm telling myself I can't do something, either that it's beyond my powers or that I'm now too old or stupid or silly to do it anymore. *Can't*—a powerful word. Once I recognize what I'm telling myself, once I hear that word *can't*, I work to turn it around into *can*. From experience, I know I can change my thinking; I can identify what it is I'd like to do; and then I can empower myself to make an intelligent choice. What I want to do is usually good for me or even admirable, but it is also often fearful or difficult. So I can remove my depressed feelings by doing whatever I'd like to do or by deciding that it is not worth the risk. Deciding either to go ahead or to forget it, invariably, frees me of my depressed feelings.

Despite this self-knowledge, however, I'm still shaking my head in surprise over this massive change in my life; I'm still asking myself how I managed to move from a comfortable place, where I had such a good life, to Utah to begin a new career at my advanced age. When my incredulous Atlanta friends challenged me this past summer to explain my planned move, I jokingly told them that it was easy to understand: I was moving from the garden to the lone and dreary world. But returning to my favorite mountain has eased my longing for place; no matter where I've lived or traveled, Utah has always felt like home. Each day now as I look at Mount Timpanogos, I can tell in its many aspects how my day will go. That splendid mountain was the anchor of my early years, and it blesses me again with its beauty and solid presence. Nowhere else lately have I felt on such sure ground. But I am not deluded; I know that place is relatively unimportant; I can be happy anywhere if I choose to be.

And I am happy. I've titled this paper "Finding Peace and Purpose in the Valley" because I believe that is what I've found. I don't have to whip myself up anymore into a falsely upbeat state just so I can get out of bed and get through the day; I don't have to manufacture any particular feeling. Instead, now I feel authentic, grateful to be alive, and blessed by my opportunity to teach at BYU. I truly feel a Fiona-like joy. I have a compelling need to be useful, to be a change agent, to make a difference in the lives of my students. What I have learned about needing to live on the brink, to feel passion about ideas and people and the gospel can make me a better teacher because I can help students to be open to experience, to question, and to seek the virtuous and the lovely and the praiseworthy. Because of my climb out of that ravine, because of my commitment to find purpose in life again, I can help students to be happy in their own quest, to feel contented with their choices, and to be passionate in their efforts to lead righteous lives.

At this very moment, I realize with amazement how few regrets I have about my major decisions in life. For someone who struggles over which orange to pick from the pile of identical plump juicy oranges, I have made incredibly quick and decisive major choices. One technique that has helped me is to try to step into the future, imagining what it would be like for me to have chosen or not to have chosen a particular path. I knew at eighteen that I was too young to marry, but I also knew I didn't want to miss being married to my husband. That decision turned out to be a very good one. When we went to Western Samoa for three years with three small children, I was only twenty-three; I got on a plane for the first time in my life for that trip. And I had never expected to live anywhere but Utah Valley. Choosing to continue my education and graduating just ten years late, getting two master's degrees in six years taking one evening class each quarter while teaching full-time, and then deciding to get a Ph.D. and using as my research focus the relationship between theater and politics in Northern Ireland—all of these are risky choices that I'd readily make again. Even returning to Utah—perhaps my riskiest choice—is turning out to be one of my best. True, no other decision in my life required that I be slammed down into a gully before realizing I needed to take another path. But I'm especially grateful for that graphic message. I don't have time anymore to ask the pitiful question—"Is this all there is?" I'm having too much fun. I had forgotten how wonderful it is to really enjoy your work. Thanks to my students and co-workers, my life again has meaning, heart, vitality, passion.

Of course, I still have heartsinking moments, especially when I go home to a silent house, wishing Chet were there to share my day. Recently I was savoring a particularly lovely memory of my husband when unbidden came the thought of how much I will enjoy being with him again. But then I heard the clear message in my mind—"So why don't you allow yourself to take comfort in the gospel then? Why don't you let yourself feel the peace that the promise of eternity offers you?" At that moment, I realized how aloof I've needed to be from the promise of the next life; I've been holding myself aloof because at any thought of reunion I've wanted to be there, not just with my husband but with all of the loved ones I've lost recently—my mothers, my grandmother, my nephew Dale, my niece LeAnn, my sister Mary, her husband, and both of her sons. To think of the glory of the next life and not yearn to step over into it had been too hard. But now that I know what purpose my life still holds, I can allow myself to be comforted by that blessed, peaceful promise of what is to come. So I have found peace and purpose in the valley, and I thank God for that blessing.

Making a Paradigm Shift: The Cranky, Creaky, Perilous, and Absolutely Crucial Process

SHARON LEE SWENSON

Let me tell you about morning at my house. *This* morning. First, you have to visualize our house. Any real estate agent could tell you that it's a modest, two-story, yellow-brick bungalow in Salt Lake City on First South. Even from the outside, you can tell that it's a family house. There's a garden hose tied around a major branch of the tree in the front yard. This is where Jonathan, our nine-year-old, plays Tarzan. There are a couple of bikes kicked up against the porch. It's obvious that home repairs are going on — the front steps are new, unpainted wood, and the railing isn't up yet. In fact, if you look closely, you could see that that unpainted wood is starting to weather, so maybe the home repairs have been in process for some time. There seems to be an unusual number of telephone wires going into the upstairs bedroom window. That's where our thirteen-year-old daughter, Caitlin, single-handedly holds together the entire social structure of her junior high. There's a cat sitting in the front window. And if you open the front door, our blond, blue-eyed dog will leap forward and embrace you.

And what is that delicious odor wafting from the kitchen? Whole wheat toast with homemade jelly? No, more like pop-'em-in-the-toaster Eggo waffles. And who's this, charging out the door in a dressed-for-success suit carrying a briefcase? It's not Dad, it's Mom. Well, what's going on at the Swenson house?

Sharon Lee Swenson, assistant professor of theater and film, has served as the film program administrator at Brigham Young University. She focuses on critical studies in film theory and is interested in gender and family in film. Sister Swensen has served as Relief Society president and has taught the Gospel Doctrine class in her Salt Lake City ward. She and her husband, Paul, are the parents of two children.

I'll tell you: it's a living, breathing, hands-on laboratory experiment in the construction and refinement of paradigms.

A paradigm is the way we see the world—an image or a model that includes rules about how things operate. If you're an ancient Hawaiian, then your paradigm explains volcanos: Pele, goddess of fire, is going to get furious and spit lava all over the island every so often if a virgin princess doesn't drop a black rooster into the caldera. If you're a modern Hawaiian, you still have a paradigm that explains volcanos, but this time it includes plate tectonics and sea-floor rifts. And even though you would cheerfully sacrifice any number of virgin tourists, the lava's gonna flow where the lava's gonna flow until the vent closes again.

Well, we're not ancient Hawaiians but modern American LDS women, for the most part. And we have paradigms that explain our families and our marriages. I want to define two of them—two paradigms that are often in conflict and that often leave us confused and bewildered because the universal rules that come with our models just don't seem to work. These two paradigms are kin-value and market-value.[1]

I played off your sense of the LDS paradigm when I described our house—a single-family dwelling in a modest residential neighborhood where children play and relate to their friends and are fed breakfast every morning. This is the kin-value paradigm. It says that the family is the most important unit of society, that no success can compensate for failure in the home, that the best way to make human beings is in loving, nurturing, value-clear families, that children need to be raised with a full-time, breadwinning dad and a full-time, breadmaking mom and family home evening every Monday night. And if they do, this paradigm continues, those children will grow up to be solid citizens, good mothers and fathers themselves, the kind of women and men who will become Primary presidents and Scoutmasters and a light on the hill to the heathen nations.

Well, we all believe this, don't we? We see models of these families in the *Ensign* every month and hear about them on

241

Mother's Day and at general conference. Some of us grew up in those kinds of homes. If we didn't, we wish we did. Some of us have those kinds of homes. And if we don't, we wish we did.

The second kind of paradigm, which I'll call the market-value paradigm, comes to us mostly from our society. It says that the most important unit of society is the individual — that each individual has inalienable rights, that each one of us has the right to try and make as much of our lives as we can, that we exchange our skills and abilities and time for the highest possible rate of cash return, which we then have a right to use in any way we want that isn't illegal. These individuals can be organized into families and care about each other, but they don't have to be, because our society deals with them as individuals. The schools exist to teach individual children. The economy is geared to contracting with individual workers. And our society works best when each individual has as much freedom and as many options as possible.

Well, we also believe this, don't we? We get expensive college educations so that we can get better jobs. We know we're succeeding at work because we get a fatter pay check. When we have a headache, we want a choice between two different strengths of ibuprofen, either in capsule or in tablet form. We know that we're teaching our children correct principles when we intone, "The idler shall not eat the bread nor wear the clothes of the laborer, and you're not getting your allowance until you clean your room, and that includes vacuuming up that three-year's supply of dust bunnies under the bed." We get terribly outraged if our seven-year-old slouches home and says, "I'm not going to learn multiplication. It's boring." We paint a terrifying picture of long-term penury and social disadvantage; and the next time we drive past someone sleeping on a bus bench, we say, "Look, Jonathan. Somebody who didn't learn his times tables. Do you want this to happen to you? Your dad and I aren't going to be around forever, you know." And we also remind ourselves that each individual needs a healthy testimony, that we can't be saved with borrowed light, and that nobody is going to ride into heaven on her husband's coattails or — and in my heart of hearts, I have trouble believing this — on his mother's apron strings.

So we have these two paradigms — kinship-value and market-value. We see evidence in our lives that both of them work. The rules really do explain how our world operates. They both make sense. The problem is that they're mutually exclusive in some ways.

Now, let's go back to the Swenson household this morning. There's something else you need to understand about this modest family dwelling on First South. It has experienced some very dramatic changes in the last three years. Shortly after I received my appointment at BYU — and that was not long after I was called to be my ward's Relief Society president — my husband left his job. He has now been free-lancing for about three years. So four or five times a week I drive to Provo to work, and Paul is home with the children. He carpools to school. He co-ops in the classroom. He manages his work in the pieces of time when the children are at school. He shops, he launders, he cooks — not all of it, but quite a lot of it.

I get up early to put dinner in the Crock-Pot before I leave. On the way home, I plot how to have quality time around the supper table, teaching moments doing homework, and families-are-forever bonding at bedtime. But the inevitable happens. I get home and see that the Crock-Pot didn't get plugged in this morning. So we go out to McDonald's and the kids fight over whose drink has the most ice in it. Or I have a day I can barely crawl home from, and our evening of intensive and creative bonding consists in watching cable TV on the bed until the dog's snoring wakes us all up.

I know that no success can compensate for failure in the home — I mean, I *know* that. It's one of the cornerstones of my universe. But I'm a logical person. Doesn't that also mean that success outside the home has to be purchased at the price of failure in the home? Now I didn't expect to enjoy work. I expected to do a good job and be a responsible, competent, and conscientious faculty member. But I didn't expect to love it, to be wildly excited about my teaching, to even relish faculty and committee meetings. I go to work willingly, even joyously. I like spending time at BYU. My teaching is rewarding. People respect me. I have an assistant who answers my phone, takes messages, and handles routine things for me. Students may whine a little when they come into the office, but they don't lie down on the floor and have tantrums. They don't whimper, "Everybody else in the class gets to turn papers in late." They don't ask me, "Where did you put my backpack?" And every month, the university gives me a very respectable check, and the janitors clean my office every night. I feel respected, valued, appreciated. This is the market-value paradigm, and boy! does it work for me!

But back to this morning at the Swenson household. I was getting ready to leave. It was late. I was frantically charging around. I went thundering into the basement to yank my blouse off the clothesline — feeling proud because I was doing it myself instead of making someone else do it for me — and yelling up the stairs, "You guys are just going to have to have cereal this morning. I don't have time to fix you breakfast." The breakfast I had in mind, the Real Breakfast made by all Real Mothers, was a dainty dish of kiwi-fruit and orange slices, hot oat bran muffins and mother love, with a scrambled egg and a cheery song. Clearly I couldn't pull that off this morning and these kids should recognize it and just be grateful they've got a mother who has a job at BYU.

Then my husband, who is popping the Eggo waffles into the toaster, mutters to my son, "I wish she'd hush up. We're just fine." And my son chased me all the way to the car to say, "Do you know what Dad just said about you?" And he told me!

Well, I peeled away from the house with a good head of steam; but by the time I got on the freeway, I was crying. I cried halfway here. What did he mean, "We're just fine"? How dare he? How can they be just fine without *me?* I'm the mother.

Aren't my kids damaged psychically if they have Eggo waffles instead of kiwi and orange slices? So there I was, plowing through the traffic, tears pouring down my cheeks—until I realized something.

The kin-value paradigm had turned into a club I was beating myself with. It's *wonderful* that this morning my husband was the nurturing parent who got breakfast on and that I was the parent who got in the car with a briefcase full of work. Neither one of us is a bad person or a bad parent. Our children have two full-time parents. Both of us work and both of us nurture. Caitlin and Jonathan are learning great lessons about what it means to be women and men.

But if I say to myself—and this is what I was doing out of the kin-value paradigm—"I am a loving wife and mother and that means the kids can't leave the house without me," then I've destroyed myself as both a mother and a worker. I've destroyed my husband as a nurturer. And I've turned our children into dependent, whining, helpless little twerps that nobody, not even a mother, could love.

So, the first point I want to make, my dear sisters, is that we need to identify the paradigm we're operating from and recognize its limitations. We don't have the luxury in our culture of having one simple paradigm that explains everything. We do not live in an environment that allows us to uncomplicatedly subscribe to one of these paradigms and ignore the other. We have, as a minimum, these two; and they frequently conflict with each. Each paradigm contains within it excesses that can be deadly, if taken to extremes.

For example, one of the excesses of the market-value paradigm that we are saturated with today is the equation between commercial products and personal happiness. You know the assumption behind the ads: "Buy Pledge and you, too, will have gorgeous antique furniture. Not only that, but your hair will suddenly be fantastic and you'll lose twenty pounds and see your cheekbones again." Or think about modeling your family after the Cosbys. If you had to parent for only thirty minutes a day, your family might look like the Cosbys, too. But your family and my family lasts twenty-three and a half hours longer every day than the Cosbys.

Now, let me give you a parallel example about the excesses of the kin-value paradigm, a trap that I think Mormon women are particularly susceptible to. Sometimes we feel that the gospel tells us to sacrifice the self—that attention to the self is *selfish*. Well, we all know that isn't so. You can't have a healthy family if you don't have healthy individuals—individuals with a strong sense of self—in that family. But you have to be sure that *everyone* in the family has it—including you. I am very good at respecting the individualism of my husband and my children. Hey, I'm *great* at respecting the individualism of the dog. But I don't respect my own individuality very much. I've struggled with the challenge of finding my self and taking care of that self in ways that are neither self-indulgent nor self-obliterating.

I don't think Mormon women are self-indulgent, but I think we sometimes suffer from a syndrome of pathological sacrifice. Now, in a strict market-value paradigm, sacrifice is just stupid. It doesn't make sense to give up any advantage you have to anyone else—whether it's your mother or your child. And in a pure kin-value paradigm, sacrifice is truly ideal. But we don't live in pure models of either. We have to work out a more complicated way of relating to this ideal. We have a martyr tradition in our family—my grandmother, my mother, and myself. I've seen it early enough that I'm trying to head it off in my daughter, but there is no doubt about it. She'll have it, too. And the other day, I heard Jonathan grumbling, "I do everything in this house." He's nine years old, and already he's convinced that he suffers more and works harder than anyone else.

The danger connected to pathological sacrifice is great. Women should not be the only ones practicing kin-value while the rest of the world and the rest of the family are operating from a market-value paradigm. I was very good at doing things for my kids until I found out that they didn't like it and it made them uncomfortable. Now, you have to understand that my children are normal. They don't like being asked to *do* things, either; but I prefer the kind of human being they are when they're learning to do things for themselves, so that's a discomfort I'm willing to tolerate, and it's a discomfort that I'm willing to help them tolerate.

The second point I want to make is logically connected to the first. After we identify the paradigm we're operating from and become aware of its dangers, we should work for intelligent change, not simply swap one paradigm with its excesses for another. Beware of setting up an either-or dichotomy — of saying, "Well, the kin-value paradigm is real-reality and the market-value paradigm is pseudo-reality," and then trying to run our lives according to only one paradigm.

It just won't work. Parts of both are true all the time. Parts of both are false some of the time. Different parts are true at different seasons of our lives. Whatever private paradigm we construct from these larger social paradigms, we have to build in flexibility, avoid rigid categories, and be willing to look at our own changing needs.

For example, the kin-value paradigm prizes togetherness, insists that we exist best and most fully in families, that we discover who we are only in relationships. The market-value paradigm exalts the lonely individual, defines groups as competition, and says that you discover who you are best by struggling against the obdurate and hostile personalities of others. Where does reality lie? Obviously between them both, but the exact point of reality is different for each individual. Maybe you're one of those people who need a lot of personal space. I like carpooling to BYU, but I also like driving alone. I like the feeling of just spending time with me, between leaving intensive family relationships and jumping into equally intensive work relationships. I love bustling around the house on Saturday with the kids and two or three of their friends, organizing projects and parties. But I also like to get up at five

247

in the morning and cook by myself. It's kind of soothing. You clank around the kitchen and whip eggs and mutter. Capitalize on your extrovert strengths, but don't deny your introvert needs. Kin-value needs to accommodate that range of personalities and meet those different needs.

Let me give you another example. At the university, you'd think I operate strictly from the market-value paradigm. Students exchange tuition for classes, time for knowledge, and tests for grades. As a teacher, I see different classes every semester: same desks, different faces, same papers, same grades. Right? Yes, all of that happens, but the explanation is too simple. I love my students. They're almost my children. I have a caring relationship with them. They're not just a series of faces, rotating through my office, my grade book, my classroom. They're individuals that I care about, think about, sometimes pray for. So, it's natural for me to apply the kin-value paradigm in my work.

But it wouldn't work—this is the either-or trap I was mentioning—if I tried to apply only kin values at work. For example, one of my students came in and told me how very much he wanted to make a film. He's a beautiful young man, a charming fellow from a very talented family. But he just hadn't done his homework, and he wasn't prepared. He didn't know what was involved in making a film. He didn't have the technical skills. He didn't have the financial skills. He didn't have the writing skills. Now, as a teacher, I had some choices. I could say to him, "In the market-value paradigm, which is what we use in this university, you haven't taken the right classes, acquired the right experience, or done the preliminary projects. Get out of my office and don't come back until you have." I could be rigid and punishing. Or I could take the kin-value approach and pat his hand and say, "Oh, Ned, dear, I really wish you'd taken those classes the catalogue says you have to take. I really am sorry. I know how disappointed you must be."

Either-or won't work. This situation calls for a combination of paradigms. The reality is that he's *not* prepared, no matter how much I like him or want to help him. He needs to face that reality, but maybe the way I explain the parameters and the reasons for them can help him understand not only his individual preference and desires, his personal dreams, but also the dynamics of our film program and the students involved. He hasn't been there. He hasn't made their kind of commitment and connection. Obviously he has a paradigm of the inspired young artist triumphing over all odds — Luke Skywalker as filmmaker. Well, he needs to change that paradigm and see himself as an intelligent, hard-working apprentice first.

I've had to learn how to see standards and apply them as a teacher in a market-value setting; and that's been very good for me. Basically I'm a cozy, let's-all-hug, motherly type. I think we should be happy all the time, and I've had to learn how to say, "No, that won't work, and here's why." It's been a hard skill for me to learn, but an important one, and I find myself being a better parent because of it. I used to think the most important thing was for us to be happy all the time as a family. Well, if people aren't doing their fair share and learning the basic skills it takes to survive as a human being, happiness pretty much depends on being able to deny reality. And nobody gets to do that very long.

As a consequence, I'm a real proponent of avoiding either-or dichotomies. Instead I'm an advocate of transferring tools from one paradigm to another and finding ways to combine the values of both. Let me give you another example. Sometimes we think that the gospel is telling us to reject the material world and the market-value paradigm that interprets it. That's not so. I think the gospel tells us rather how to relate to the material world in a kin-value way. One of the faculty members on this campus is Joe Bennion, a potter. He gets glossy reviews in national magazines about his pots. He gets invited to exhibit in the Soviet Union. In the pottery world, Joe is right up there. He's married to a portrait painter, Lee. She has received state art awards and has exhibits in important regional galleries. Her portraits command spiffy prices, and critics write perceptive and profound essays about her technique. Joe and Lee have three daughters and live in Spring City, Utah. They grow a big garden, and Joe usually has dirt under his fingernails from crawling down the rows thinning lettuce with his girls. Lee has her easel set up where the steam from canning tomatoes and applesauce won't wreck the canvas.

My point is that they're both pretty high rollers in the national and international art world; but they live in a small Utah town, raise a lot of their own food, and are full-time parents to three very active and demanding youngsters. They don't have a cash relationship with their world. They have a personal relationship. They have transferred kinship values to the earth. They're making a synthesis of the best parts of creative and productive paradigms. Sometimes we're tempted just to reject the material world. Well, that's the either-or trap again. Do not reject the material but revise your relationship to it.

My third point is that change is necessary but very, very hard. After we identify the paradigm that we're using, after we've learned about its limitations, after we see how to modify our paradigm by subtracting parts of it and adding parts from other paradigms that fit our situation better—after we see all that, we'd still better be braced for a long, hard process of change.

We get extremely uncomfortable when we try to change our behavior to match the more workable paradigms. Let's understand that these paradigms are deeply inbred patterns. We learned them at our mother's and father's knees. We've practiced them. We hear them from authority figures like parents, teachers, and church leaders. We literally see the world through them. What happens in our skulls shapes what happens to us in the world. Sometimes we have to bump up against our own experience pretty painfully before we realize that the map in our head is leading us into a brick wall.

But when we try to avoid the brick wall—when we begin to make changes—it will still hurt. We will become uncomfortable. Other people will be uncomfortable. We get a lot of negative messages, and what do we say to ourselves? "I guess this is the wrong thing. The Spirit is telling me not to do it." Now, the Spirit may, in fact, be telling us not to do it; but I want you to promise me to actually work on finding out if the discomfort is coming from the Spirit or from the paradigm shift. If it's really paradigm shift discomfort, the Spirit will say, "Go ahead." If it's the Spirit saying, "Whoops! It isn't the right time," then you can stop. But don't let the fact that it doesn't feel right stop you from examining your existing paradigm and working on changing it. It won't feel right when you start, and it will keep on feeling uncomfortable for a long time.

Let me give you an example of how deeply entrenched these paradigms can be. Before I started working for BYU, I always did the shopping. This is what a good mom does, right? When you send a man to the supermarket with thirty dollars, what have you got to eat? You have a bunch of Twinkies and boxes of Cap'n Crunch.

"How did this happen?" you ask in disbelief.

"Er, I had the kids along."

"Ah, that explains it."

And then he virtuously adds, "I didn't get the Cap'n Crunch with the crunch berries. I want them to be healthy."

"Oh, good."

Well, the good-mom-as-shopper behavior is a part of the kin-value paradigm that has long ago bitten the dust at our house. But when I was called as the Relief Society president, I was bustling down the aisles in the supermarket, full of the spirit of my calling, and I saw my hand reach out and pick up the quart-size can of yeast and put it in the cart. I wheeled that yeast to the check-out counter and I paid for it. Then I took it home and put it on my shelf. And it didn't hit me until later how crazy that was. Now, every fall, I buy yeast in those little triple-envelope packs, and every spring I throw away two of them. My mother was a bread baker. I love the smell of that fresh-baked stuff. But until the market economy allows me to buy one of those bread machines where you put everything in, set the timer, go to bed, and take it out of the oven in the morning when you wake up, *I* am not going to be a bread baker. So when I picked up the biggest yeast container known to woman, I was clearly making a symbolic gesture. I was acting on a paradigm about Relief Society presidents that I didn't even know I had.

Watch out for the internalized models you get from television, family, and movies. They will sabotage you quicker than anything else. My mother is a great mother. I thought I would become my mother when I had children. Well, it didn't happen and hasn't happened yet. I'm me. Learning to adjust that paradigm labeled "mother" so that it fits the real me is a job I work on every day.

In conclusion, sisters, I think we're here on earth during a kind of historic confrontation between paradigms. We are all struggling to match paradigms that were created in time by time-bound creatures to eternal principles. It's true that work is love made visible. In order to give the miraculous love that expresses kin-value, we have to work—and work very hard. But in the work itself we feel and express the love.

Note

1. I am indebted to Kathleen S. Bahr, assistant professor of family sciences at BYU, for defining these two paradigms. Her writings on the value of family work as ritual are central to my comments, although she is not responsible for my interpretations. She describes two contrasting patterns: "the world" (the non–kin-sphere) and "the family" (the kin-sphere). In Bahr's model, the non–kin-sphere is governed by individualism and focuses on profits and products. The kin-sphere is governed by altruistic love and focuses on fostering growth. Non–kin-sphere activities prioritize management and control of resources; they are linear and prioritize reason. Kin-sphere activities prioritize stewardship and respect for individual agency; they are synchronous and prioritize caring.

BOUNDARIES OF BELONGING

Nothing pleases God more than to have his children seek greater light and knowledge.

—Hugh Nibley

Instead of putting us on the defensive, questions ought to encourage us to talk with one another more, to acknowledge that we as people have a lot to learn.

—Kate L. Kirkham

Dilemmas of Stewardship:
Being in Charge and Being One

KATE L. KIRKHAM

"I say unto you, be one; and if ye are not one ye are not mine." (D&C 38:27.) We all experience systems of governance. As citizens involved in politics, as volunteers in the PTA, as workers in Primary, Young Women, or Relief Society, as employees and employers, as parents and children, all of us have numerous occasions to observe authority, influence, power, and leadership in secular as well as family and church settings. The scriptural injunction that we "be one" seems to pose a dilemma: how may we be in charge and be one? Or to put the question in more pragmatic terms, as we come together in our callings, as we interact in the congregation, what principles and skills might we learn that would help us work more effectively together?

The Apostle Paul addresses this question in his epistle to the saints at Ephesus: "Now therefore ye are no more strangers and foreigners," he instructs them, "but fellowcitizens with the saints, and of the household of God; and are built upon the foundation of the apostles and prophets, Jesus Christ himself being the chief corner stone; in whom all the building fitly framed together groweth unto an holy temple in the Lord: in whom ye also are builded together for an habitation of God through the Spirit." (Ephesians 2:19–22.) So as a congregation, as fellow citizens, we are fitted together in our many callings

Kate L. Kirkham, associate professor of organizational behavior at Brigham Young University, has served on the general board of the Relief Society. Her research has focused on race and gender diversity in organizations. She has written educational materials on institutional racism and discrimination and has been a consultant to government, education, volunteer, and business organizations.

and capacities and we are "builded together"—a wonderful verb. We are builded together in order that we might grow into something more: in fact, into an habitation worthy of God through the Spirit. That ideal should be the context for our work together in the congregation and for our effort to be together as a community.

How we image authority is the cornerstone of becoming "builded together." I want to discuss how we define authority and how we experience it in our interactions with others. What is your image of what is going on as women and men work together in their callings? What is your vision of what is happening and of what each contributes?

Of all the images that affect our work within a congregation, the most crucial are those that reveal our ideas about authority. Influence, leadership, stewardship, priesthood: all of these flow from our understanding of authority as a religious concept and from personal experiences, which shape our attitudes about people in authority positions. Our images of authority differ widely.

Two opposed images of authority are illustrated by two separate experiences I have had. One image comes from an experience I had in Washington, D.C., when I was called up for jury duty. This call to civic duty came at a most inopportune time. (I know many people say that about jury duty, but it did.) I had spent the preceding four months working with the local Girl Scout unit to prepare a national conference in which I played a central role. There was no second-in-command. No one was prepared to take over my responsibilities. When I went to the court to explain my situation, the clerk said, "Well, if you want to be excused from jury duty, you have to go before The Judge." I had forty-five minutes to wait to see him, which meant forty-five minutes to explain my situation to the others waiting or working there. Every time I mentioned his name, people would say, "Oh!" Shaking their heads sympathetically, they would explain, "The Judge rarely excuses *anyone* from jury duty. And you will have to stand in front of *everyone* to tell why you want to be excused." Then they would shake their heads again, sorry for me, anticipating my experience. Forty-five minutes of waiting with people shaking their heads, "Oh." As I became more and more intimidated, I thought, "I'll never be able to stand up and state my request. This person has absolute authority over me. He can intimidate me, make fun of me, ridicule me."

When I was finally ushered into the room, sure enough, I was one of a very sizable crowd of people petitioning to be excused from jury duty. When my name was called, I stood up and said, "I am working with the Girl Scouts, and I really need to be absent to finish a national conference we have been planning."

Everything fit the image—the stern face, the glasses, the double chins, the black robe. He looked at me and growled, "Can you get me Girl Scout cookies?"

I answered cautiously, "Yes—if that's appropriate."

To everyone's amazement, I was excused. He would excuse me, he explained, because of the community rather than the personal interest of my request and because of his interest in fostering what Girl Scouting was accomplishing. People around me were again shaking their heads, this time muttering, "I don't believe it."

Had I not gone to that authority to make that petition, I would not, of course, have had the opportunity to finish my responsibilities with Girl Scouting. In one way, the outcome was favorable, but that intimidating image of The Judge has stayed with me: the absolute authority of the person who is inaccessible, the person who is arbitrary. Many of us have a similar image of authority.

A very different image of authority comes from an experience I had a few years ago. I was in the Lion House during conference time having a conversation with a general authority, a member of an area presidency in the British Isles. The time was short before the next session, and he was interested in the insights about race and gender issues that I could offer from my training in organizational behavior. At one point he remarked in obvious frustration, "I wish we could follow up on this conversation." I offered, "Well, it just so happens I'm going to Europe for a conference." He was pleased. "Could you drop by our area offices?" he asked. I agreed to do so. Several weeks later I wandered into the area office not really having any official invitation, or appointment. The office staff wasn't sure what to do. No appointment, I wasn't a visiting dignitary, I could only state my name and home ward and that I wanted to complete a conversation that had started in Salt Lake.

What interests me about this experience is how totally inviting and approachable this general authority was. He invited me into his office, invited me to talk openly about the difficult issues of race and gender and how we might understand them in a Church context. Both at lunch in the Lion House and in his London office, our exchange was the most accepting conversation with a person in authority that I have ever had.

So here are the extremes: on the one hand, the most inviting, clear, and wonderful spirit and, on the other hand, the distant, intimidating authority. Authority is necessary and exists in every organization. It is inextricably meshed with responsibility. My concern is with how each of us relates to it. How do our experiences with authority influence how we relate to the next person in authority? What images of authority do I have that will affect my working with someone in authority? If I thought of everyone in authority as The Judge, my expectations would be both inaccurate and counterproductive. Yet, if I expect everyone to be as warm and inviting as that member of the area presidency, I will be disappointed. Each of us must investigate and clarify our day-to-day expectations of authority.

Our image of authority is also formed by our definition. In the behavioral science literature, authority is generally discussed as legitimate power. Legitimate power is power that an individual acquires because she or he fills a position within a structured, role-defined organization, such as a government, a corporation, or an institutionalized church. This legitimate power is actually conferred upon a person by subordinates who accept the organizationally defined value that persons in certain positions should have authority. For example, when I meet with students in the classroom they recognize that I have authority to grade their performance.

In a church setting, God is the ultimate source of authority; however, we have the somewhat unusual opportunity to enhance the authority of church leaders: we do not *confer* authority on others; we *sustain* authority. We are in relationship with that authority and legitimize a person's power by sustaining him or her in a church position. So there is, in the Church, a consistent type of authority that does not depend on us to be conferred and yet very much depends upon us to be sustained and legitimized.

The distinction is profoundly important. In secular organizations I may be totally dependent on a person's authority. She or he could hire, fire, encourage, or mistreat me, and even determine my worth to others in the organization. But in church settings, I am *both* independent and dependent. To understand this requires "bifocal ability." Let me explain. I used to wear contact lenses. Because I have aged, the opthalmologist discussed with me the option of correcting the vision in each eye separately, adjusting one eye for distance and the other eye for close-up. After a period of adjustment, this division of tasks allows the contacts wearer to see both close up and far away without having to shut one eye or consciously shift from one or the other eye to do so. My understanding of authority resembles a type of bifocal vision because, on the one hand, I believe in the absolute authority of the priesthood of God. I believe that my worthiness is very much connected to my sustaining that power and authority from God. At the same time, I believe in my absolute worth as a daughter of God, and I believe that nothing about differences in our individual authority as members makes me less valuable to the Lord. So, I define authority with one lens focused on my absolute worth and another lens focused on the fact of the absolute authority of God. So, to say that I sustain authority is *not* to imply that I am submissive or of less value or have no right to petition. It is to say that I am of absolute, paramount worth, irrespective of any office I may or may not hold in the kingdom, yet also to say that there is an orderliness in the authority of God's priesthood that makes offices of authority beneficial and necessary. Both these statements are congruent. This bifocal vision is basic to my understanding of how we are meant to be "fitly framed together" as a congregation.

For one thing, the orderliness that authority implies is very important. For most of my life, I have been directed by authority. Only lately—a side benefit of age and maturity, I suppose—am I on occasion "in charge" some place. From being in charge, I have acquired a different view of authority. At present, I am directing a major organizational change project. Twelve people report to me as the project manager. People react to my being the authority in that program in different ways. Some people don't share anything with me. If I contact them for information about decisions they have made, they say, "Oh, I thought you wouldn't be interested in that, Kate," or "I didn't think you needed to know that." In essence, they act as if I have no authority in my role as project manager. They have no use for a director. Others will say, "I think I could do that, but I'd like to check with Kate first." And, of course, I feel better about that. Ego aside, I simply feel the support of people who will make sure I know what's going on. My experiences as project manager have led me to wonder, "Maybe this is how some of the men and women that I have worked with in the Church have felt. As I have reported to them, maybe this is what they wanted: more of my *alignment* with their authority. They didn't want to be authoritarian personalities; they simply wanted me to join with them and share information—to acknowledge in an orderly way who had what responsibilities and what was being done. Their wish to be informed leaders did not mean that they wanted to be dominant, in control, or acknowledged as more important than me. (Of course, there are some who may want something else — to gain personally at the expense of others, to exercise dominion over the lives of others. We can learn to distinguish differences in the uses of authority.) I now better realize the need for authority and the value of orderliness as we coordinate responsibilities in a way which will allow us to be "builded together for an habitation of God through the Spirit."

Another insight about authority that I have found useful is that there is a difference between one's heart and one's style. I have worked with some men and women in the Church who have very odd styles but very pure hearts. We ought not to confuse the two. We should take care not to assume that a man or a woman with a poor communication style or an uninviting manner is being arbitrary or distant in his or her exercise of authority. Often their hearts are in the right place, but they don't yet have some important skills of talking and working with others. If we are generous in our sustaining, we can look to their hearts and relate warmly to these less inviting personalities in authority.

There is an interesting paradox in group dynamics related to authority. The science of group dynamics[1] includes the study of authority in groups. As a group matures it will begin to authorize its members to do different tasks without having those assignments be experienced as de-authorizing someone else. In other words, in the beginning people in a group are often intimidated by authority and rarely act creatively and autonomously; furthermore, those in authority may fear loss of control or the misguided actions of group members. But as the common purpose of the group develops, more people can and do act autonomously to achieve group goals without anyone regarding this as taking away from someone else's authority. We can see this in congregations. As we gain maturity in our callings, we can take more initiative, take more action, without it registering with anyone as de-authorizing someone else or encroaching on their authority. Instead, we are seen as acting with the authority of our calling and our capacity in the congregation. We are "builded together," having a common purpose but different roles and responsibilities. But finding that mature balance is part of the dilemma. When is it appropriate to feel authorized to do your own work, and when are actions viewed as de-authorizing somebody else because you are seen as taking away activities or leadership others associate with their authority or stewardship?

In this context, consider our interactions, especially when women interact with those who hold priesthood authority. Many people feel uncomfortable with this topic because some views of feminism are interpreted as critical of all male authority. However, we should welcome questions. As Mormon scholar Hugh Nibley observes, "Nothing pleases God more than to have his children seek greater light and knowledge."[2] He goes on to say that in many ways he observes Latter-day Saints not petitioning enough, not trying to seek more knowledge. He encourages us to investigate and seek wisdom and knowledge, quoting from Nephi, "And because that I have spoken one word ye need not suppose that I cannot speak another; for my work is not yet finished; neither shall it be until the end of man." (2 Nephi 29:8–9.) We should continue to expect more insight and light and knowledge. So when I am asked, "How do you explain the differences between men and women?" or "Why do women in your church not hold the priesthood?" I am not discomfited by the question, because I believe that a sincere attempt to understand is, in fact, a petition to God for greater knowledge. Instead of putting us on the defensive, questions ought to encourage us to talk with one another more, to acknowledge that we as people have a lot to learn. As women, we can investigate what it means to men to hold the priesthood, to sustain it, and to experience ourselves in relationship to it. As women we can also learn what it is like to serve in callings authorized by the power of God and to experience how our leadership affects other women and men.

Conversely, priesthood holders have much to learn from women because women can mirror to men in priesthood positions how they affect women. If I were a man holding the priesthood and I had the task of being able to exercise power "only by persuasion, by long-suffering, by gentleness and meekness, and by love unfeigned; by kindness, and pure knowledge" (D&C 121:41–42), who might perceive how I am doing? Those who do not have the priesthood. So as I attempt to understand how we might work together as men and women—with men holding priesthood and women having callings and authority but not holding the priesthood as men do—I make sense of the situation in this way: it is the ideal condition for *oneness*. What makes it ideal? To put it in very simple terms, because each has something the other lacks. If you combine people who have some attribute or experience with people who don't, you have the basis for a strong, vital, working relationship. If all have the same experiences or gifts, there is less likely to be growth in the relationship.

For an individual to exercise the priesthood in righteousness, then, the view of those who do not hold the priesthood is very important. Part of sustaining priesthood, I believe, is to volunteer a lot of information to priesthood leaders about their interactions with us. Of course, awkward moments will arise if you announce to someone, "Excuse me, this is *not* love unfeigned!" Styles of communication can make a difference.

The Church as a vehicle for bringing women and men together in organized effort, then, provides a very important learning relationship for both. Men—having the opportunity to exercise authority—more often must personally learn the capacity to yield, to be gentle, to be long-suffering; and women—having more often been schooled in gentleness and long-suffering—must learn to claim personal authority, to petition, to ask and enquire, to be met as an equal. In a relationship, then, each must learn from the other's experiences and nature. Such a state of inherent difference is the perfect condition for oneness. In my mind and heart, nothing about our male-female differences equates with subordination or with diminished value of either gender. Instead, our gender differences and our authority differences offer the greatest opportunity to learn what Christ is trying to teach us through his gospel: that charity and oneness are available to us; that the pursuit of our individual salvation is inextricably linked to others'; that this life is a time of opportunities to teach and learn from one another.

Now let's investigate some interactions and skills that would enable us to grow toward that holy community of oneness described by the Apostle Paul. We can do a lot to create a spirit in which learning can take place by using what organizational behaviorists call "third-party" roles. The third party is someone who observes a relationship but is less directly involved. For example, a bishop's counselor is in a good position to observe how the Relief Society president relates to her bishop. Third-party information is invaluable. We ought to ask people more often about what they are perceiving. We should ask questions, explore, and discuss so that we can benefit from their observations. Once you establish the third-party role, you can ask about how you are working with someone. "Am I coming across as too submissive?" "Am I too rigid or authoritarian?" "Do I appear to be irritable?" Generally a third party has fewer vested interests, so opinions can be more accurate. Strengthen those third-party roles and take advantage of this useful source of feedback.

Of course, sometimes feedback can be painful. What should you do when you are in a position to give feedback that is potentially painful? First of all, we need to distinguish between two types of criticism. Elder Dallin H. Oaks, in an LDSSA fireside about criticism, said, "I do not refer to the kind of criticism the dictionary defines as 'the act of passing judgment as to the merits of anything.' " Instead, he was referring to criticism that has another meaning, which is "the act of passing severe judgment; censure; faultfinding." Faultfinding involves pointing out faults, especially "faults of a petty nature."[3]

In interactions our first responsibility should be to examine our own hearts. After some experience, I have become a little clearer on knowing when I am being appropriately critical: when I have information or an observation I want to offer, and when I have worked to develop a relationship where I can say to that person, "I don't know why you did that," expecting a laugh and an explanation. When I am, on the other hand, backbiting or faultfinding, I am generally feeling not so much puzzled by their behavior as superior. I am feeling, "If he had only asked me, he would have shown better judgment," implying a more perfect knowledge. So, there is, I am afraid, a not very subtle difference between being critical and giving helpful feedback. Yet we often mask, even to ourselves, faultfinding as constructive criticism. Tone and attitude usually determine whether or not you will be perceived as sustaining and contributing or as seeking to "counsel the brethren."

When we go to someone in authority with a problem to be solved, we should think through what it is we are hoping he or she will do. At times, for instance, when I have felt very excluded or alienated in a ward, I have gone to a bishop, hoping he would make me feel more comfortable. If I had thought more realistically about the bishop's position, I would have realized that he could, of course, provide sympathy and spiritual comfort, but to solve my problem permanently I should have been approaching those in the congregation with whom I hoped to improve relations. At other times, I have gone to a priesthood authority hoping for understanding that I should have been seeking from someone I had wronged. So we should clarify what it is we are seeking when we approach a person in authority. Is this something we should be working on more autonomously? If not, then our next step should be to identify what we expect or hope the authority will do. We can go prepared to say, "I want more elderly sisters to work in Primary so we can benefit from their experience and break down the Relief Society/Primary age barrier. I was hoping you might call Sister Cromar to be a Merrie Miss teacher. She helped teach a class on short notice and remarked how much she enjoyed the opportunity." Be as clear as you can: here is what I'd like to have happen and this is what I hoped you might do to make it happen. Then invite some discussion of your hopes.

I am convinced that as a Church congregation we are moving steadily forward toward Joseph's counsel of teaching principles and allowing people to govern themselves.[4] As we do so, fewer programs will come from a central Church headquarters. More and more often, principles will be emphasized and application will devolve on local initiative and inspiration. As Elaine L. Jack, general president of Relief Society, explained in a 1990 open house to Relief Society leaders: "You are the harbor pilots. We are bringing you the ship of Relief Society, and we know that you have the ability and you have the inspiration to take the program of Relief Society to your sisters because you know the local conditions, you know their special needs. We want Relief Society to bless the sisters."[5] Because of increasing emphasis on local initiative and inspiration, we must strengthen our skills in interaction within our congregations. We will require more interaction and more occasions to discuss and engage in dialogue to understand principles as they relate to the needs of the people that we work with.

If our image of authority is that of The Judge and if we assume that those who hold callings don't want to hear our comments or our concerns, we may miss opportunities to learn and bless the lives of others. For instance, as the visiting teaching supervisor, I may have ideas to offer both my Relief Society president and my bishop about how to serve ward members with this specific Relief Society program, given the people currently in the ward.

It will also become more important to understand what sustaining means. Some of us think that sustaining the priesthood or sustaining a calling means that you agree with that person and that you don't give them too much "grief" while they are in that position. Yet the definition of priesthood authority specifies that it is exercised only under conditions of long-suffering, gentleness, and meekness. If so, then what you are sustaining is someone's opportunity to have those experiences. Each of us sustains that potential in our leaders. At times, my sense of self-worth necessitates that I raise questions and encourage others to share their viewpoints. At other times, my sense of worthiness necessitates my compliance with direction or decisions made by those in authority over me.

How can we sustain our leaders if we never give them the chance to enlarge their souls by being honest and open in our interactions with them? Elder Dean L. Larsen said, "The Savior attempted to impress his questioners with the fact that the real power in the kingdom of God is not represented in outwardly observable things. Its strength is in the quality of the lives of its members. It is in the depth of their purity, their charity, their faith, their integrity, and their devotion to truth."[6] If we keep that vision alive when we work with one another, we will in fact be builded together as a congregation and be a place the Spirit of God can inhabit.

Notes
1. Kenwyn K. Smith and David N. Berg, *Paradoxes of Group Life* (San Francisco: Jossey Bass Publishers, 1987).
2. Hugh W. Nibley, "Priesthood," *Sunstone* (December 1990): 10–11.
3. Dallin H. Oaks, "Criticism," *Ensign*, Feb. 1987, pp. 68–73.
4. Joseph Smith, as quoted in John Taylor, "The Organization of the Church," *Millenial Star*, 15 Nov. 1851, p. 339.
5. Elaine L. Jack, "The Mission of Relief Society," open house address, 27 Sept. 1990, unpublished manuscript on file in Relief Society Offices, Salt Lake City, Utah.
6. Dean L. Larsen, "The Strength of the Kingdom Is Within," *Ensign*, Nov. 1981, p. 25.

Real Women

DONNA LEE BOWEN

A few years ago I spoke at women's conference about power and spirituality within the gospel. At one point, using as an example my two-year-old divorce, I shared the events that had led up to the death of the marriage. The audience listened receptively, and I felt that some of my points connected.

That year, the conference evaluations included a number of comments that expressed the following wish: We want to hear from "real women," not from all these M.A.s and Ph.D.s — women with letters after their names. My heart was pierced, for I had exposed myself in my talk. I had taken a chance and trusted the audience with my sorrows and the faith that pulled me through. Did the letters after my name (which represented more discipline than I thought I had, more work than I thought I could ever do, and abilities I wasn't always sure I had) mean that I was not a real woman? These questions still echo in my mind.

A few weeks ago, in conversation with a group of friends, one woman, Nancy, spoke with devastating honesty about the isolation she had felt when she was raising her children. She had felt that she was no longer a "real person any more" but was just filling various roles: mother, wife, Primary president. Then, after my ears had perked up at that word *real*, she went on to explain how badly she had longed at that time to hear

Donna Lee Bowen, associate professor of political science at Brigham Young University, has served as associate director of the BYU Women's Research Institute. Interested in the intersection of family issues and govenment policy, she has conducted extensive fieldwork in the Middle East and North Africa and is coeditor of the forthcoming book Everyday Life in the Middle East.

from *real women* in Women's Conference. She said, "I wanted a *real woman*, not one with a degree but a woman who had experiences like me: home, kids, isolation, doubts, a need for greater self-value. I wanted to hear from women like my everyday neighbors, women who have confronted these problems and found some answers." (Note that she said she didn't feel "real" and then turned right around and defined "real women" as ones like her.)

Why is this issue important? The cutting question here for me is whether I am a "real woman" as judged by other women whose lives have taken turns different from mine. Underlying the adjective *real* is another word—*valuable*. If I am not a real woman, then do I have any value? Do other women consider me a valuable sister—or, by not conforming in some way, am I irrelevant, disposable, a person who doesn't matter to her sisters? Nancy was voicing the same question, only from another point of view: I'm a mother; I've been staying home with no adults to talk to all day; I'm lonely; I'm isolated. Am I real? Do I have any value? Is my life worthwhile?

Opposites: Real and False

The need to feel valued poses a great temptation for each of us to find an example to copy. Although we all need examples as models to guide us in our growth, making ourselves over to fit an already existing model can be counterproductive. If we lose sight of who we are—our individuality and the unique strengths we have to offer in service—we may simply, in wholesale pursuit of our chosen model, become what we think others want us to be.

Another great temptation is to characterize others according to one model or another. We label, we stereotype: she is a doctor, she is a psychologist, she is a mother of ten, she is a beauty queen. That is helpful information, but partial: one aspect, not the whole person. To see the whole person, we must integrate all the pieces that make an individual uniquely her.

That is difficult to do, for generalization is both necessary and easy. Proceeding upon bits of information is part of our imperfect social universe. But when these pieces are believed to be the whole person, divisiveness and pain often result.

Rachel, a Korean-American BYU student in one of my courses, told me last year of her frustration that her race always seems to be an issue in relationships. "I'm Korean, but I don't think I look different. In my California high school no one treated me as different; however, here at BYU no one has got to the point where they see *me*, not my Asian features. I am one of 'those people,' Oriental. This was a shock to me, because I wasn't aware that I was different."

Melani, a student from Hawaii, spoke vehemently about how her family's wealth and other superficial characteristics affect the way people treat her. "What counts is how much my father makes, if I attend a fancy school, what my ACT scores are, if I am Mormon or not, if my clothes are expensive, fashionable, or ordinary, whether I wear the right T-shirt, if inside my shirt is the right label. My looks matter: if I have zits, if I am fat, what my hair looks like. They treat me differently if I am driving my dad's Mercedes or my sister's ten-year-old Subaru. They don't care that the Subaru gets you where you are going. They care about appearances."

Both Rachel and Melani dislike being defined by characteristics that are superficial and at best only a partial reflection of who they are. Another way to characterize these social interactions is as false opposites. Rachel is Oriental; I am not. Melani has high ACT scores; Janene doesn't. To concentrate on one particular aspect of a person's life, a label or a stereotype, allows us to conveniently pigeonhole and relate to that person. Stereotypes are easy to deal with, whereas people may not be. We are seeing ourselves and them in terms of opposition rather than in terms of connections. We remain divided from each other, seldom trusting, easily threatened.

A second false opposition may exist *within* ourselves. If we attempt to emulate a model, if we try to become what we think our friends, our workplace, the Church, or our families want us to be—rather than what we really are—then we create an opposition within ourselves. Divided within, we may pit one part of our identity against another, creating confused and conflicting feelings.

How many of you at one time or another have compared yourself to the Mormon stereotype and felt chastened if you didn't quilt, bottle, bake, cook, do crafts, give birth to congregations of children? General Relief Society president Elaine L. Jack, concerned that "sisters compare themselves to others," said at the women's broadcast that there is no single template for the perfect Mormon woman. "If I could have the desire of my heart for you, it would be that you feel valued for your own goodness," she said. We are each, with *all* our individual differences, "a typical Relief Society woman."[1]

In the Book of Mormon, Lehi teaches the need for opposition in all things. (2 Nephi 2:11.) Life stems from genuine opposites: life and death, good and evil, joy and grief, pain and pleasure, chaos and calm, peace and turmoil. The existence of opposites precedes the ability to choose—the priceless gift of agency.

The true doctrine of opposition allows us to grow, to change, to develop in the light of God. Opposition is not meant to be divisive, to isolate, to alienate one person from another. Opposition between individuals is a false dualism, for the only duality God ordains is that between good and evil, truth and falsehood. Individuals are not good or evil, true or false; rather we are capable of *doing* good or evil, *speaking* truth or falsehood.

We each—like a cut diamond—have multiple facets to our personalities; we respond to different situations as the diamond reflects different lights. The trick is to recognize and value the combination of facets in each of us and not judge ourselves, or others, by only one facet of personality.

A Reintroduction Experiment

All of us are uncomfortable with one-faceted descriptions

of ourselves, yet we are far too easily content to label others in monochromatic stereotypes. Let me pose two questions to illustrate my point: First, how do you describe yourself to others? If I asked who you are, what would you say?

Second, when you are introduced to another, what questions do you pose in your mind about them? Do you check out their clothes? Their hair? Their professions? Do you need some signal about what they do or how they fit into society or what their husband does in order to know how to relate to them?

I have for two years been on the women's conference planning committee. The committee spends hours debating the brief program blurbs that introduce the participants each year. How can we describe each other? Should we omit the descriptions? If we do, will the audience decide that they have no reason to listen to a speaker, for she seemingly has no expertise? It is a difficult problem to furnish necessary information and yet not alienate those who read it. A blurb that notes that I am an associate professor of political science, for instance, separates us more than it pulls us together.

So let me reintroduce myself. As an experiment let me try to show all the pieces that make up my whole in terms of what I think really matters about me. Of course, I remember my failures and pain longer than my triumphs. Most achievements mean more to me when I am working toward them; once achieved, they decline in importance. Failure, however, registers for a long time, because I have developed the ability to dwell upon it properly.

You know already that I am a professor. I enjoy teaching; at times I enjoy writing. I never enjoy grading papers.

I read murder mysteries — piles and piles of them. I once inadvertently disconcerted my Cultural Refinement leader, who had invited me to share books that I loved with the other Relief Society sisters. I turned up with a stack of murder mysteries and spent ten minutes telling sisters of the joys of Dorothy Sayers and Elizabeth Peters as escapist reading.

I am an oldest child. I feel responsible for the whole world, not just my brothers and sisters.

I always weigh at least ten pounds too much. Always.

I have been divorced; I watched a marriage formed with high hopes and purpose die.

I love my friends.

I love my family and have difficulty telling them how much.

I have breast cancer. Two years ago, I had a breast removed and a new one built.

I was not invited to join the pep club in high school.

I was forced to withdraw from a lifesaving class because the men were too heavy in the water for me to drag across the pool.

I am married, for a second time, and in this marriage I gained three stepdaughters; I worked at learning to love when I feared I was not loved, and I have been rewarded with relationships that mean more to me than I can say.

I have had only miscarriages, no children.

I don't exercise enough.

I need to be in the mountains from time to time to look at the tops of the trees.

I don't always listen to what goes on. I daydream.

I seldom find Sunday School interesting.

I love working in the soil, even if I forget to weed what I plant.

I procrastinate. Always.

I can work very hard with great concentration.

I love my husband but find marriage to be one of the most challenging jobs I've undertaken; to respond to those challenges requires new parts of me that I was not conscious of before.

When I look at myself, I see few successes. I see isolation, self-doubt, fear, attempts to keep valuing myself, to understand how I fit into God's world.

My greatest successes keep coming through the hardest

times: getting a Ph.D. in a hostile environment; getting through the divorce; surviving breast cancer; working on my marriage.

Does knowing more about me diminish the space between us? Can I now be a real woman to you?

I have done most of my fieldwork and research overseas in the Middle East. I often find women in the villages surprisingly easy to know and care about, although we have little in common. They are often illiterate and can't share my favorite books or discuss world politics, but we share other things. We can share small vanities of fingernail polish, scarves, and eye makeup. We can talk about food and cooking, about menstrual cramps, about our husbands, about divorce, about children, and about our beliefs in God.

Given that we have an ability to relate to most people on several grounds, why do we use labels and stereotypes to defend ourselves from closeness?

And why do we set up images of ourselves and then try to conform to them at the risk of losing sight of the more integrated whole person we really are?

Fear and Our Hidden Selves

In living our lives and relating to others around us, we protectively draw false distinctions, sometimes between ourselves and others, sometimes between different parts of the self, but all the same with devastating results: the pain of separation — our personal separation from members of our community, our community's separation from all others, and most of all, our own separation, or alienation, from other parts of ourselves, and the concomitant confusion over which part of us is real. In doing so, we negate the type of community Christ teaches us to create — a society that is one in Christ.

So why, instead of seeking ways to connect, do we prefer to maintain distance by stereotyping each other and ourselves by profession, by clothing, by education, by income, by appearance, or by some other factor of the whole self? I believe many of the reasons boil down to fear: fear of intimacy, fear of being rejected, fear of showing weakness or emotion.

Putting each other into pigeonholes serves to keep others away from us by defining our own place as somehow different, somehow superior. We feel safer keeping others at a distance. What lies behind our strong aversion to intimacy?

Part of our discomfort may result from the fact that we automatically associate the word *intimacy* with sexuality. If we are truly intimate, we trust others with knowledge of and access to our most sensitive selves, our feelings, and — in the marriage relationship — our bodies. In the United States, as in many cultures, we are unfamiliar and not totally comfortable with our bodies. So, even in same-sex relationships, some people fear and avoid close, intimate friendships because of the strong social taboos against physical intimacy. Fearing the one, they avoid the other. It is easier to keep one's distance than to take a chance. There are good reasons for caution, but I believe we worry too much that a sexual relationship may evolve from intimacy and hesitate to show affection and trust freely, even among friends.

Another inhibitor of openness and intimacy is the new ethic of professionalism in business, which defines women and men in terms of their functions: secretary, teacher, physician, patient, executive. This practice maximizes efficiency, promotes profits, and observes the civil rights and equal protection statutes, but it is also somewhat dehumanizing. To comply, part of our essential being, our sexuality and legitimate gender differences, must be buried.

But even outside professional settings, we avoid intimacy when it would be appropriate and healthy. What are the fears that keep women from getting close to each other?

Ask yourself, are there times when you do not call your best friend even though you are troubled and need to talk? Why not? Perhaps you do not trust your friend enough to risk sharing this information that would be too potentially harmful, too precious to trust to her. You may worry, "What if she misused it? What if she betrayed me in some way? I could not bear that."

Or perhaps we are afraid of disapproval or disagreement? Intimacy with spouse, family members, or friends can turn threatening if that closeness does not spell agreement on all issues. Yet often closeness will trigger dissent because it exposes our natural lack of consensus on issues — some of them fundamental. If we dare to speak our minds, tempers may flare, and we may disagree. Many of us fear anger, aggression, or a show of real emotions, so we shun closeness to protect ourselves from the pain that can be engendered by conflict.

Our willingness to take that risk is, however, a matter of deepest integrity. How can we be truly honest with another person when we refuse to take the chance of being angry, hurt, or conflictual?

Another reason for maintaining emotional distance may be that we are reluctant to admit we have problems. We prefer to keep our all-is-well mask firmly in place. After all, much of what we do in life is directed at garnering admiration from those around us. Admiration, however, is usually at odds with love. If we seek to be admired, we seek an audience. An audience lacks the close involvement that generates love. In wanting admiration, we want to be perfect. Love, however, tolerates and even welcomes imperfections. My mother tells me that we love those who need us. Seemingly flawless people are hard to relate to, much less love. Our hearts go out to those who struggle and honestly admit it. So although we try to hide our messy houses and infested gardens, the burnt cookies and the imperfect Sunday School lessons, such failings make us human and unite us.

Underlying many of our actions is another self-defeating supposition. In his movie *Annie Hall*, the fretful, pessimistic Woody Allen character quotes an old Groucho Marx joke, "I would never want to belong to any club that would have me for a member." Putting another spin on the line, we get: "If you really knew me, you wouldn't like me." The logic proceeds conversely, "So if I don't let you know me, then you will like me." We fear letting people get close enough to the real "me" — a me that gets angry, that has inappropriate thoughts, that makes mistakes, that doesn't have all the answers. In our attempts to *control* other people's reactions to us, then, we deny them access to who we really are. We assume, "Since you won't like the real me, I'll give you a label or a stereotype that you will relate to much better, and I'll keep this stereotype sufficiently distant so that our relationship won't be endangered by reality."

Wholeness in Christ

The most serious consequences of hiding thoughts and censoring feelings is that we will lose touch with them ourselves. Psychologist Alice Miller has said: "Depression can be understood as the loss of the self and consists of a denial of one's own emotional reactions and feelings."[2] According to her analysis, depression is a result of suppressing authentic emotions — emotions that may not always be pleasant, but emotions that are real. If we can recognize authentic emotions — admitting we are sad when we grieve, fearful when frightened, angry when furious, as well as joyful when happy — we stop hiding from ourselves and admit what is real to us at a fundamental level. This sounds simple, but it is tremendously difficult because it implies understanding ourselves, including seeing what underlies our own suppositions about ourselves and analyzing our own labels and discerning what we use those labels for.

This is a life work. Know yourself. "To your own self be true" — such easy-sounding advice, until we begin. And then it is as perilous as the most dangerous course strewn with dragon's teeth. For we don't always follow what is in our best interests.

These matters frighten me; perhaps they do some of you. They challenge my identity: whether I am a real person or not, and if I am real, to whom am I real? To whom do I reveal my authentic self in all its complexity and imperfection?

Consider these preliminary questions: Who can I be a real person with?

Myself? Can I admit who I am and how I really feel about matters? Or do I live behind labels, deceiving myself about what really bothers me?

My spouse? Friends? Family? Can I afford to let them know who I am and how I really feel? Or do I live behind labels, quietly ordering my relationships with others into proper or appropriate boxes so that I keep all the facades well-maintained?

Does anyone know who I really am? Do I know? Do I fool myself into ignoring what is most important to me? Do I ignore the treasures that I have and run after others that appear more exciting or more valuable from a distance? Knowing oneself, a difficult task, is one of the fundamental purposes of mortality.

The traits that really matter, that determine who we are — spirituality, access to the Lord through prayer, humility, obedience, patience, charity — are traits that are largely invisible to the outsider. Only as we reach out to a person in love do we discern those traits.

In the gospel we have no ranks, no hierarchies. We all serve each other as we are best suited to serve. I believe this sense of community without hierarchies is both the essence of humility and basic to the self-love and wholeness we are expected to have as a starting point in the gospel.

The wholeness we seek is founded on the ideal of a community in Christ. If we recognize Christ's greatness and what he does for us, we can only respond in humility, hoping to deal with others with the same Christlike generosity. When we approach Christ, we can use no facades, no stereotypes, no labels, for we approach him as his sisters, as children of God.

Lehi taught us about the real opposition that Eve bought for us with a high price. It is by recognizing these real oppositions — by experiencing joy and sadness, by shunning evil, by embracing the good, by working to substitute calm for turmoil, peace for warfare — that we become authentically ourselves. We defeat depression because nothing is suppressed; we embrace our feelings and emotions and find that we can gain strength by sharing them with others. We—you and I— are united in our work, and in our lives, sometimes in joy and sometimes in grief, but together, not divided against each other or against ourselves.

Life is essentially a process, not a product: we will take from our lives what we have learned and have become as a result of all we do and experience. We learn from each step in the process. But we cannot learn if we deal only in falseness—if we get caught in false oppositions and refuse to recognize the importance of the real ones.

The most damaging result of defining ourselves in terms of false oppositions is that we only own and develop a piece of ourselves—for me, a professor or a researcher, instead of Donna Lee, who has experienced so much. If I set up opposition to myself, then I lose who I really am to inessentials. If we keep essentials bright in front of us, and use hope to press forward, then we are united in ourselves, in our sisterhood, in the body of Christ, and we cannot be defeated.

Notes

1. Elaine L. Jack, "These Things Are Manifested unto Us Plainly," *Ensign*, Nov. 1990, pp. 88, 90.
2. Alice Miller, *The Drama of the Gifted Child* (New York: Basic Books, 1981), p. 45.

A View from the Inner City

HATTIE M. SOIL

The first step in the process of knowing and serving others is discovering one's self. I must discover myself and my personal proclivities in order to recognize and *value* the uniqueness of others. I am a distinct individual with my own needs, ideals, and priorities—in part, a result of my background.

Let me sketch my background. I was born in rural Mississippi to parents who were sharecroppers. A sharecropper is a farmer who cultivates a part of another's land. This practice was popular in the thirties, forties, and fifties. In return for the use of the land, the sharecropper must share his crops, usually on a fifty-fifty basis, with the landowner. In the South, sharecroppers were almost universally poor—and we were no exception.

My parents moved to Memphis, Tennessee. After their eleventh child, my mother became tired of the constant burden of giving birth and my father's drinking, so she put him out. His drinking problem had caused a number of embarrassing moments for the family, and my mother felt that life would be easier without him. After he left, his financial contributions to the family stopped, and Mother had to work long hours trying to make ends meet.

She did not believe in welfare, so that was not an option for her. Mother's two jobs and long hours kept her away from home, and lack of adult supervision kept us in trouble with

A convert to the Church, Hattie M. Soil has served as Relief Society president of the Hyde Park Ward in Chicago, Illinois. She is employed as human resources assistant for the City Colleges of Chicago, and she volunteers assistance to minority students seeking and applying for college grants. She and her husband, Victor, are the parents of six children.

the authorities. Some of us were arrested for loitering, fighting, and disturbing the peace. Some of us had problems with morality, and I was a mother at seventeen.

We lived in dilapidated dwellings in neighborhoods that were rated so poorly that most policemen hated to answer calls from them. My mother decided that she was working too hard and not making economic progress, so she decided to move her large family up north.

We moved to Chicago, Illinois, and found life easier. There were plenty of jobs for us as well as for Mother. Because she could not read nor write, she found a job as a cook in a nursing home. Life was better in Chicago. We were fed and clothed properly. I started to enjoy life.

I married at age eighteen and was divorced with three small boys by age twenty. I had no high school diploma and no skills. At age twenty-five, I married Victor, who had a bachelor's degree in criminal justice. I complained to him of how ashamed I was for not finishing high school. He works for the board of education and one Christmas, the school faculties and staffs had a party. I told Victor that I could not attend that party with him because I wouldn't feel comfortable. He said, "You are just as smart as those people there, and I want you to attend this party with me." I did, and we had a good time. After that party, he encouraged me to get my G.E.D., and I did. He then encouraged me to enroll in a junior college, and two years later I received an associate of arts degree. I next enrolled in a university and earned a bachelor's degree.

As I have considered my background, I see how my past has influenced my life and attitudes. For example, I don't care to visit the South because it brings back memories of my childhood. I never drank, probably because my father was an alcoholic. I have a strong testimony of the law of chastity because of the pain and embarrassment that I suffered as an unwed teenage mother (I have stressed to my children almost since birth the importance of chastity). I know how important a good education is because my mother never received one

(I have seen that even though education will not solve all problems, it will often ease them).

My experiences and my background shaped my outlook on life and my personality. Others from different backgrounds have been shaped by different circumstances.

Let me illustrate my point. When my family and I first joined the Church a number of years ago, our branch was composed of students from the University of Chicago. My husband and I used to sit in amazement and listen to their stories of hardship. Their idea of a hard time was struggling with their studies or living in an area other than what they were used to. My husband and I, with three young sons, often wondered what these university students would do if they had to struggle for their next meal or worry about their children surviving from day to day in a gang-infested neighborhood or in the Chicago public school system. It was years before I began to realize that their problems were just as serious to them as mine were to me. When I received that enlightenment, I was on the road to understanding others.

After we acknowledge our own experiences and backgrounds, we can seek to understand others'. I have always found service to be a key to discovering needs and understanding others. People seem to open up to those who serve them and love them.

Several years ago a less-active sister in our ward was seriously ill. When I learned of her illness, I went to visit her. I took along a dinner that I had prepared and some vegetables from my garden. I noticed that her bedroom was in a state of disarray. As I cleaned it up, we began talking, and I mentioned to her how much we loved her and missed her at church. I looked directly into her eyes and asked her why she hadn't been coming to church. She stated that she didn't have "pretty dresses like the rest of the sisters." I was surprised that this sister had been so proud that she hadn't told anyone of her financial problem. I was also gratified that she saw fit to trust me. I told her that the Lord didn't care what she wore to church.

Nevertheless, someone anonymously gave this sister two dresses. My husband and another priesthood holder gave her a blessing, and after her health improved, she returned to church.

I visited another less-active sister recently who had been baptized a few weeks previous to my visit. She hadn't been to church since her baptism. My companion and I sat down and began to converse with her. Through the course of our conversation, we learned that she had no food in the house. She hadn't the money to ride the bus to church, and her older son had no shoes. We were able to solve her most immediate problems, and she returned to church the next week and has since attended regularly.

Let me stress the importance of service as the way to discover needs and discover others. Service rendered lovingly works miracles in overcoming the barriers of race and class, such as those in my home ward. As I have mentioned, when I first joined the Church, the Hyde Park branch was essentially a student unit with only about six black members. Of the branch members, 95 percent were students or alumni of the University of Chicago. In classes and in conversation, I soon saw that many members assumed I didn't have the intelligence to understand what they were talking about. They also thought that the most meaningful service I could render was cooking and cleaning. I like to do these things, but I felt I could contribute in other areas just as well. I survived this period with testimony and a truckload of tact. And I even found some humor in the situation. For instance, one day a white sister walked up to me and said, "You know I've always liked you, but today a black person snatched my purse, and now I am afraid of you."

"I know how you feel," I answered, "because for hundreds of years your people held mine in slavery, so I have *always* been afraid of you." This insight caused her to think, and we later became close friends.

On another occasion, about six years ago when Victor was in the bishopric of our ward, he had just finished conducting a meeting when a white brother visiting from Utah hugged him and said, "You are a credit to your race." I could see that my husband was angered by this remark, but he kept himself under control and replied, "I'm quite average, thank you." On the surface, the visitor's remark may seem inoffensive, but it implies that blacks as a race are somehow inferior. He would have done better to say, "You are a credit to the human race."

These are not rare, isolated incidents. In fact, Afro-American converts in Chicago must learn to cope with a flood of blacks-scare-me-to-death or U-Haul stories, as we call them, in fast and testimony meetings. The speakers, usually white Westerners, relate how they first felt when they drove their U-Haul into Chicago and how afraid they were of blacks until they came to know them. Many blacks are offended by these stories, and some go inactive.

On another Sunday I was introduced to a new sister who had just moved into our ward. I could tell that she had little experience with black people. I introduced myself and extended my hand, and she shook it. Then she inspected her hand. She looked at the front and then the back. I watched her and then told her that my blackness was a skin color and not a paint. She was embarrassed and apologized. Stereotyping is not the Lord's way. And I have been guilty of stereotyping as well.

Our ward is now about 40 percent black, and we had a hundred and fifty baptisms last year. Since the 1978 revelation that all worthy men could receive the priesthood, the Hyde Park Ward in Chicago, Illinois, has been growing rapidly. Blacks, who had before seen the Mormon church as antiblack, have investigated and joined the Church in great numbers. Twenty-two missionaries are assigned to our ward, whose boundaries include more than a million people.

You may wonder why we haven't split into two or more wards. During the last five years only five Melchizedek Priesthood holders have been ordained. The vast majority of new members are women and children. In fact, single women with children are about 47 percent of our new converts. We have a big job serving these sisters. Because of their backgrounds and economic status, the needs of our newly baptized sisters are great and the problems are many. Some of these black, single sisters have been married and divorced, but the majority have *never* been married. You can see that when we talk about the priesthood being in every home, we must seek inspiration and be creative in the Hyde Park Ward. These sisters must be taught how vital a part the priesthood plays in their salvation and then they must be taught to respect the men that hold the priesthood because most of them have a very low opinion of men. This poor opinion arises naturally from the situation of our many new sisters who are unwed mothers and feel overwhelmed by the responsibilities of parenthood. They resent the fact that they have no male in the home to assist them.

One of the big problems in our ward is retention. We can't seem to keep the sisters that we are baptizing. As Relief Society president, I have visited all the less-active sisters. They give various reasons for leaving the Church. Some have Word of Wisdom problems. Some can't understand the Relief Society lesson. The problem is not intelligence but educational background. They are not familiar with academic or with Church vocabulary. Some find the music not to their liking. Afro-Americans have a rich musical heritage and a love for gospel music because they can easily relate to its subject matter: the story in song of the black experience in America and how they discovered the Lord. Most Afro-Americans find LDS music dull and uninspiring. (Let me note that I personally feel that if a person joins any church for its music, he or she has joined for the wrong reason.) Some have law of chastity problems, and a few claim to have been insulted by more established Church members.

Church manuals and instructional materials address the needs and concerns of rural and suburban areas of the country, rather than inner-city wards struggling with high crime rates, poor housing, poor quality public education, and high unemployment. As a Relief Society president, I could use home-making lessons on big-city survival training. We need classes that teach both the problem-solving skills and attitudes necessary for independent living, including topics such as how to manage money, rent an apartment, locate and use community resources, how to maintain health as adults as well as safeguard the health of children, and how to understand the many legal and contractual requirements that occur in everyday life. I know these may seem elementary, but believe me, surviving in a big city is not a simple task, and these skills need to be taught. For many new members, knowing that they can work out solutions to their problems may encourage them to take greater responsibility for their lives and to be less vulnerable to the temptations of drug abuse, gambling, and failure to live the law of chastity.

In addition, we must not let the influx of new sisters make us forget or neglect the needs of the more established sisters. That is a real balancing act.

The Prophet Joseph Smith, when he addressed the Relief Society on 9 June 1842, in Nauvoo, Illinois, said: "Christ said he came to call sinners to repentance, to save them. Christ was condemned by the self-righteous Jews because He took sinners into His society; He took them upon the principle that they repented of their sins. It is the object of this society to reform persons, not to take those that are corrupt and foster them in their wickedness; but if they repent, we are bound to take them, and by kindness sanctify and cleanse them from all unrighteousness by our influence in watching over them."[1]

People are coming into the Church from third-world countries and from the inner cities of this country with major problems. May I be so brash as to suggest some ways of dealing with this situation. First, we need to pray for guidance from our Heavenly Father for the ability to love all of his children despite their diversity. Second, we need to try not to offend anyone through ignorance of their customs or culture. Third, we need to be bold enough before baptism to teach the gospel and communicate the basic requirements for membership in God's kingdom. Missionaries and members must tell new converts before baptism that selling illegal drugs, for instance, is no longer an acceptable way to earn a living. We must be frank and direct in our teaching of the gospel because new members will not understand anything else. Fourth, we should "by kindness sanctify and cleanse them from all unrighteousness by our influence in watching over them."

I thank the Lord that he has provided the principles for dealing with our problems of diversity. These principles work regardless of race, class, or educational level. Joseph Smith said, "Nothing is so much calculated to lead people to forsake sin as to take them by the hand, and watch over them with tenderness. When persons manifest the least kindness and love to me, O what power it has over my mind, while the opposite course has a tendency to harrow up all the harsh feelings and depress the human mind."[2] If we love each other, serve each other, and are supportive and nonjudgmental, we will be following the teachings of Jesus, especially his admonition to "feed my sheep." (John 21:17.) We should always remember to feed his sheep. We should never forget that we are sheep as well and also need to be fed.

Notes

1. Joseph Smith, *Teachings of the Prophet Joseph Smith,* sel. Joseph Fielding Smith (Salt Lake City: Deseret Book Co., 1956), p. 240.
2. Ibid.

Language and Labeling:
Tunes for a Dancing Bear

DELMONT R. OSWALD

In my high school, I had a classmate called Rosie who was very plain and very overweight. Children in their teens are unusually weight conscious and can be very cruel. Rosie was teased everywhere she went, whether in school or out, even in seminary classes. What began as statements behind her back soon became statements made to her face. At first she cried, and then she stopped. I never said anything directly to Rosie, but I was just as guilty as the rest of the class in inventing new labels. It became a standard joke to say to friends, "Have you got a date with Rosie tonight?" or "Are you taking Rosie to the prom?" And, of course, the teasing didn't stop there. As the dating and weight jokes got stale, sexual innuendos crept in and were shouted down the halls. We had two major labels for Rosie. The spoken label was "You're fat!" The unspoken label was "You're a joke!" Both were believed.

I never really knew Rosie; not very many people did. Most did not want to be seen with her. She had a couple of girlfriends from her neighborhood, but not many and not close.

About five years ago, I met an old high school friend who still lived in my hometown, and as we talked about fellow classmates, Rosie's name came up. He told me she had become one of the town prostitutes. Because of her physical appearance, her clientele was not the most savory, even among the types

Delmont R. Oswald has served as executive director of the Utah Humanities Council and as a member of the board of the National Federation of State Humanities Councils. He has taught history at Brigham Young University and at Westminster College in Salt Lake City. He is the author of The Life and Adventures of James P. Beckworth *and is the father of two children.*

288

who solicited these services. Rosie died at about age forty-five from some form of cancer. She never married, never had a family, never had friends, never had joy. She was labeled early in life, and everyone accepted the labels. The worst thing was she accepted them and believed them herself.

We still label people—you and I—but as adults we are much more subtle and educated in the way we do it. Hopefully we are much more caring and Christian. We will continue to label—it is a basic means of communication—but I pray we will learn the destructive power of words and teach it to our children. We all need to be aware of just how dangerous and complex labeling can be.

I wish to dedicate this essay to Rosana for all the guilt I feel for helping to eliminate joy from her life.

Something wonderful happened to me the other day. Usually when I go somewhere and meet someone, they will say, "Didn't you attend BYU?" "Do you have any children?" or "Aren't you the director of the Utah Humanities Council?"—defining me in terms of my position, family, or accomplishments. This time I met a person who said, "Aren't you Sarah Oswald's father?" I proudly said, "Yes, I am." Suddenly I was no longer defining my children; they were defining me. I had assumed a new label, one I was very proud to have. In Japan, mothers are defined by their children, and fathers are defined by the company for whom they work. They are not necessarily bad labels, but because they are so dominant, they become restrictive. Sometimes we are guilty of labeling an acquaintance with a description such as *insensitive, homely, funny, divorced, single*, etc. When we make the label dominant, it also becomes restrictive.

Labeling is something we all do and something we all have done to us. There are both positive and negative aspects to this act, but because there seems to be no better way of defining people, we need to understand its benefits, dangers, and complexities. Commenting on the human tendency to make snap judgments and never revise them, Friedrich Nietzsche said, "When you first meet someone, you know all about him; on subsequent meetings, you blind yourself to your own wisdom."[1]

Some modern psychiatrists, interpreting him literally, use this quotation to verify the theory that first impressions are more accurate than later ones. They feel people do not initially put up a strong guard to protect their true selves.[2] I disagree with both that theory and the interpretation of Nietzsche. Any reader of Nietzsche knows there is considerable sarcasm and cynicism in his writing, especially in his references to women. Futhermore, people are generally more guarded with the unknown than with the known. They may change or adjust their guard as they get to know individuals, but the initial protective device is usually the strongest. Trained psychiatrists may see things differently, but I interpret this quotation from Nietzsche to mean that when you and I—untrained ordinary people— meet someone, we tend to stick with our first impressions. If we allow ourselves to accept more and more truth as we come to know the person better, we might change our judgments. That generally does not happen, because in doing so, we are questioning the original authority—ourselves. We usually prefer to prove ourselves right rather than prove ourselves wrong. We set ourselves up as judges, and we like the role and its power so much that we are usually willing to maintain it at the other's expense.

When we hear the term *label*, we usually think of it as something negative. If you are labeled, you are tied to a specific image and viewed as that image. If it is a label you like, that is no problem. If it is a label you do not like, then it can be a problem. The system is even more complex, however, because even labels we like, or are comfortable with, can limit us and thus become destructive. Irvin D. Yalom, in his book *Love's Executioner*, describes three problems we must confront in really knowing someone. First he says, in defining someone we must break down the barrier between image and language.

Our minds think in images, which can only be verbalized as labels. To communicate with one another, we have to transform images into thought and thought into language. Those microseconds from image to thought to language are treacherous. Calamity can occur because the texture, depth, emotion, plasticity, and flexibility of image can be lost when it is crammed into language. Great writers and artists often use metaphor or imitation to evoke from their audiences the images they see. We frequently do this in our own minds, but metaphor and imitation are certainly not infallible. The author of *Madame Bovary*, Gustave Flaubert, best describes the weakness of this process: "No one can ever express the exact measure of his needs, or conceptions, or sorrows. The human language is like a cracked kettle on which we beat out a tune for a dancing bear, when we hope with our music to move the stars."[3]

Second, to really know others, we must recognize we are judging them only from the information they choose to disclose. We may think we know someone for a period of time and suddenly something that person says or does will change our interpretation or view of that person completely. That happens even in marriages, but undisclosed information is even more likely to be a factor in relating to those we are not as intimate with as a mate.

Third, to know someone, we, the viewer, must reverse any sequence of information given to us: we must translate language back into thought and then into image—the script the mind can read. Because we also have our own bias and our own unique ways of thinking and seeing, it is very doubtful that the receiver's image will ever match exactly the sender's information. Marcel Proust describes this process beautifully when he says: "We pack the physical outline of the creature we see with all the ideas we already formed about him, and in the complete picture of him which we compose in our minds, those ideas have certainly the principal place. In the end they come to fill out so completely the curve of his cheeks, to follow so exactly the line of his nose, they blend so harmoniously in the sound of his voice that these seem to be no more than a transparent envelope, so that each time we see the face or hear the voice it is our own ideas of him which we recognize and to which we listen."[4] Because we still label, regardless of our lack of accurate information, we need to recognize that a person is many things at one time. If we can allow for the complexities of many roles, then we do not tend to lock someone into one implacable image. If we must label, it is much better to give several labels rather than just one. You are safest when you define or label someone by several categories: accomplishments, physical attributes, spouse, family, money, work, actions, morals, and so forth. Being defined by only one attribute takes away that person's freedom, especially if the label is picked up by others or, even worse, if the person comes to believe exclusively in that label of himself or herself. We have all been told that we are what we eat or what we read or what we think. What we really are, however, is what we believe. What we eat, read, or think is the material we build from. What we believe we are is truly what we become.

More dangerous than labeling from others is labeling ourselves negatively and believing it. There is usually no other authority we accept as readily as ourselves, even God's. To provide ourselves with healthy labels, then, becomes the challenge. We may do that by prioritizing options that we like, from which we may then select and believe. In latter-day scripture we are told that we are daughters and sons of God and sisters and brothers to Christ. I find nothing negative here; in fact, these labels give me self-respect, self-assurance, and confidence. I'm in the very best of company, and what a pedigree. Even though my next prioritized selections may not show me as a perfect being, these first two labels should counterbalance any weaknesses.

Next, I am labeled by my earthly roles: father, son, husband, brother, neighbor, Mormon, priesthood holder, citizen, and so on. Adjectives such as "honest," "good," "better," "great," "ethical," or "moral," are added, as in "good neighbor," "faithful Mormon," and "responsible citizen." When we believe these good or at least credible things about ourselves, we become them. Our confidence and self-respect then leads to positive thinking, and we continue to improve. Now, being honest — one of our high-priority labels — we acknowledge that we have faults, but we should place these less positive labels further down the priority scale. We accept them because they are also real but in a context of "areas for improvement."

When we label others, we should start with the same priorities. Certainly many others may not meet the standards we set for ourselves (remember "humble"), but if we always see them first as a daughter or son of God and a sister or brother to Christ, later judgments on the priority list will be counterweighted by this understanding.

So what should we look for when we begin to label someone? I recognize what we see and what we look for may be two very different things, but if we have in mind a positive priority of what to look for, our judgments will not be of the "snap" variety. Robert Henri, one of the most prominent American portrait painters from the turn of the century, taught his students how to look — really look — at people in order to convey their spirit as well as their image to a canvas. He says in his work *The Art Spirit*: "I am looking at each individual with the eager hope of finding there something of the dignity of life, the humor, the humanity, the kindness, something of the order that will rescue the race and the nation. . . . I seek only, wherever I go, for symbols of greatness . . . they may be found in the eyes of a child, in the movement of a gladiator, in the heart of a gypsy. . . . To hold the spirit of greatness is in my mind what the world was created for. The human body is beautiful as this spirit shines through, and art is great as it translates and embodies this spirit."[5]

I recently had the chance to reread two short works I had read in my early college years, works that proved again to me how important it is for us to look for the true-self instead of the false-self, or at least to recognize the difference. One was

Tolstoy's *The Death of Ivan Ilyich,* the story of a man who never examined his own life until he was confronted with death and what belated reality meant to him. Ilyich leaves this world regretting he had never made his *own* definition of himself. He had drifted through life living the labels and expectations others had given him. They were not uncomfortable labels, but they were not his selections. He dies with great remorse and anguish because he has found he had given up his freedom of making choices. He dies with the question, "What if my whole entire life, my entire conscious life, simply was not the real thing?"[6]

The other work is a brief autobiographical essay by George Orwell entitled "Shooting an Elephant."[7] When Orwell was a young man, he served as a member of the Imperial Police of the British colonial government in Burma. He tells of coming into a rural village just after an elephant had gone "must" (mad) and killed a man and wrecked some huts. Orwell knew he was hated by the villagers as representing an alien government, and he didn't like himself in the position he held because he felt the colonial policies were wrong. In other words, he was not certain about his own true-self, because what he was doing and what he really believed were different. Another interesting complication was that the village was very poor and the elephant was desperately needed for work. Yet the villagers began to egg him on to shoot the elephant because he had a gun and represented authority. There was also a perverse reason for their actions in that they knew he was young and hesitant and they could show power by forcing the issue. When Orwell got to the elephant, the period of madness had ended and the elephant was calmly eating and gently swaying back and forth in the middle of a field. As you might guess, everyone acts out the designated roles: *Orwell remains a figure of authority designated to maintain order.* Young Orwell shoots a calm elephant and with a terribly pained conscience watches it die.

Both these works illustrate how decisions are often made

in complex situations. When we make such decisions, what we really believe within ourselves should be the deciding factor, much more than external labels or expectations.

This strength of self-knowledge and confidence in each of us should mean we are always able to stand up for our own principles and values in ways that would never allow outside influences to coerce us into evil decisions such as wrongful discrimination, or, as an extreme case, a Jewish holocaust.

I will close with one caution especially relevant to you and me as Mormons. We come from a tradition of believing we have absolute truth through the gospel. When we meet and label strangers or those who believe differently from the way we believe, we need to be very careful that we allow their image, the way they see themselves, to be transmitted to us. We must be fair and not label them by only Mormon standards. Labeling them in that way becomes a judgment that separates rather than brings us together. We, in effect, take away their freedom of choice. To maintain communication, we must tolerate diversity and not label unfairly. Also, to maintain humility, we must remember we have been given some of the truth, but not all of the truth. We are to be rewarded with more truth as we are worthy to receive it.

Concerning ourselves and the labels we take on, we can always pray to God for confirmation. We control our own destinies by what we choose to do or say. Observers may interpret our choices differently, and as we make choices, we do have an obligation to carefully think through all the implications concerning other people, but they are *our* choices. And there will always be other choices. God does not dogmatically label us and then lock us into that definition. To do so would remove all the blessings of agency.

When we label or when we are labeled, we should always look for the true-self—and the true-self, remember, is whatever we actually believe. Whether we want to or not, we must continually examine our labels and be willing to change them, both for ourselves and for others. We should always look for the positive aspects to believe first, then, if there are negative aspects, at least we have given the total a fair hearing and balance. Although others may impose their definitions on us, just as we do on them, what is most important is what we believe about ourselves. When it comes to self-knowledge and self-evaluation, we should be our own key authorities. Our lives are like theater that others watch, and usually we are playing from someone else's script. We should always strive to be more than actors, however, and aim for the role of writer when it comes to our individual life drama.

Notes

1. Friedrich Nietzsche, as quoted in Irvin D. Yalom, *Love's Executioner* (New York: Basic Books, 1989), p. 183.
2. Irvin D. Yalom, *Love's Executioner* (New York: Basic Books, 1989), p. 183.
3. Gustave Flaubert, *Madame Bovary*, trans. Mildred Marmur (New York: New American Library, 1964), [Part II, Book XII] p. 188.
4. Marcel Proust, as quoted in Irvin D. Yalom, *Love's Executioner* (New York: Basic Books, 1989), p. 182.
5. Robert Henri, *The Art Spirit* (New York: Harper and Row Publishers, 1984), pp. 149, 148.
6. Leo Tolstoy, *The Death of Ivan Ilyich*, trans. Lynn Solotaroff (New York: Bantam Books, 1981), p. 126.
7. George Orwell, "Shooting an Elephant," *A Collection of Essays* (San Diego: Harcourt, Brace and Jovanovich, 1981), pp. 148–56.

Thank You Very Much, Rock Hudson and Doris Day

LOUISE PLUMMER

I first learned about sex in the sixth grade from Dawn Grow. Dawn, spelled D-A-W-N, was my best friend, and her brother had given her a book that explained "it" using explicit language and very few euphemisms.

I was appalled that the human race procreated by means of such a grotesque act.

But I was thrilled too. It made all of childhood seem boring. Still I was positive that my parents, who by then had six or seven children, would not do anything so disgusting. Dawn Grow and I decided quickly that it must be true (her brother's book seemed so authoritative, after all), but it was something a married couple only had to do once, and then an indiscriminate number of children would appear over the next twenty years.

It wasn't until I was thirteen that sex began to make more sense to me. I sat behind the world's most handsome boy in American History, and I had the strongest urge, a physical urge, to lean forward and kiss the back of his gorgeous neck, which always smelled of Old Spice after-shave.

What was a young girl to do with all this new, hormonal energy?

I received the answer at Mutual at the yearly "Chastity

Louise Plummer has taught writing at Brigham Young University. She received her master's degree in English literature from the University of Minnesota and is the author of two young-adult novels, The Romantic Obsessions and Humiliations of Annie Sehlmeier *and* My Name is Sus5an Smith. The Five is Silent, *and a book of essays,* Thoughts of a Grasshopper. *She and her husband, Tom, are the parents of four sons.*

Nights," as my friends and I called them. The answer was that I was to do absolutely nothing until I was married. I was to save "it" for my husband. This was demonstrated with various metaphorical examples: "Would we want to be," the speaker asked, "like a rose that had been passed around the room and examined by curious fingers poking at us, noses sniffling at us, until our petals were limp and discolored, until we were faded before our time? Would we want to present ourselves to our future husbands as toast with all the butter licked off by others?"

For me, in 1956, the answer was a definite no.

So I repeat the question. What was a young woman to do with all this new hormonal energy until she married?

I know what I did. I began to look for a husband at age thirteen. This had its drawbacks, because every attractive boy then became a prospective husband, that is, a prospective sexual partner. The result of this embarrassing dilemma was that I could no longer talk to attractive boys. I became tongue-tied.

I sought help from the only models available to me in 1956: Rock Hudson and Doris Day. You will remember that Rock Hudson and Doris Day were the leading box office draws in the fifties. Their romantic comedies showed us how male-female relationships worked, and I studied them religiously.

I thought the two of them were so witty: "I know I've sown a few wild oats," Rock says to Doris at the end of *Lover Come Back*.

"A few wild oats!" Doris exclaims. "You could apply for a farm loan with the wild oats you've sown."

I loved Rock Hudson, who was handsome as Apollo. He was humorous and a little naughty, but he always ended up committed, if it was the right girl. Doris Day was always the right girl. She was pure and upstanding and pretty—she wore those cute boxy suits with the matching hats designed by "Irene" of Hollywood.

I wanted to be like Doris Day to Rock Hudson: glamorous, witty, rich, and in love. The disparity between my life then and those romantic comedies, that I idolized, was so great that the only choices were suicide or a sense of humor. I chose humor. It was a good choice, because I have since realized that I never was the romantic heroine of my own life. I was never Doris Day. I was Thelma Ritter, her comic maid. I was Eve Arden, Rosalind Russell's quipping friend. I was never Mary Richards, played by Mary Tyler Moore. I was Rhoda Morgenstern. I wasn't even Lucy. I was Ethel. I have always been the sidekick: Sancho Panza, Gabby Hayes, and Jingles, all rolled into one.

To illustrate the disparity of my life and the movies, I will describe the worst date I ever went on. It was a blind date, and it was set up by the sister of my friend Ruth. Three boys needed three dates. Ruth said she would get two of her friends to go along.

I did not want to go. Ruth said it would be fun. I said no, I would not go.

"Please," she said, "it will be fun."

I said, "Don't ask me again. It will be awful."

But Ruth insisted it would be fun. *She* would be there. *Joyce* would be there. What was there to worry about?

I don't know how she got me to go. Maybe she said something like, "You don't have to marry him, for pity's sake!" Maybe she said, "Are you going to be one of those girls who just plays volleyball all of your life?" In any case, I went.

We waited, the three of us, in Ruth's second-story bedroom, which had a window looking out onto the street. I was tremulous with expectation. There was always a chance, albeit slim, that someone *nice* looking with a *nice* personality would show up.

A Chevy with a low-slung back end and an open muffler stopped in front of the house. This did not bode well. Nice boys did not have their mufflers open.

The driver got out first. He was a tall, athletic-looking blond boy wearing a letter jacket from a school across town. He wasn't bad. "He's mine," said Ruth, "I've seen a picture of him."

Then another boy, dark and swarthy, but also not bad, got out. "He's Joyce's," Ruth said with absolute authority.

I waited, holding my breath. Out stepped a short, under-nourished boy, his shoulders hunched into a black vinyl jacket, his hair swept up off his neck in an oily ducktail.

"He's awful!" I cried.

"He's yours," said Ruth.

He was, I learned down in the living room, about five inches shorter than I—a fact that I considered catastrophic. His name was Paul, and he was clueless. I handed him my coat, and I could tell from the blank look on his face that he had not an idea in the world of what to do with it. "Could you help me on with my coat?" I prodded. He looked at me blankly. His friend, the blond athelete, nudged him into action.

The six of us went to the all-state high school basketball tournament. My high school was playing, so everyone I knew in the world was there. Everyone in my high school would see me with this little, greasy dork. What I know now, and didn't know then, is that no one was looking. No one cared who I was with. They were all worrying about themselves. But not knowing this important fact then, I was miserable.

The basketball game was exciting, and we were on our feet most of the time. While we were standing, Ruth elbowed me. Nodding toward Paul, my date, she whispered out of the side of her mouth, "Look, he's standing on his toes."

Sure enough, Paul was standing on his toes, and he remained there for the rest of the night, not just at the basketball game, but later, in downtown Salt Lake, on the way to the Capitol Theater, he still walked on tippy toes. I was mortified. The best part of the date was when he fell asleep during the movie.

Perhaps, somewhere right now, at a *man's* conference—it might be in a bar—Paul is describing the worst date he ever had, a date with a girl the size of a skyscraper.

I saw the humor of the date afterwards. I stayed the night with Ruth, and we laughed about Tall Paul—a name we coined that night and forever. We laughed about a boy who walked on his toes.

I had enough sense of humor to save my own face, but now I wish I could have saved Paul's face as well.

I wish I'd been nicer to you, Paul. I wish I'd asked you questions like those articles on dating in Seventeen *magazine suggested. I wish I'd asked you how many brothers and sisters you had. What was your favorite color, Paul? I never asked you any questions. I never spoke to you at all. I wish I'd poked you in the ribs and made you laugh with a joke:*

— Hey Paul, did you know that they're now replacing laboratory rats with lawyers? There are some things a rat just won't do.

— Knock, knock, Paul.

— Who's there?

— Dwayne.

— Dwayne who?

— Dwayne the bathtub, I'm dwowning.

There was a precedent, Paul, for the way you and I looked together. Sophia Loren married Carlo Ponti, who was a whole head shorter than she was. And speaking of Sophia Loren, do you remember that movie with her and Alan Ladd? He was so much shorter than she, that they dug a trench for her to walk in so that he would appear taller on screen.

We should have dug a trench, Paul, you and I, or I could have walked in the gutter while you walked on the curb with your arm slung loosely around my shoulder. We should have laughed together. I never asked your last name. I wish I knew what it was now. I wish I'd been nicer to you, Paul, wherever you are.

I did not marry anyone remotely resembling Rock Hudson or Tall Paul. I married Tom Plummer. We grew up in the same ward, in the same neighborhood, but he was three years older than I, and so we didn't run in the same circles. He went on his mission when I was a junior in high school. I thought about him while he was gone. I was already attracted to him. He appealed to me for four reasons:

301

1. He was smart.
2. He was kind to the old ladies in our ward.
3. He played the piano beautifully.
4. He had a perverse sense of humor.

Even now, these seem like pretty good criteria for finding a mate.

He gave his missionary homecoming talk on my twentieth birthday. I wore a red paisley dress with a matching belt—it was a dress that made me feel as beautiful as Doris Day. I sat at the far left side of the chapel next to the window about six rows back. Tom's talk was built around the parable of the sower. It was the best missionary homecoming talk I had ever heard. I was smitten.

But I didn't get his attention until almost a year later. It was after Mutual—we still had M-Men and Gleaners then. I knew Tom was in the building, so I asked Harley Busby if he would accompany me while I sang—I often did that. I sang loud. Maybe I sang "Embraceable You" or "Night and Day" or "You're Just Too Marvelous for Words." I sang and knew that Tom would come. And soon he stood in the doorway of the chapel, and I could see that he saw me for the first time. He saw exactly what I wanted him to see: I was one sexy woman.

That Saturday night we went on our first date. We went to the movies at the Tower Theater, which was then in its artsy period—they served coffee in the lobby. We saw an Ingmar Bergman picture, where a woman confronts a priest who is also her lover and says, "You don't love me anymore, do you? It's my eczema, isn't it?" And she holds out her hands, which are covered with an ugly, lumpy rash.

Tom and I snorted and stifled our laughter.

The next day a sister stood up in testimony meeting and said she was grateful to the Lord for curing her eczema.

From the back of the chapel I looked at Tom, who was sitting at the organ, and we shared a silent guffaw. In that moment I knew we would marry.

To have a sense of humor is to see the disparity between

fantasy and reality. It means seeing the pretense, the contradictions and imperfections in our lives. It is realizing that unlike Doris Day and Sophia Loren, we have no script to give us clever lines and no direction in italics to tell us how to act. We have no dress rehearsals.

To have a sense of humor is also seeing our sadness. I was sad that I was never as popular, as smart, as articulate, as beautiful as the girl seated in the next aisle. I am sad now that I let opportunities slip by, that I am no longer young, that I am still flawed, and that I too must die.

Laughter is a reaction to being alive in an imperfect and mortal world, a world where even Rock Hudson was not what we thought he was. I am thankful to all those people who forced me to distinguish between fantasy and reality:

— Thank you, Rock Hudson and Doris Day.

— Thank you, Dawn Grow.

— Thank you, handsome boy in American history class.

— Thanks a whole bunch, Ruth.

— Thank you, Tall Paul.

— But especially, thank you, Tom Plummer.

Index

Index

Israelite law, 105

Jack, Dave, 11
Jack, Elaine, 65, 266; and the "perfect" Mormon woman, 271
Jacob, story of, 124–25
Jacobs, Presendia, 60–61
Jacobs, Zina Diantha, 60
Jephthah, 126–27
Jesus Christ, a steadfastness in, 3–5; as our hope, 12; a personal knowledge of, 13; and being alone, 22; descends below all things, 96–97; marriage of, 97; spiritual suffering of, 97–98; education of, 106–8; relationship with women, 108; as rabbi, 108–9; appears to women, 109; gives Peter direct revelation, 111; and compassion, 184–85; and responsibility, 288–89; works of, 204; and community, 274, 278
Johnson, Richard E., 162
Johnson, Samuel, on solitude, 22
Johnston's Army, 64
John the Baptist, 106
Joy, 234, 238
Judges, setting ourselves up as, 290
Judgments, snap, 289–90

Keats, John, 30
Kimball, Sarah, 35–39, 47
Kimball, Spencer W., 59–60
Kindergarten, establishing a, 76
Kin-sphere, 252 n. 1
Kin-value paradigm, 241, 246
Knitting during meetings, 86
Kovářová, Olga, 65
Krause, Edith, 65–66

Krejcí, Miloslava, 143

Labels, 274, 277, 288–90, 292
Lang, Eugene, 170–71
Language, spiritual, 94
Larsen, Dean L., 267
"Last days," the, 166
Lee, Rex E., 4
Lejontieva, Nina, 50
L'Engle, Madeleine, 94
Levinas, Emmanuel, 182
Listening, 28–29
Literature: women and, 69; importance of, 226
Loneliness, 22
Lord, waiting for the, 27–28
Loss, empathizing with, 200–201
Lyman, Amy Brown, 50, 65

Madsen, Carol, 55
Malnourished children, 163–64, 169
Manifesto, 1890, 75
Marital statue, and value, 223
Market-value paradigm, 241, 244–46
Marriage, 9; planning for, 222–23
Marxist-Leninist philosophy, 139
Materialism: emphasis on, 159–60, 162–63, 173–74; and morality, 167–68; attitudes and, 177–78; and pride, 182; rejecting, 250
McConkie, Bruce R., 58, 106–7
McHugh, Olive, 85–86
Memorial Shrine, 213
Mentally disturbed homeless, 169
Metaphors for spiritual reality, stories as, 91
Midrash, 104
Millennium, 166
Miller, Alice, 277